RACISM

RACISM
Reality Built on a Myth

John Lovchik

RESOURCE *Publications* · Eugene, Oregon

RACISM
Reality Built on a Myth

Resource Publications
An Imprint of Wipf and Stock Publishers
199 W. 8th Ave., Suite 3
Eugene, OR 97401

www.wipfandstock.com

PAPERBACK ISBN: 978-1-5326-4822-9
HARDCOVER ISBN: 978-1-5326-4823-6
EBOOK ISBN: 978-1-5326-4824-3

Manufactured in the U.S.A.   10/09/18

To those on whose shoulders we stand.
We don't start at the beginning, but we have a long way to go.

Contents

Acknowledgments

I want to acknowledge and thank first and foremost, Mr. Ronald Chisom, co-founder of The People's Institute for Survival and Beyond, who is one of those on whose shoulders I stand. He has been in the struggle a long time; yet he retains his good humor and youthful enthusiasm. I have been educated, inspired and challenged by him and by the results of his work. I also want to thank all of the trainers I have had the honor of working with, and learning from, at The People's Institute For Survival and Beyond workshops, especially Mary Flowers and Dustin Washington who initially threw me into the deep end of the pool. I am honored by their friendship and their faith, not in what I knew, but in my willingness to learn. This work is about organizing and motivating people, and you will not meet more skilled organizers than Ron, Mary, and Dustin.

I also want to thank Diana Bender, Julie Nelson, Colleen Kelly, Martin Friedman and Scott Winn who were among the first white people through whom I got involved in this work. They remain as committed as they were when I first met them. Through them I have learned, been inspired, and been supported. They are true friends who help make this difficult work enjoyable, though we all wish it were not necessary. Martin is also a trainer with the People's Institute for Survival and Beyond, and his knowledgeable presentations on the history of racism led to my realization of how our general ignorance about that past has distorted our view of the present.

I want to thank the members of the Seattle Race Conference Planning Committee, past and present. As members of a committee organizing conferences around racism, we began to recognize the extent to which the committee itself has manifested the ills of society as a whole. Our efforts to heal ourselves have drawn us closer and taught me a lot. I do want to thank individually Dr. Pamela Taylor, whose knowledge and wisdom on this subject, and grace in sharing that wisdom, have influenced me more than she could know. A special thank you is also due to AngaLee Alexander who read several versions of the manuscript. Her genuine interest in this project and her constant encouragement were invaluable, particularly during those inevitable periods of uncertainty.

Bryan Tomasovich of The Publishing World provided developmental guidance and editing that helped bring a first draft by a novice to an organized and readable end product. This book would not have been possible without his participation. I am grateful for his support and encouragement that went far beyond merely doing a job.

I feel I must also acknowledge the many authors who I have referenced and quoted throughout this book. Some are long gone, but many are still with us, continuing the work. We definitely stand on their shoulders. Their extensive research ensures the past will never be forgotten. It also allowed me to present this book as an overview, in no way intended to either diminish or bury the past. The horrors are in the details and, though it serves no purpose to dwell on them, we must be aware of the realities of our past. I highly recommend all of the books listed in the bibliography, especially those published most recently.

I also want to thank my incredibly supportive family. My daughter, Jennifer, was always ready to provide research materials for me, or assist me in locating what I needed. My sister, Kathy Devine, read an early draft and proofread the final copy. Her guidance early in the process and her review at the end, as well as her constant encouragement throughout, were helpful beyond measure. Finally, but most importantly, I thank my wife Vicky. From the first tentative drafts through every new and challenging step of the process she has been my sounding board, my counsel, and my most honest critic. A project such as this involves many years of distractions from the normal routines of life. She cheerfully endured the distractions and never wavered in her support.

Introduction

This book reviews the long history of racism from its origin in colonial times through its evolution and intentional promotion and use in subsequent periods. It is also the story of how I became aware of the importance of knowing this history in order to understand racism in our time and how each of us is connected to it. I am a white man who was completing my education and beginning my career and family during the civil rights movement in the 1960s. I was naturally troubled by the plight of people struggling for their basic rights. But I saw it as their struggle. I was detached from it by where I lived and by my focus on my own family and career. I did not see a role for myself, either in the underlying problem or in the solution.

But while I did not join in the struggle, I did try to understand it, and had continued to do so over my lifetime. What was this thing that regularly bubbled up in small incidents and major events? Needless to say, hundreds of such incidents and events have occurred in my lifetime. As I neared retirement, and with our daughter grown, I had time to pay more attention to current events and public policy regarding racism. I began writing letters to the editor, expressing my views. When a syndicated columnist demeaned the work of Malcolm X by writing that he had "spent most of his adulthood describing the racial problems of America, not doing the hard work of creating solutions,"[1] I was reminded that the only thing victims of racism can do is describe the problem; white people must do the hard work of creating solutions.[2]

I saw the attention I was paying to the subject, and the critiques I was able to get printed in the newspaper, as part of that hard work. I also felt I was becoming much more knowledgeable about the subject of racism. When I read a letter to the editor signed by a group of white people calling

---

1. McCarthy, "Malcolm's message."
2. John Lovchik, letter to the editor, *Seattle Times*, December 4, 1992.

1

themselves "European-Americans Against Racism,"[3] I saw the opportunity to expand my efforts by working with other like-minded white people, and in turn share what I had learned. I write that with some embarrassment now, because the first thing I learned from my new friends was how little I really knew about racism.

But that discovery did change my life. That small group of white people has expanded into a network of white friends and acquaintances who continue to provide support and encouragement as we continue this work together. They also connected me with a number organizations led by People of Color that helped me gain a perspective not available in my all-white world.

Most importantly, they introduced me to the People's Institute for Survival and Beyond, an organization founded and led by People of Color that has been conducting Undoing Racism® workshops since 1980. Part of each workshop addresses the history of racism, and that brief exposure encouraged me to follow up with my own in-depth research into the subject. The more I read, the more the pieces began to fall into place in the mosaic of racism. As a white man I did not experience racism and all of my knowledge had come from outside sources in random bits. I don't easily process random bits of information like some people do, but when I began looking at the history of racism chronologically, the random bits of information began to make sense to me, and the true nature of racism became more clear.

That is not to say that I have learned all there is to know. There is a wealth of good material available, and every book and article adds some new insight to help understand the present. We, white people especially, need to do our homework and there is always more to learn. We also need to be involved in the work of finding solutions and creating change.

Like most people, when I am confronted with a problem I want to solve the problem and put it behind me. But racism is not the sort of problem that can be solved easily. This must be a lifelong commitment. The most we can hope for is to make some progress in stopping and reversing this legacy of our past.

For me, as for most white people, racism can be ignored. I choose not to do that. Hopefully you will too.

The Importance of History

There is a symbol from the Akan people of Ghana in West Africa of a bird standing or flying forward while its head is turned backward. The symbol is

3. Bender, et al., "European-Americans Against Racism"

called *Sankofa* and it represents the importance of looking at the past while moving forward.

We have all heard the adage that we study history to avoid making the mistakes of the past. But while history does offer lessons on mistakes best avoided by people in subsequent times, a more important reason to study history is to understand the present. The present is but a moment in time, but it did not just happen. It would seem that those of us living in the present would be in the best position to understand and describe the times we live in. But much of what is done by us, and by the others we share this present with, is done without conscious thought. And much of what we see and experience is simply accepted without question or analysis.

The present is a moment in a progression of changing attitudes and events. Understanding where we are in that progression is key to understanding ourselves and our time.

Nowhere is this more evident than in attempting to understand and combat racism. All of human history consists of disputes between groups of people: by tribe, by religion, by ethnicity, or by countless other lines of division that we have been capable of imagining. In many of those cases the "other" was viewed as inferior to one's own group. How any, or all, of those disputes are characterized can be debated, and some could reasonably be included under the various definitions of racism. But for this book, I use a much more narrow definition of racism.

At its core, racism is a system of *ranking human beings* for the purpose of gaining and justifying an unequal distribution of political and economic power. Racism takes its name from race, and this book will review the process by which that occurred. But it must be emphasized at the outset that there is no such thing as race, or races of humans. There never has been. It is a myth. The myth of race continues to affect our thinking to this day.

This review shows when the fallacy of races of humans came into being and how its use from the very beginning was to justify treating some people as inferior to others. Race did not lead to racism; it was simply a convenient justification for the ranking of human beings that has come to be called racism.

Racism was intentionally created and the process required the active support and participation of government bodies from colonial lawmakers to the United States Supreme Court. The racism that directly affects the daily lives of millions of People of Color is the racism backed by the power of government—certainly in the past, but also continuing in the present. The racism supported by the myth of race and backed by the power of government is the racism that continues to plague this country and is the focus of this book. This is the racism that is best understood by looking at the past to understand the present.

*

Part I looks at slavery from ancient times to the U.S. Civil War that brought about the end of slavery in the United States. Though slavery existed in ancient times as a result of warfare, slavery for the specific purpose of providing free labor was a much more recent development. The capture of slaves for free labor began with sugar plantations in the eastern Mediterranean; later, Europeans adopted this form of slavery for sugar plantations in the islands off the coasts of Europe and Africa.

The advances in shipbuilding that allowed Europeans to cross the Atlantic also made possible the massive expansion of the African slave trade, which in turn made the colonization of the American continents economically feasible. The process began in Central and South America a century before the first English settlement in North America. That period, between the arrival of Columbus in 1492 and the founding of Jamestown in 1607, is often overlooked in United States history lessons. Yet, that period laid the groundwork for the expansion of slavery into the English colonies that became the United States.

Indentured servants, laborers who worked for a master for a set number of years, originally filled labor needs in the English colonies. As the colonies grew and the need for laborers increased, the colonies gradually turned to the importation of slaves to fill that need. Indentured servants and slaves worked side by side, and other than the term of service, their treatment and working conditions were the same. Their common concerns and grievances posed a threat to the plantation owners and their families.

Racism provided the wedge that separated the two groups of workers and diminished their ability to organize together to demand better working conditions and more humane treatment. Racism did not arise naturally, but had to be introduced and nurtured by the lawmakers and wealthy landowners who reaped the benefits. There was a deliberate process by which workers were divided by color—the origin of modern-day racism.

Racism filled another need as well. Where warfare had been seen as moral justification for the enslavement of prisoners of war, there was a need for moral justification of slavery for free labor as well. Creating a hierarchy of humans allowed for the argument that lower forms of humans were only suited for slavery and would remain primitive and uncivilized without the control that slavery provided. Both religion and science were manipulated to "prove" a racial hierarchy that was both God's will and a fact of nature.

The founding of the United States in 1776 and the people, who we refer to as the *fathers of our country*, warrant special consideration in the review of racism. It is important to look critically at some of the erroneous assumptions we make about our founding, not to lay blame, but to see how they affect our understanding of the present. The founding of a new nation by combining thirteen separate colonies was a truly remarkable accomplishment. The Constitution that was written at the time has guided this country for over two centuries and has accommodated immense changes during that time.

But we do no dishonor to those accomplishments by noting what was left undone. By overlooking what was not done, we delude ourselves into believing that more was done than actually was. And that distorts our perception of the present. The words of the Declaration of Independence, "We hold these truths to be self evident, that all men are created equal," had to have a different meaning to men who owned slaves than they mean to us today. Unless we can admit that our country really was not founded on that principle, we cannot admit that our country has not achieved that noble goal to this day.

Though the founders of our country allowed slavery to continue, the war for independence from England intensified the debate about the lack of freedom for the people held in slavery. Northern states, with economies not dependent on slave labor, began enacting emancipation legislation. In the South, though, the invention of the cotton gin led to a massive expansion of cotton production and a corresponding greater dependence on slave labor. That regional difference led to political disagreements that grew and intensified during the eighty-five-year period between the founding of the country and the Civil War that almost ended it. That period of political maneuvering regarding slavery was very instrumental in the development of the racism that has survived and thrived long after the end of the slavery that gave birth to it.

Twenty-one states were added during that period, each addition increasing the representation in Congress for the region in which the state was located. For the people of the South, the fear was that if the North gained too much power, slavery might be abolished nationwide.

Initially the people of the North had no intent to interfere with slavery in the South. They were more concerned with their own issues. As each northern state ended slavery they found themselves confronted with the reality of former slaves, all of African descent, being incorporated into a free society that was primarily white. Emancipation did not automatically change the attitudes toward Blacks that had developed during slavery. So, while an effort could have been made to overcome the stereotypes created by slavery, the stereotypes were instead commonly accepted as real, and the focus was on how to exclude free Blacks from white society. That focus ultimately began to affect how the people in the North viewed the expansion of slavery in the South. Their concern was not ending slavery in the South, but preventing its spread, which they saw as increasing the number of Blacks in this country.

That regional debate among white men about black slaves fueled the growing view of Blacks as distinctly separate from, and inferior to, Whites. The arguments by people of the South in support of slavery that insisted on the inferiority of Blacks, while not sufficient for the people of the North to support slavery, did reinforce their negative attitudes toward Blacks. And the arguments by people in the North about excluding Blacks from White society reinforced the attitudes in the South about Blacks being an inferior race. As slavery was nearing its end, racism was gaining momentum.

Part II presents the history from the Civil War to the present and shows how racism, originally a justification for slavery, took on a life of its own. Like the plantation owners, the people in power in subsequent times found that the continued divisions caused by racism benefited their political and economic interests. The process of nurturing racism was as deliberate and as actively supported as the process of implementing it.

The relatively short period from the Civil War to the end of the nineteenth century presented many opportunities to overcome the racism created by slavery. Instead, the widespread legal—and sometimes illegal but officially sanctioned—efforts to keep the freed slaves subordinate to Whites served to reinforce it. Particularly harmful were the *convict leasing programs* initiated by many of the southern states by which corrupt sheriffs and judges falsely accused and convicted Blacks of crimes so they could be leased to plantation and mine owners as cheap labor. The massive conviction of Blacks in turn supported the argument that all Blacks were lawless and irresponsible and had in fact *needed* the control of slavery.

The scientific study of humans, which got its start in the eighteenth century, was used extensively before and after the Civil War to support the ranking of human beings. Throughout the nineteenth century, prominent doctors and scientists committed themselves to proving that certain groups of people, particularly those of African descent, were inferior to those of European descent. The outcomes of their research were biased by their preconceived conclusions, but were nevertheless presented as scientific fact in classrooms everywhere for almost a century. The misinformation they propagated had a significant impact on public opinion that continues to this day.

A look at the history of the twentieth century shows the unfortunate truth of W. E. B. Du Bois' 1903 warning that "the problem of the Twentieth Century is the problem of the color-line."[4] The first half of the century, generally remembered only for its Jim Crow segregation, was actually a period of violence against Blacks as bad as any in our past. The legally sanctioned segregation and the condoned violence against Blacks and other People of Color impressed on the public subconscious the inferior status of Non-Whites. A major war and concern about enemy propaganda, not concern about the victims of the violence, finally brought about some changes in policy.

The second half of the century, in the aftermath of the Second World War and the revelation of Nazi atrocities in the name of racial purity, began with a re-evaluation of our treatment of African Americans and other People of Color in this country. That re-evaluation did not originate with policy makers, but with the courageous non-violent protests of those being discriminated against. The extensive media coverage of the civil rights movement in the South and the civil unrest throughout the nation forced lawmakers and the public to take note of the racism that was an integral part of public policy everywhere.

Legislation was passed to outlaw segregation in the South and housing and employment discrimination nationwide. But legislation could not eliminate the racism that had been fostered by previous policy. And the commitment to change immediately came under attack by policy makers. Within a few decades almost all progress had stopped and racism continued on, transformed. A review of the role language played in that transformation shows the adaptability of racism and how the appearance of change is very different than real change.

The United States Supreme Court has played, and continues to play, a significant role in validating and supporting racism. The Supreme Court, with its power to interpret the Constitution and to endorse or overturn state and federal laws based on those interpretations, influences public policy to a much greater degree than generally recognized. A review of some significant cases shows the role of the Supreme Court in allowing unequal treatment for different groups of citizens under supposedly neutral laws. As the final arbiter of our justice system, the Court's rulings can result in legally sanctioned unequal treatment of People of Color that lasts for decades.

Part III covers the present and the future. Policies of the past continue to affect us in the present and connecting the past to the present guides our understanding of the time we live in. It also shows how we have been

---

4. Du Bois, *The Souls of Black Folk*, 3.

socialized to overlook some of the realities of the present. It is important to be aware of that socialization so we are able to reflect on how our perspective affects how we see racism.

The disproportional incarceration of young black men resulting from the war on drugs was neither justified nor accidental. It has been tolerated because the lingering effects of racism in the past have distorted our perception of what is actually taking place. At the same time, it is adding to the racism of the present by creating a false image of black men as prone to criminality, much like happened during the era of convict leasing. That false image affects all aspects of our criminal justice system, the society we live in, and our own thinking.

For white people, a careful look at the concept of whiteness is also helpful in understanding racism. Since we all expect to be judged as individuals, white people rarely consider themselves as part of a collective. Yet the term "White" as it relates to humans has been a part of national and state laws from the very beginning of our country. Because of racism, those of us who meet the artificial category of "White" have a very definite collective identity. *White privilege* is not just the latest catch phrase. It is very real. Discussing the benefits white people take for granted helps white people see how we are all connected to racism. All Whites, not just white racists, are affected by racism, just as all People of Color are affected. The effect on Whites, though, is positive so we have an incentive to not notice.

While the primary goal of this book is to give clarity to the present, that does logically lead to a consideration of how to use that information in moving forward. The review of the lengthy evolution of racism leads to the inevitable conclusion that there are no easy answers or quick fixes. Eliminating racism will require a commitment by a large number of people to understanding racism and to supporting actions aimed at ending it. The key for white people is to do the internal work needed to really understand racism and our connection to it. We can't change the past; but we can change ourselves, and by doing so we can change the future.

The lessons of the past regarding white superiority linger in all of us. That internalized sense of knowing more and being more qualified leads white people to attempt to control any activity in which they participate. We must be honest about recognizing and overcoming that tendency. In the work of ending racism, white people—who are not negatively affected by it—must take leadership from People of Color who are; and we must hold ourselves accountable to them. There is much work to be done, and it is critically important that white people get involved. Much of the work involves white people interacting with white communities and white-controlled institutions.

For those of us not harmed by racism, our interest ebbs and flows depending on events in the news. But the news events are just the manifestations of racism. Racism remains constant. Recent events have renewed interest in racism by news reporters, news analysts, and the general public. This moment of public interest presents an opportunity that must not be missed. The opportunity lies in taking advantage of public attention to broaden awareness of the realities of racism and the commitment needed to end it. Centuries of carefully nurtured racism will take a very long time to overcome. The public commitment to change must be nurtured as diligently as racism itself was.

Some Comments On Terminology

Because the subject of racism is often misunderstood, and always viewed from a variety of perspectives, the words we use can have different meanings to different people. As noted above, race is a myth, so I try to avoid the use of that word. But because we are dealing with events of the past when races were believed to be real, and because it is still so ingrained in our thinking, there are times when it seems awkward to avoid the word. It is my hope that soon we will find a way to talk about racism, and retain our commitment to ending it, while seeing the concept of *race* as we see the concept of a *flat earth.*

The impact of the past on us in the present is very real, but we are not conscious of it. The illustration of how that happened, and how it affects us, is the goal of this book. There are many ways of looking at and describing that process. Chapter 13, covering racism in the present, discusses the process in terms of brainwashing and internalizing ideas of inferiority and superiority. But it is important to recognize that this is a normal and necessary process called *socialization.* Socialization is generally positive, but it can also be negative.

In their book, *Beyond Inclusion, Beyond Empowerment: A Developmental Strategy To Liberate Everyone,* Leticia Nieto, et al. describe socialization like this:

> All societies lean on social conventions. . . . Socialization is the process of absorbing, internalizing, and adapting to the social norms of any society while remaining oblivious to them. . . . Participation in any society requires a degree of unconscious conformity to dominant values.[5]

---

5. Nieto, et al., *Beyond Inclusion, Beyond Empowerment,* 3.

Learning when to say *please* and *thank you*, and appropriate behavior at the dinner table or in a public place are examples of that socialization. This book examines some negative aspects of socialization that operate at that level, as unconscious conformity to what we have been taught. While the word *unconscious*, is generally used in this context, it also has the secondary meaning of not being conscious at all. I have chosen instead to use the word *subconscious* to emphasize that, though not operating on a conscious level, our socialization definitely comes into play when we are very much awake and in control.

Because racism is about groups of people, how we identify and discuss those groups of people can be problematic. With full recognition of the importance of honoring the preferences of those being referred to, I have made some general choices that I hope will be understandable and at the same time respectful. Racism is about groups, but it affects individuals. Racism is brutal, physically and emotionally, and for many even the discussion of it can be very painful. Whatever we do, we must never forget that we are talking about real people and their very real lives.

Racism has always been arbitrary and based on nothing more than appearance. The terms *Black* and *White* demonstrate that arbitrariness and are used as a simple reference to two major groups. Where I use white and black as adjectives I use lower case. Where I use them as nouns to designate groups of people I capitalize them.

Those of us who meet the arbitrary designation of White should self-identify as such, not in the old self-serving way but in the new, accountable, way. Any other application of those designations should be solely to suggest likely differences in life experiences, not as labels. There are no valid labels, but there are very real differences in life experiences because of appearance.

There are also loving relationships between people of very different ancestries. In discussions about racism, the children of those relationships can be made to feel that they must choose between their two parents in how they identify and in how they should understand racism. We must be very sensitive to the infinite complexity of the subject, and the infinite variety among humans.

The term *People of Color* reminds us that racism isn't just about Blacks and Whites. But it is also disrespectful in a way because it totally disregards hundreds of separate and distinct ethnicities, cultures, and experiences, and presents them as one homogenous pool. Yet, in the effort to be succinct, I have often used that shortcut. I mean no disrespect and beg the indulgence of those being referred to in this way. I capitalize People of Color because I am referring to a specific group of people—those who are not White.

This too is not intended as a label, but to suggest likely differences in life experiences.

A similar situation exists for the original inhabitants of the American continents. They also consisted of hundreds of unique individual groups, and pooling them, regardless of the name used, disregards their varied histories before and after the Europeans arrived. Still, again in the effort to be brief, I have used the shortcut name "Native Americans" in their case. I hope they will understand and accept my explanation. I also hope that readers will make a special effort to see the effects on those people and their ancestors through our entire history with racism.

In many ways, people of Native American ancestry are often the most invisible in discussions of racism, yet their history was as brutal and devastating as slavery. We use the terms *discovery* and *colonization* to describe Europeans' connection with these continents, but they in fact came as conquerors. An honest look at history shows the extent to which attitudes and policies regarding the original inhabitants have reflected, and continue to reflect, that reality.

2016 Presidential Election

As I was completing my writing, the 2016 presidential election presented an excellent example of the racism described in this book. Donald Trump's entire campaign was supported by the following ideas, and his acceptance speech at the Republican Convention provides a simple outline of how the process works.[6]

In the speech, Trump included some comments about the issue of "illegal immigrants." He then told the story of one undocumented man who had caused the death of a young woman because of an auto accident resulting from his driving while intoxicated. The effect on his audience was that the one drunk driver represented every Mexican immigrant. Trump also spoke of "Islamic terrorists" and referred to the attack on the World Trade Center and several individual bombings and shootings by radicals. Again, the effect was to identify every Muslim in the United States and around the world with those few radicals.

Finally, he accused President Obama of dividing us by "race and color." He referred to unemployment and crime in the inner cities and identified himself as the "law and order candidate." Divisions by race and color were blamed on Obama, our first African American president, and every black inner city resident was connected with social disorder and crime.

6. Trump, "Read: Donald Trump's Acceptance Speech."

Whether or not that approach helped Trump win the election is beside the point. He must have thought it would help or he would not have used it. We can never know with certainty how much effect it had, though it must have had some. More important is the illustration it provides regarding how racism is used and how we are affected by it.

The examples Trump used were obviously intended to represent the groups he was talking about. That is the purpose of examples. Consider the outrage we would have heard if his comments about people who wanted to shake up the federal government had been followed with Timothy McVeigh as an example. But since the identification of every group of non-whites with the actions of each member of the group has been in place since the days of slavery, his examples were hardly noticed. The white supremacist groups noticed. Their enthusiastic response shows there was no doubt in their minds regarding the intent of Trump's words. There should be no doubt in our minds either. Creating a negative image of whole groups of people by misleading means, such as connecting the group to the flaws of individual members of the group, is racism. That was clearly the intent.

A closer look at the effects is also informative. The primary objective of racism was, and continues to be, to divide people. That is exactly what happened during this election. The people who didn't support Trump saw his rhetoric as racist and accused all who voted for him of racism.

On the other hand, those who voted for him saw themselves as ignored in public policy and accepted Trump's portrayal of himself as a populist who would address their concerns. They felt their problems had been ignored while immigrants, Muslims, and the inner cities were getting all of the attention. Some had voted for Obama in the past but, regardless of whether they had voted for Obama, they all resented being called racist.

That is how racism works. The voting public was left bitterly divided, arguing over who was the most forgotten and whose issues were most important. One side resented an outcome they saw as driven by racism, while the other side resented the suggestion that they were motivated by racism. And People of Color were once again outsiders—the center of the debate, but not consulted or included in it.

So who benefited? Trump was elected and given significant political power. He and many of his cabinet appointees are wealthy individuals whose lives, careers, and financial interests are far different than those of average citizens. It's probably a safe assumption that the demographic of Trump and his appointees will do well.

It's also entirely possible that Trump's policies will help improve the lives of those who voted for him. But someone who ran as a populist, while excluding the large groups of people he demeaned in his speeches, is unlikely to unify the country or benefit everyone equally. It's probably more likely that the divisions will be hardened and we will again have taken a step backward.

The divisions promoted by Trump were by color, by country of origin, and by religion. They were not by the old categories of race. But the old race categories remain in the background reinforcing the new categories. It is just another change in terminology. Racism continues to adapt.

PART I

Slavery from Ancient Times to the Civil War

1

Slavery

To understand the origins of racism, it is important to look at the history of slavery. Racism didn't bring about slavery; slavery brought about racism. Slavery has existed since ancient times. But the use of slavery in this country was unique in its magnitude and in the color divide that existed from the start, when people of European descent began importing people of African descent as slaves. That color divide was then exploited to justify and protect the whole system of slavery. The process of pitting white workers against black slaves was the origin of the racism of today.

Ancient Slavery

In ancient times, warfare was often a matter of conquest. When one army was defeated, their territory and its inhabitants were taken over by the victors. There was no way to repatriate prisoners of war, so they were made slaves.[1] Ancient slavery took many forms, but generally there were protections for the rights of slaves and often the slaves were allowed to eventually become accepted members of society.[2]

It was not until the development of large-scale agricultural production, which created a need for many laborers, that raids to capture large numbers of slaves began. Sugar production was very labor intensive and lent itself to the creation of plantations with many slaves. Sugar plantations

1. Smedley, *Race in North America*, 129.
2. Ibid., 128–37.

began in the islands of the eastern Mediterranean,[3] and were then copied by Europeans on Cyprus and the islands off the coasts of Europe and Africa.[4] This development was the first step in the process of enslaving people—not as a necessary result of wars, but specifically as a source of free labor.

Moral Justification For The Slave Trade

Slavery from warfare was common and generally recognized as a necessity. The only moral issue was the treatment of the slaves.[5] With the advent of slavery solely for free labor, some began to see a need for moral justification for the raids. The premises that captives were people who were only capable of performing slave labor, or that they were barbarians who needed to be civilized, were sometimes used as that justification.[6] For Europeans especially, the conversion of the captives to the religion of the raiders provided the best moral justification.[7]

That was the situation in 1455 when Spain and Portugal had developed shipbuilding to the stage where they could venture farther from their homeports and begin exploring the west coast of Africa. In that year, Pope Nicholas V issued a papal bull, Romanus Pontifex, reaffirming that, by his authority, all rights to the explored and conquered lands of West Africa, and the captured "enemies of Christ," belonged to King Alfonso V of Portugal. The section of the papal bull itemizing the rights previously granted reads as follows:

> We [therefore] weighing all and singular the premises with due meditation, and noting that since we had formerly by other letters of ours granted among other things free and ample faculty to the aforesaid King Alfonso—to invade, search out, capture, vanquish, and subdue all Saracens and pagans whatsoever, and other enemies of Christ wheresoever placed, and the kingdoms, dukedoms, principalities, dominions, possessions, and all movable and immovable goods whatsoever held and possessed by them and to reduce their persons to perpetual slavery . . . .[8]

3. Ibid., 133.

4. Reese, "The Slave Trade," 347.

5. Smedley, *Race in North America*, 133–34.

6. Ibid., 134.

7. Franklin and Moss, *From Slavery to Freedom*, 35.

8. Davenport, *European Treaties*, 23.

Another section of the papal bull recapped some of the explorations and conquests undertaken by Portugal under the authority of the earlier letters and, as the following excerpt shows, makes it clear that the justification was the conversion of captives to the "Catholic faith":

> Thence also many Guineamen and other negroes, taken by force, and some by barter of unprohibited articles, or by other lawful contract of purchase, have been sent to the said kingdoms. A large number of these have been converted to the Catholic faith, and it is hoped, by the help of divine mercy, that if such progress be continued with them, either those peoples will be converted to the faith or at least the souls of many of them will be gained for Christ.[9]

Though the objective was conversion, the reference to "perpetual slavery" suggests that conversion wouldn't necessarily lead to freedom. And while enslaved Africans were taken to Europe for various uses, and many were converted as indicated in the papal bull, most were taken to the islands of the Atlantic: the Canary Islands, Madeira, the Azores, and the Cape Verde Islands to provide free labor for the sugar plantations that were being established there in the latter half of the fifteenth century. This was the beginning of the Atlantic slave trade that ultimately spread to the Americas.[10]

Slavery in the Americas

Thirty-seven years after Romanus Pontifex, when Christopher Columbus sailed west to the Americas under the sponsorship of the Spanish king, his discoveries led to a similar dispute between Portugal and Spain regarding the rights to those newly discovered lands. To resolve that dispute, in 1493 Pope Alexander VI issued a papal bull, "Inter Caetera," by which he awarded Spain the rights to all those lands "together with all their dominions, cities, camps, places, and villages, and all rights jurisdictions, and appurtenances"[11] west of a line "distant one hundred leagues towards the west and south from any of the islands commonly known as the Azores and Cape Verde."[12]

"Inter Caetera" did not resolve all issues between Spain and Portugal, so they entered into their own independent negotiations. In 1494, they signed the Treaty of Tordesillas, changing the line to 370 leagues west of

9. Ibid., 22.
10. Reese, "The Slave Trade."
11. Davenport, *European Treaties*, 77.
12. Ibid.

the Cape Verde islands, and specified that Portugal was entitled to all newly discovered lands east of that line.[13] Pope Julius II confirmed the treaty in 1506 in a papal bull, "Ea quae."[14] The treaty became the controlling agreement regarding claimed ownership of the Americas by European nations, with Spain claiming all except a portion of South America; that territory was claimed by Portugal and named *Brazil*.

While it is clear from the papal bulls that conversion of non-Christians was the justification for those ventures, history is also clear the real purpose was financial. The purpose of Columbus' initial journey was to find a new trade route to the East Indies to more efficiently and reliably acquire the spices that commanded high prices and produced large profits in Europe. It was this potential for large financial gains that induced the King of Spain to finance the trip. And, though access to the spice markets was the primary goal, the following entry in Columbus' log from that trip, as quoted by Howard Zinn in his book, *A People's History of the United States*, shows that the potential financial benefit of enslaving the natives was also on his mind:

> They were well-built, with good bodies and handsome features
> . . . They do not bear arms, and do not know them, for I showed
> them a sword, they took it by the edge and cut themselves out of
> ignorance. They have no iron. Their spears are made of cane. . .
> . They would make fine servants. . . . With fifty men we could
> subjugate them all and make them do whatever we want.[15]

Though the presentation of U.S. history often skips from the 1492 voyage of Columbus to the 1607 founding of Jamestown, the first permanent English settlement in what is now the United States, the intervening 115 years saw significant events occurring in the Caribbean islands and in Central and South America that must be considered in order to give context to what happened in the English colonies after the founding of Jamestown.

As in the case of the first voyage of Columbus, subsequent voyages by him and others were primarily economic ventures. Columbus had landed in the islands of the Caribbean, not the East Indies as planned, and consequently there were no lucrative spice markets to recoup the costs of the trips. There were, however, the spoils of war, mainly gold, and the possibility of enslaving the natives. Over the next one hundred years, Spain conquered and colonized the Caribbean islands and Central and South America. The conquered peoples were enslaved from the start, but their value as items of trade and export was limited. Their value as free labor, though, made

13. Ibid, 85, 95.
14. Ibid., 107–11.
15. Zinn, *A People's History*, 1.

the production of agricultural products for export to Europe economically viable.

The islands of the Caribbean and some parts of South America proved to be well suited for the growing of sugar cane, and as sugar was in much demand in Europe, large sugar cane plantations were quickly established. The demand for free labor grew quickly. So quickly, in fact, that the demand soon exceeded the supply of enslaved natives. The indigenous people of the Americas had no natural immunity to the diseases brought by the Europeans, and the resulting epidemics killed thousands. The reduced populations contributed to the relative ease of their conquest, but also reduced the number of natives available for slave labor. The growing need for additional free labor for the sugar plantations provided the impetus for the expansion of the African slave trade across the Atlantic to the Americas. The importation of enslaved people from Africa began in 1517[16] and by 1540 numbered about ten thousand per year.[17]

16. Franklin and Moss, *From Slavery to Freedom,* 40.

17. Ibid.

2

Slavery in the English Colonies

In the British colonies that ultimately became the United States of America, the poor from England and other European countries initially filled the labor needs. When that labor supply proved insufficient, the wealthy landowners began to turn to slavery. The same shipbuilding skills that allowed worldwide exploration and colonization also enabled the transport of massive numbers of captives from Africa to the Americas.

It was in the English colonies that slavery evolved into what is commonly known as chattel slavery, the treatment of slaves as property, no different than farm animals. The colonists' justification of placing other human beings at that level led to the attitude that Africans were an inferior form of humanity. That was the origin of the ranking of human groups that became known as racism.

In the transition to slavery, laborers from Europe and slaves from Africa worked side by side on the plantations. Working conditions were harsh, and their treatment was often brutal. When it became apparent that the two classes of workers would join forces in resisting their abusive treatment, lawmakers and the plantation owners found a way to create a wedge between the two groups. The color divide already existed because of the sources of the two labor pools. It was just a matter of exploiting that division. That color difference continues to support the racism that divides us.

The Early Years of the English Colonies

By the latter part of the sixteenth century, other European nations began to challenge Spain's exclusive rights to all of the lands in the Americas. England made several unsuccessful attempts to establish colonies before the successful founding of Jamestown in 1607. Spain's settlement, St. Augustine in what is now Florida, predated the founding of Jamestown, and within the next century other European countries also established colonies in what is now the United States. But the English controlled the original thirteen colonies and were a major influence in the ultimate formation of the United States.

Slavery was practiced within the countries of Europe, but there was also widespread opposition to the owning and trading of human beings. That was the case in England. A court ruling there in 1569 stated that slavery was not allowed under English law,[1] although later cases considered the rights of slave owners and slaves without addressing the legality of the institution.[2] The later cases show that slavery continued to exist in England despite the earlier court ruling, but also suggest that it was not widespread.

In the early years of English colonization in America, labor was provided by indentured servants—Europeans who agreed to pay for their passage to the colonies by working for a master for a specified number of years, usually five to seven. Howard Zinn describes the situation at the time:

> In England, the development of commerce and capitalism in the 1500s and 1600s, the enclosing of land for the production of wool, filled cities with vagrant poor, and from the reign of Elizabeth on, laws were passed to punish them, imprison them in workhouses, or exile them. . . . In the 1600s and 1700s, by forced exile, by lures, promises, and lies, by kidnapping, by their urgent need to escape the living conditions of the home country, poor people wanting to go to America became commodities of profit for merchants, traders, ship captains, and eventually their masters in America."[3]

The first record of people of African descent arriving in Virginia was in 1619, twelve years after its founding, as noted in the writings of John Smith: "About the last of August, came a dutch man of warre that sold us twenty Negars."[4]

---

1. Higginbotham, *In the Matter of Color*, 321.
2. Ibid., 321–24.
3. Zinn, *A People's History*, 42.
4. Arber, *Travels and Works of Captain John Smith*, 541.

Judge A. Leon Higginbotham, Jr. conducted a review of laws and court rulings in Virginia and five other colonies in his book, *In The Matter of Color*. He points out that the exact status of those original twenty Africans cannot be known with certainty.[5] They clearly were not free since they were sold, but they may well have been treated like any other indentured servant of that time. Historians John Hope Franklin and Alfred A. Moss, Jr. point out that they were listed as servants in the census counts of 1623 and 1624.[6] They also point out that:

> As late as 1651 some blacks whose period of service had expired were being assigned land in much the same way that it was being assigned to whites who had completed their indenture. During its first half-century of existence Virginia had many black indentured servants, and the records reveal an increasing number of free blacks.[7]

Transition from Indentured Servitude to Slavery

Judge Higginbotham's research shows how attitudes and the treatment of Blacks evolved during the middle of the seventeenth century, ultimately leading to two hundred years of slavery and over three hundred and fifty years of racism. In 1624, the General Court of Virginia allowed a black man to give testimony because he qualified as "a free man and Christian" due to having been christened twelve years earlier in England.[8] The reference to him as a free man indicates that other blacks were not free, though it's not certain whether any were actually slaves. Christian baptism conferred the privileges of a free person under English law at the time, and this case shows the influence that was having on the colony and its General Court.[9]

Later, as Virginia began to experience the problem of a shortage of labor not unlike that experienced by the Caribbean sugar plantations one hundred years earlier, this began to change. Tobacco was the main item of export for Virginia, and it required labor to grow and harvest. The total number of indentured servants was limited and they had to be replaced at the end of the indenture period. While Virginia had no direct connection

---

5. Higginbotham, *In the Matter of Color,* 20.
6. Franklin and Moss, *From Slavery to Freedom,* 65.
7. Ibid.
8. McIlwaine, *Minutes of the Council,* 33; Higginbotham, *In the Matter of Color,* 21.
9. Higginbotham, *In the Matter of Color,* 21.

with the Spanish colonies, they were aware of those colonies' use of enslaved Africans as a permanent solution to their labor needs.

Two cases in 1640 show the beginnings of the shift from indentured servitude to slavery in Virginia. The two cases also show that, from the start, slavery applied only to those of African descent, never to those of European descent. The rulings are brief, and lack some relevant details, but some reasonable inferences can be drawn. The first case involved three men who ran away from their master. The punishment for the two white men was as follows:

> One called Victor, a Dutchman, the other a Scotchman called James Gregory, shall first serve out their times with their master according to their Indentures, and one whole year apiece after the time of their service is Expired . . . and after that service . . . to serve the colony for three whole years apiece.[10]

The punishment for the black man: "The third being a negro named John Punch shall serve his said master or his assigns for the time of his natural Life here or elsewhere."[11]

Punch's previous status was not distinguished from the other two men; they were referred to as "three servants."[12] If he had already been a slave, this punishment would have returned him to his previous situation with no additional penalty. What is more likely is that his previous status was similar to that of the white men, but that the judge chose to treat him differently for the same offense, and instead of sentencing him to additional years of service sentenced him to slavery for life.

The other case from 1640 involved a black man and six white men who ran away from their master. Upon capture and conviction, some of the white men were branded, some whipped, some required to wear shackles for a period of time. Most were required to serve additional time. The black man, Emmanuel, was whipped, branded with an *R* on his cheek and required to wear shackles for a year. Though his punishment was among the most severe, it included no additional time.[13] While it is not stated in the judgment that was handed down, it is likely no additional time was possible because he was already a slave for life.

---

10. McIlwaine, *Minutes of the Council*, 466.
11. Ibid.
12. Ibid.
13. Ibid., 467.

By 1659, the transition to slave labor had progressed to the point that a law was passed encouraging the importation of slaves by awarding reduced tariffs to foreign merchants who imported slaves. The following wording of the law makes it clear that slavery was to be limited to people of African descent.

> . . . provided, that if the said Dutch or other forreiners shall import any negro slaves, They the said Dutch or others shall, for the tobacco really produced by the sale of the said negro, pay only the impost of two shillings per hogshead, the like being paid by our owne nation.[14]

Creating The Color Divide

As the number of slaves increased, an old problem took on a new dimension. As demonstrated by the two cases above, masters always had to contend with the problem of runaways. With indentured servants, the captured runaway would simply be required to serve the entire term of the indenture by making up for the time when absent, and then serve additional time as a penalty. No comparable way of making up for time absent or serving additional time was available in the case of a captured runaway slave. The initial approach to dealing with the problem was to require that any indentured servants escaping with a slave make up the time of the slaves absence as well as their own. The following law was enacted in 1660:

> "Bee it enacted That in case any English servant shall run away in company with any negroes who are incapable of makeing satisfaction by addition of time . . . that the English so running away in company with them shall serve for the time of the said negroes absence as they are to do for their owne by a former act."[15]

The following year another law addressed the possibility of the death of the slave:

> . . . and if the negroes be lost or dye in such time of their being run away, the christian servants in company with them shall by proportion among them, either pay fower thousand five

14. Hening, *Statutes*, vol. 1, 540.
15. Hening, *Statutes*, vol. 2, 26.

hundred pounds of tobacco and caske or fower yeares service
for every negroe soe lost or dead.[16]

One of the objectives of the laws was to protect the plantation owners
from financial loss by allowing the master to recover the time lost by the
slave's absence. But the laws also began to create a divide between indentured servants and slaves, since indentured servants incurred greater risks
escaping in the company of slaves than escaping alone. The clear distinction
between servants and slaves written into the laws also served to remind indentured servants of the importance of not risking that distinction.

While the 1660 law allowed for the indentured servant to serve for the
time lost by a runaway slave who was recaptured, the 1661 law did not allow
for the indentured servant to serve as a slave for life in the place of a slave
who died. The treatment of indentured servants was often harsh and the
Emmanuel case shows that they were subject to punishments that included
whipping, branding, and the wearing of shackles. The one punishment indentured servants of European descent were not subjected to was slavery.

By common practice and understanding as well as by law, indentured
servitude was being reserved for people of European descent and slavery
was being reserved for people of African descent. The divide between indentured servants and slaves was also becoming a divide along color lines.
Creating and reinforcing that divide became very intentional as the total
number of workers began to pose a safety risk, as well as a financial one.

The significant number of workers on each plantation greatly outnumbered the plantation owners and their families. Though their status differed,
the indentured servants and slaves worked side by side, and would have had
common grievances regarding treatment by the owners. The possibility of a
joint uprising that would have endangered the safety and lives of the owners and their families was a risk that was mitigated by keeping the workers
divided.

A review of Bacon's Rebellion, an uprising that occurred in 1676,
shows how the economic and social conditions of the time created a situation that posed a substantial risk to the wealthy landowners of the colony.
By then, more than two generations after the founding of Jamestown, all of
the desirable land had been distributed and the only land available for those
completing their indenture was farther out on the frontier. When the inevitable confrontations and conflicts with Native Americans resulted, the new
landowners objected to what they saw as an inadequate response against
the Native Americans by the ruling class. Further, crop prices were controlled by England, so small landowners were having difficulty supporting

16. Ibid., 117.

themselves. Those free men who were not landowners found it even more difficult. And then there were, of course, the substantial number of indentured servants and slaves.

Nathaniel Bacon was a young man who was born into the ruling class, but whose personal agenda seems to have been all out war against the Native Americans on the frontier, an aggression opposed by the ruling class. Because of this disagreement, he became a symbol for the general opposition to the ruling class and he rallied a rebel force consisting of poor whites, indentured servants, and slaves. Though their individual objectives likely varied, they nonetheless were willing to fight and die together. In the end, when their chief garrison was overcome, it consisted of four hundred men—a mix of free men, indentured servants, and slaves. The last to disarm were eighty black men and twenty indentured servants.[17]

Creating and reinforcing the color divide was seen as an effective way to reduce the risk without abandoning the lucrative practice of slavery. Two laws passed in 1691 demonstrate the intent of the lawmakers to reinforce the divide between people of African descent and people of European descent. The first was a prohibition against intermarrying under penalty of banishment:

> Whatsoever English or other white man or woman being free
> shall intermarry with a negroe, mulatto, or Indian man or wom-
> an bond or free shall within three months after such marriage be
> banished and removed from this dominion forever.[18]

It is important to note the appearance of the term "white" in laws being enacted at this time. A Maryland law prohibiting intermarriage, enacted in 1681 shortly after Bacon's rebellion, was the first legal use of the term "white" in the colonies,[19] and the Virginia law of 1691 adopted the same language. From the beginning, people of African descent had been identified as "Negro," a color designation, but this was the first time that people of European descent had been identified as "white." It is also important to note that the prohibition in the Virginia law also prohibited intermarriages with free Blacks or Indians, as well as with slaves. The color divide, even among free men and women, was becoming an essential element of the system of slavery and the holding of people in perpetual bondage.

The same 1691 Virginia law prohibited the freeing of slaves without paying for their transportation out of the colony.

---

17. Zinn, *A People's History*, 41.

18. Hening, *Statutes*, vol. 3, 87.

19. Browne, *Archives of Maryland*, 204; Battalora, *Birth of a White Nation*, 21.

". . . it is hereby enacted, That no negro or mulatto be . . . set free by any person or persons whatsoever, unless such person or persons . . . pay for the transportation of such negro or negroes out of the countery within six months after such setting them free . . . ."[20]

The lawmakers were not prepared to tell the slave owner that he could not free his slaves, but they could limit the number of free Blacks in the colony by decreeing that freed slaves be removed from the colony. Blacks who were already free were not affected, but they were clearly treated differently than whites under the law. A 1705 law prohibited any "negro, mulatto, or Indian, bond or free," from lifting his or her hand at any time, against any "christian, not being negro, mulatto or Indian," under penalty of thirty lashes.[21] Regardless of circumstances, no free Black or Native could defend himself or herself from assault by a white person. Another 1705 law absolutely prohibited the marriage between a white man or woman and a "negro" under penalty of six months in prison and a fine of ten pounds. Any minister performing such a marriage was fined ten thousand pounds of tobacco.[22]

Those 1705 laws were part of a comprehensive set of laws primarily dealing with indentured servants and slaves. The law spelled out the rights and remedies available to indentured servants, while at the same time spelling out the rights of slave owners and leaving no doubt that slaves had absolutely no rights.[23] Those laws were clearly intended to appease indentured servants by addressing some of their concerns. The laws were equally intent on refining and maintaining the system of slavery.

Those laws, enacted just two years shy of one hundred years after the founding of Jamestown, mark the completion of the transition from indentured servitude to slavery as the principal form of labor in the colony of Virginia. In the next seventy years prior to the Revolutionary War, those slave laws were amended ten times, always to refine and preserve the system, never out of concern for the people in bondage.[24] In fact, the brutality sanctioned in those laws demonstrates the extreme measures the lawmakers were willing to accept in order to preserve that unnatural system of perpetual bondage for their own financial benefit.

20. Hening, *Statutes*, vol. 3, 87–88.

21. Ibid.., 459.

22. Ibid., 453–54.

23. Higginbotham, *In the Matter of Color*, 53–57.

24. Ibid., 58.

Human Beings As Property

There are many variables in relations between human beings, but the ownership of some individuals by others is not at all natural. Maintaining that unnatural system required laws to enforce it and rationalizations to justify it. One rationalization was that Blacks were lesser human beings, or not really human beings at all. The way slaves were treated helped support that rationalization. Since slaves were owned by plantation owners, the lawmakers determined that the rights of the owner superceded any rights that the slave might have had as a human being. A law passed in 1669 shows lawmakers were more concerned about the rights of the slave owner than any rights of the slave, including the right to life:

> An Act about the casuall killings of slaves.
>
> Whereas the only law in force for the punishment of refractory servants resisting their master, mistris or overseer cannot be inflicted upon negroes, nor the obstinacy of many of them by other then violent meanes supprest, Be it enacted and declared by this grand assembly, if any slave resist his master (or other by his masters order correcting him) and by the extremity of the correction should chance to die, that his death shall not be accompted felony, but the master (or that other person appointed by the master to punish him) be acquit from molestation, since it cannot be presumed that prepensed malice (which alone makes murder felony) should induce any man to destroy his owne estate.[25]

Under the law, murder only applied to the life of a free person. The life of an enslaved person was valued only in regard to his or her economic value to the slave owner. Only the slave owner had any rights regarding the life of the slave. As property, the slave was no longer entitled to human rights.

And since the slaves were property, lawmakers also had to deal with how slaves were to be passed down to heirs or used to satisfy creditors' claims. The following law recognized that slaves were being treated as animals, but also had to allow for the uniqueness of individual slaves. Yet their humanity was never considered. The slaves were simply part of the assets of the estate to be indiscriminately sold at auction if that produced the best economic benefit for the heir.

---

25. Hening, *Statutes*, vol. 2, 270.

In the former act . . . it is provided that sheep, horses, and cattle should be delivered in kind to the orphan when they came of age . . . to which some have desired that negroes may be added; this assembly considering the difficulty of procureing negroes in kind as also the value and hazard of their lives have doubted whether any sufficient men would be found who would engage themselves to deliver negroes of equall ages if the specificall negroes should dye, or become by age or accident unserviceable; be it therefore enacted . . . that the consideration of this be referred to the county courts who are hereby authorized and empowred either to cause such negroes to be duly apprized, sold at an outcry, or preserved in kind, as they then find it most expedient for preservation, improvement or advancement of the estate and interest of such orphans.[26]

Since the slaves were property, additional laws were required to define the specific type of property. A 1705 law, part of the comprehensive set of laws concerning slavery enacted that year determined that slaves would be considered the same as real estate.

All negro, mulatto, and Indian slaves . . . within this dominion, shall be held, taken, and adjudged, to be real estate (and not chattels;) and shall descend unto heirs and widows . . . according to the manner and custom of land of inheritance, held in fee simple.[27]

The law made an exception for slave merchants, who owned slaves as personal property, and also specified that though slaves were owned as real estate this didn't qualify the owner as a landowner for voting purposes.[28]

A court ruling in 1730, Tucker v. Sweney, determined that slaves held by executors of estates were also considered personal property. "So that in this Case they are considered no otherwise than Horses or Cattle."[29] In 1748, the law was changed to classify all slaves as personal property rather than as real estate.[30] In all those laws and rulings, the concern was always how to make the system work; the humanity of the slaves was never a factor. In fact, whether slaves were treated as real estate or as "no otherwise than horses or cattle," the lawmakers, and the laws of the colony, clearly separated them from the human race.

26. Ibid., 288.
27. Hening, *Statutes,* vol. 3, 333.
28. Ibid., 333–34.
29. Barton, *Virginia Colonial Decisions,* R39.
30. Hening, *Statutes,* vol. 5, 432–48.

Slavery in the other Twelve Colonies

All of the other twelve colonies allowed slavery at the time of the Revolutionary War. The other colonies, all founded after Virginia, each followed a somewhat different path in the evolution of slavery.

South Carolina, for instance, was founded in 1663 by plantation owners who came from the British Island of Barbados, which previously had been settled by the British in 1627. Slavery existed in Barbados from its beginning, as the British settlers there came with the intent to set up plantations and brought slaves with them. Those Barbados plantation owners who subsequently founded South Carolina initially relied on indentured servants to fill their labor needs, as had Virginia.[31] Unlike Virginia though, the transition from indentured servants to slaves as the principal form of labor in South Carolina happened very quickly. The development of rice as the major agricultural product of the colony by the 1690s created a need for workers that could not be filled by the limited number of indentured servants; within a decade there were more black slaves in the colony than Whites.[32] As documented by Higginbotham, the evolution of laws regulating slavery, and the treatment of Blacks in general, then followed a pattern very similar to that in Virginia.

Georgia, founded much later in 1732, was chartered with the specific intent of providing employment and economic opportunity for the poor of England and also to provide protection to South Carolina from the Spanish and the Native Americans to the south. Slavery was inconsistent with both of those objectives and was expressly prohibited by a law passed in 1735.[33] Slave labor would have reduced the number of jobs available for the English poor who were to be given the opportunity for employment in the colony. Also, slaves could not be used in the militias needed to provide protection from the Spanish and the Native Americans, as well as from slave uprisings. The large numbers of slaves and limited number of Whites in South Carolina resulted in its inability to raise the military force needed to protect itself against those threats. The founders of Georgia were determined not to duplicate that situation; instead, they populated their colony primarily with Whites, who were then capable of providing a strong military.

The 1735 law was enacted solely to implement the initial objectives of the colony and had nothing to do with protecting slaves or free Blacks. In fact, the experiences and attitudes of the other colonies were clearly

31. Higginbotham, *In the Matter of Color,* 152.

32. Ibid., 166.

33. Candler, *Colonial Records,* 49–52.

reflected in the provisions of the law. For instance, while the law prohibited the importation or use of slaves in the colony, it also contained a fugitive slave provision where any fugitive slaves from any other colonies, apprehended in Georgia, had to be returned to their owners upon payment of the costs of apprehension.[34] Further, the law also prohibited the importation of free Blacks as well as slaves because, according to the preamble to the law, in other colonies the presence of "Black Slaves or Negroes" had "Obstructed the Increase of English and Christian Inhabitants."[35]

For a variety of reasons, the prohibition of slavery was widely opposed, ignored and un-enforced from the beginning, and within fifteen years it had been repealed.[36] According to Higginbotham's research, despite Georgia's late acceptance of slavery "with the writing and passage of slave codes of 1755, 1765, and 1770, Georgia quickly became as strict as any other American colony in the prohibitions on freedom enforced against enslaved blacks."[37]

The actual numbers of enslaved people in the northern colonies were generally significantly less than in the southern agricultural colonies, but the practice was condoned and regulated and slaves were held in every colony. Further, the wealthy merchants of the northern colonies were directly involved in the slave trade and had strong business ties to the plantation owners in the southern colonies and in the Caribbean. Those merchants owned the ships that made regular sailings to Africa to acquire as many captives as could be squeezed into their holds. The ships were also used to provide supplies to the plantation owners and to bring the products of the plantations to the markets in the north. In his book, *Ebony and Ivy*, historian Craig Steven Wilder provides this summary:

> New Englanders were partners in the rise of Atlantic slavery. Puritan merchants carried food, timber, animals and other supplies to the expanding markets of the English, French, Spanish, and Dutch colonies . . . Puritans also supplied the Carolinas and Virginia and brought the products of slave labor and other materials back to New England, where they built new ships and launched new ventures. New Englanders entered the Atlantic slave economy as shippers, insurers, manufacturers, and investors. For two centuries the Caribbean and southern markets buoyed the New England economy, and ships from

34. Ibid., 51–52.
35. Ibid., 50.
36. Higginbotham, *In the Matter of Color*, 241–49; Candler, *Colonial Records*, 57.
37. Higginbotham, *In the Matter of Color*, 217.

Massachusetts, Connecticut, Rhode Island, and New Hampshire filled West Indian ports.[38]

The Role of Universities

Wilder's book also explores the role of universities during the colonial period and some general comments on the subject are appropriate at this point. While the Ivy League is actually a grouping for intercollegiate sports competitions, the term is also commonly used to reflect the schools' status as among the most elite in the country. Of the eight universities in the Ivy League, seven were chartered before the revolutionary war: Harvard in Massachusetts in 1636, Yale in Connecticut in 1701, Princeton in New Jersey in 1746, University of Pennsylvania in Pennsylvania in 1749, Columbia University in New York in 1754, Brown University in Rhode Island in 1764, and Dartmouth in New Hampshire in 1769. Two other highly regarded Universities, though not in the Ivy League, had also been chartered prior to the revolution: William and Mary in Virginia in 1693 and Rutgers in New Jersey in 1766.[39]

One of the primary purposes of the earliest universities was the training of missionaries to spread Christianity among the Native Americans. Relations between the colonists and the many Native American nations varied significantly over time and by region, ranging from friendly alliances, to tolerance, to periodic raids conducted by both sides, to outright war. The steady westward expansion of the colonies created tensions and regular conflicts with the original inhabitants.

Unlike the way pre-colonial North America is often portrayed as vast areas of unoccupied, undeveloped, and underutilized forests and plains, the continent was actually covered with hundreds of separate nations and communities. Much of the forestland was groomed to attract deer and other game animals. Permanent communities were surrounded by hundreds of acres of cultivated farmland producing corn, beans, squash, potatoes, and other vegetables. The people cultivated berry patches and managed orchards of nut and fruit trees.[40] The continent was covered with hundreds of miles of roads and trade routes connecting the many communities.[41]

---

38. Wilder, *Ebony & Ivy*, 32.

39. Ibid., 17, 49.

40. Ibid., 149–179; Dunbar-Ortiz, *An Indigenous Peoples' History*, 21–25, 27–31.

41. Dunbar-Ortiz, *An Indigenous Peoples' History*, 28–30.

The regular contact between the colonists and the original inhabitants indicates the density of the local population when the Europeans arrived. The investors in England and in the colonies felt that by educating the natives in the religion and customs of the English they could be assimilated and further conflicts could be avoided.[42] Harvard and William and Mary both established separate Indian colleges for the training of Native American youths who could then be sent back to their nations to spread the English religion and customs among their people.[43] Much of the original funding for these universities came from investors in England.

The Indian colleges produced limited results and were soon discontinued, but the new universities did provide an alternative for sons of wealthy plantation owners who previously had to travel to England, Scotland, and Ireland to attend universities. And the growing numbers of wealthy merchants were able to provide domestic funding in place of that previously provided by English investors for the Indian colleges.

By the time of the revolution, nine universities had been established, all except William and Mary located in the northern colonies. All were affiliated with religious denominations,[44] and many of the graduates became ministers,[45] although the ministry did not necessarily mean poverty. Ministers often owned slaves and were landowners, as well.[46] In addition, the universities often owned plantations and plantation slaves that had been donated by wealthy benefactors. Slaves were also a normal part of university campuses, performing the many tasks needed to build and maintain the facilities for housing and teaching the students.

Despite the free labor and the sponsorship of wealthy merchants, tuition-paying students were also needed to cover the costs of operating the universities. The wealthy plantation owners in the southern colonies and the West Indies were actively solicited for their sons' enrollment. In some cases, housing was even provided for the personal slaves of those students who chose to bring them.[47] Upon graduation, armed with an education specifically designed for their roles as future leaders and with connections formed during several years of living with others similarly trained, the graduates returned home to build or enlarge their fortunes as plantation owners and merchants. The universities would then rely on them for future students

42. Wilder, *Ebony & Ivy*, 21.
43. Ibid., 26, 43–44.
44. Ibid., 17, 49.
45. Ibid., 85–86.
46. Ibid.
47. Ibid., 136

and donations. The trustees of the universities were the merchants doing business with the plantation owners, and the universities became one more business connection.

3

Religion

Though their religious affiliations and practices varied, all of the colonies considered themselves Christian. As in the Virginia laws, the laws of all of the colonies often distinguished between Christians and non-Christians. Religion and morality were important to the colonists, and many of their policies and laws were guided by religious principles. In Christianity, the Bible provided the moral guidelines, but those guidelines have always been subject to interpretation. The interpretations came from human beings whose motives were not always objective or pure.

The defenders of slavery in this country borrowed from earlier interpretations, created their own theories where necessary, and in general became quite adept at fitting the Bible verses to their cause. The biblical justification for enslaving Blacks was based on interpreting certain passages as proof that people of African descent were a deficient and cursed branch of the human family. Since those interpretations applied to all people of African ancestry, that naturally affected people's perceptions of free Blacks as well. The resulting discrimination and abuse against free Blacks during slavery, and against all Blacks since, was inevitable. An example cited in chapter 11 shows that a century after slavery ended, the Bible continued to be used as justification for discrimination against people of African descent.

Moral Justification of Slavery

It is important to emphasize at the outset that there is a difference between belief in a religion and the use of religion to rationalize behaviors that basic humanity and common sense would ordinarily condemn. The following review is not intended as a comment on Christian doctrine, or the text of the Bible. It is instead a careful look at how some humans found a way to use the Bible to justify the enslavement, and subsequent mistreatment, of other human beings.

Chapter 1 showed that one of the ways used to justify the slave raids in Africa was the conversion of pagans to Christianity. When, after several generations of slavery in the various colonies, the Christians' desire to spread the faith through baptism coincided with American born slaves' readiness and willingness to adopt the religion of their masters, the possibility that this might result in freeing the slaves created a quandary that had to be addressed. Chapter 2 cited a 1624 case where the General Court of Virginia treated a black man as free specifically because he had been baptized in England. A 1667 Virginia law addressed the concerns of slave owners:

> Whereas some doubts have risen whether children that are slaves by birth, and by the charity and pity of their owners made pertakers of the blessed sacrament of baptisme, should by virtue of their baptisme be made free, it is enacted . . . that the conferring of baptisme doth not alter the condition of the person as to his bondage or freedome . . . .[1]

The Duke of York Laws, which had been adopted by New York, Pennsylvania, and Delaware in 1665,[2] simultaneously recognized slavery for non-Christians, prohibited it for Christians, and specified that conversion to Christianity subsequent to enslavement did not lead to freedom.[3] Maryland enacted a law in 1671 expressly stating that a slave's baptism would not result in him or her being set free,[4] and South Carolina did the same in 1712.[5] The fact that so many of the colonies felt the need to address this question in their laws shows the extent of their reliance on conversion to Christianity as justification for slavery. While the new laws removed the threat to the institution of slavery, they also removed the conversion justification that had been used since the time of the Papal Bulls.

1. Hening, *Statutes,* vol. 2, 260.

2. Higginbotham, *In the Matter of Color,* 126, 270.

3. Ibid., 126–28, 270–71; *Colonial Laws of New York,* 18; Beckman, *Statutes at Large of Pennsylvania,* 78; Higginbotham, *In the Matter of Color,* 270.

4. Franklin and Moss, *From Slavery to Freedom,* 68.

5. Higginbotham, *In the Matter of Color,* 200.

Use of Bible Interpretations to Justify Slavery

Yet there was a way to use the Bible, particularly the Book of Genesis, to find alternative moral justifications for slavery and racism. The books of the original Bible are ancient writings, used first by the Jews and later adopted by both Christians and Muslims. It has gone through many translations, and survives in modern times in many versions. The study of the Bible is extremely complex, involving a study of history, religions, languages, and interpretations spanning centuries. Biblical scholars have been able to re-solve some questions with reasonable certainty, but in other cases have been limited to choosing between possible answers. David M. Goldenberg, who has a doctorate in Post-Biblical Literature and Institutions, is one of those biblical scholars. In his book, *The Curse of Ham: Race and Slavery in Early Judism, Christianity, and Islam,* he examines the Bible texts and interpreta-tions through the ages. His extensive research shows that there is nothing in the Bible that condemns Africans in any way.

> I found no indications of a negative sentiment toward Blacks in the Bible. Aside from its use in a proverb (found also among the Egyptians and Greeks), skin color is never mentioned in descriptions of biblical Kushites. That is the most significant perception, or lack of perception, in the biblical image of the black African. Color did not matter.[6]

He did find, though, that since ancient times interpretations of Bible passages have been tailored to justify conditions of the era in which they originated.[7] Interpretations connecting Africans and skin color to slavery did originate in the Middle East, but did not begin to appear until more modern times. The reliance on biblical interpretation by proponents of slavery in the United States was not new, but its widespread use shows the importance of that moral justification for many. The interpretations used to justify slavery will be discussed below.

Families of Mankind

It is helpful to look at how the Book of Genesis set the stage for group-ing human beings into distinct "races." Genesis, the first book of the Bible, gives the ancient account of the origins of the world and mankind. Accord-ing to the Bible, Adam and Eve were the first humans, but the great flood

6. Goldenberg, *The Curse of Ham,* 195.
7. Ibid., 8.

destroyed everyone except Noah and his family. Noah and his three sons and their wives were the only survivors, and all of mankind has followed from them. Chapter 9 of Genesis lists Noah's three sons:

> And the sons of Noah, that went forth of the ark, were Shem, and Ham, and Japheth: and Ham is the father of Canaan. These are the three sons of Noah: and of them was the whole earth overspread.[8]

Chapter 10 of Genesis lists the children and grandchildren of each of the three sons, indicates the territory each of the families occupied and finishes with: "These are the families of the sons of Noah, after their generations, in their nations: and by these were the nations divided in the earth after the flood."[9] This chapter is referred to as the "Table of Nations," and when plotted on a map shows Ham and his descendants occupying northern Africa, Shem and his descendants occupying the Arabian Peninsula, and Japheth and his descendants occupying the area north of that. This was the extent of the known world at the time and this chapter of Genesis was the attempt to explain the different nations living within that known area. The Bible itself gives no significance either to the individual families or to the territories they occupied.

As knowledge of the world expanded and the center of power moved to Rome, it became commonly accepted that Africans were the descendants of Ham, Europeans were the descendants of Japheth, and the people of the Middle East and the Far East were descendants of Shem.[10] This three-way division of mankind provided a credible explanation for the differences between people from the various parts of the world. The three main religions—Judaism, Christianity and Islam—all have some version of Genesis in their holy books. For a significant part of the world population, the idea of three families of mankind was, and continues to be, a matter of religious doctrine revealed by God. As a simple account of three family lines to explain the origins of the different nations of humans, this story presents no problem. The problem arose when rankings of relative worth and goodness were superimposed on the family lines. Those rankings did not exist in early times, as noted by Goldenberg:

> We today are heirs to centuries of anti-Black sentiment, which has greatly conditioned our perspective. As a consequence, people—in and out of the academic world—readily assume

8. Gen. 9:18–19 (King James Version).
9. Gen. 10:32 (King James Version).
10. Haynes, *Noah's Curse*, 5–6.

that Blacks were always viewed pejoratively. But as I immersed myself in the literary remains of ancient Judaism, it became increasingly apparent that a different way of thinking about humanity was operating in the Mediterranean and Near Eastern civilizations of earlier times . . . .

In those earlier times color did not define a person and was not a criterion for categorizing humanity.[11]

The Curse of Ham

In his book, *Noah's Curse: The Biblical Justification of American Slavery,* Stephen R. Haynes notes that starting in the second century of the Common Era there were a few references in Bible interpretations that connected Blacks with slavery.[12] But it wasn't until the seventh century that the connection was made with any regularity. According to Goldenberg, "From the seventh century onward, the Curse of Ham is commonly found in works composed in the Near East, whether in Arabic by Muslims or in Syriac by Christians. The increasing reliance on the Curse coincides with the increasing numbers of Blacks taken as slaves into the Islamic world."[13]

Defenders of slavery in this country used the Curse as one of their main arguments from the beginning, but its use is most evident in those periods when slavery came under the most aggressive attack, such as during the early nineteenth century, when abolitionists were having some success ending slavery in the northern states. According to Haynes, by the 1830s "Noah's Curse had become a stock weapon in the arsenal of slavery's apologists, and references to Genesis 9 appeared prominently in their publications."[14]

Noah's Curse, or the Curse of Ham, appears in Verses 20 to 25 of chapter 9 of Genesis, as part of the story of Noah and his three sons immediately after the flood:

> And Noah began to be an husbandman, and he planted a vineyard: And he drank of the wine, and was drunken; and he was uncovered within his tent. And Ham, the father of Canaan, saw the nakedness of his father, and told his two brethren without. And Shem and Japheth took a garment, and laid it upon both their shoulders, and went backward, and covered the nakedness of their father; and their faces were backward, and they saw not

11. Goldenberg, *The Curse of Ham*, 200.

12. Haynes, *Noah's Curse*, 7.

13. Goldenberg, *The Curse of Ham*, 174.

14. Haynes, *Noah's Curse*, 8.

their father's nakedness. And Noah awoke from his wine, and knew what his younger son had done unto him. And he said, Cursed be Canaan; a servant of servants shall he be unto his brethren.[15]

These six verses are vague in a number of ways, resulting in an endless variety of interpretations that claim to explain the exact meaning. The most obvious question is: why is it that Canaan is cursed for his father's offense? The likely answer is that the original writing—apparently from around the tenth century BCE during a period when Canaanites were being enslaved by the Israelite monarchy—was used in the same way subsequent interpretations were often used—to justify conditions at the time.[16]

Of course, for those wanting to use those verses in later times, that inconsistency presented a challenge that had to be overcome. Many different interpretations spanning centuries remain in various written records available for study by biblical scholars.[17] For this overview, I will address only those that were used in this country, and those pretty generally. Each writer had his own way of looking at the details of the story and explaining them, so there were many variations. But, in general, the underlying arguments were the same.

The first challenge was to make the verses apply specifically to Blacks. Since the Table of Nations had placed Ham and his descendants in Africa, it was assumed that all Africans were descended from Ham. The name Ham was also generally accepted to have been derived from words in various Middle Eastern languages meaning "black" or "dark" or "hot," or combinations such as "scorched." A careful study of linguistics has shown the assumed name derivatives to be in error, but at the time they helped support the idea of all Blacks descending from Ham.[18]

But the Bible passage explicitly states that the curse was on only one of Ham's sons, Canaan; and Canaan and his descendants were not black.[19] To make the curse of slavery fall on all Blacks, the curse had to be on Ham and all of his descendants. A number of creative ways were used to make that happen. Some just substituted Ham's name for Canaan, while others found ways to show a symbolism in the way the names were used that really showed the curse was on Ham. One of the more easily understood explanations was that since God had previously blessed Ham along with his broth-

15. Gen. 9:20–25 (King James Version).

16. Haynes, *Noah's Curse*, 6; Goldenberg, *The Curse of Ham*, 98.

17. Goldenberg, *The Curse of Ham*, 157–77.

18. Ibid., 141–56.

19. Ibid., 101.

ers, the only way he could be cursed was through his son, and that is how it was done.[20]

One final challenge remained: explaining how the simple act of seeing his father naked in his tent justified a curse of perpetual slavery on Ham's descendants. Haynes found that in many Middle Eastern interpretations the simple statement that Noah, "knew what his younger son had done unto him" was used to imply a sexual offense such as attempted rape or castration of his father, or incest with his mother, increasing the seriousness of the offense.[21] He also found that defenders of slavery in this country avoided the sexual implications and were more inclined to focus on the issue of honor and dishonor. They embellished a bit by suggesting that Ham's offense included mocking and ridiculing Noah, and attempting to get his brothers to do the same, rather than just failing to cover him. This then demonstrated that he was fundamentally dishonorable, a character trait that infected all of his descendants and justified their perpetual slavery.[22]

Haynes's review of the writings citing the Curse of Ham as a defense of slavery in the United States identifies three different approaches: the majority merely cited the Curse without telling the story or analyzing it; the second group told the story or paraphrased it without discussing the nature of Ham's offense; only the third group went into any detail regarding the offense that resulted in the curse.[23] The fact that in the majority of cases a simple citing of the curse was all that was necessary is an indication that most people knew about it and accepted it as moral justification of slavery. It was common knowledge that God had revealed the curse in the Bible, and there was no need to dwell on the details. It was only when there was a need to formally counter the arguments of abolitionists that all of the details had to be presented, and inconsistencies had to be explained.

20. Ibid., 158.
21. Haynes, *Noah's Curse*, 67.
22. Ibid., 70–78.
23. Ibid., 70.

4

Science

At the same time as slavery was coming into use in the English colonies, science was evolving in Europe. The same oceangoing ships that enabled colonization and the slave trade also enabled the discovery of new and different plants and animals from around the world. Science was not new, but these new discoveries dramatically increased the interest in natural science. Unfortunately, the timing of this new interest also resulted in the misuse of science to justify slavery and the ranking of groups of human beings by intelligence and worth.

In the interest of presenting the development of racism chronologically, I have separated the review of the involvement of science into two parts. This chapter shows how the stage was set for the blatant misuse of science that followed. The early scientific study of mankind had to be superimposed on the commonly held beliefs drawn from the Bible. The resistance of the general public, including the scientists themselves, to ideas counter to their long held beliefs meant the early scientific theories had to maintain some similarity to the old beliefs.

At the same time, science was supposed to be totally objective. Because of the limited amount of scientific data that were available in the early stages, and the lack of the analytical methods and technology we have today, mistakes were made. More important than the mistakes made by those early scientists is the way those mistakes were compounded by subsequent scientists. That compounding of the early errors was consciously and subconsciously done in the defense of slavery and racism.

That process occurred throughout the nineteenth century, and will be discussed in chapter 9.

The Origin of Scientific Groupings of Humans

Carl Linnaeus of Sweden, who was trained in botany and medicine, made valuable contributions to the field of science but also laid the groundwork for the misuse of science to perpetuate the idea of Blacks as inferior. Linnaeus developed the system of classifying plants and animals that is still used today. Before he died he had classified 7,700 species of plants and 4,400 species of animals.[1] In his book, *Systema Naturae* printed in 1735, he classified man with the apes and monkeys in a category he called "manlike" and divided man into four groups by color and geographic distribution: Europeus albus (white), Americanus rubescens (red), Asiaticus fuscus (brown) and Africanus niger (black).[2]

He was immediately criticized for including man with the animals. The criticism came from other scientists, but the basis of their objection was that this conflicted with the Bible teaching that man was made in the image of God and was above the animals. Linnaeus persisted, and in later editions he changed the group name to "primates" and changed the color of Asiaticus to luridus (yellow). He also expanded the definitions of the groups by adding a one-word descriptor for stature, by assigning one of the four humors of Greek and Roman medicine to each, and by adding appearance and behavior characteristics. His final categories were:

Europeus, white, sanquine, muscular
hair blond long, eyes blue, active, astute, inventive, covered with close vestments, ruled by laws.

Americanus, red, choleric, erect
hair black straight thick, wide nostrils, face harsh, beard scanty, obstinate, contented, free, paints himself with fine red lines, ruled by customs.

Asiaticus, yellow, melancholy, rigid
hair black, eyes dark, severe, haughty, avaricious, covered with loose garments, ruled by opinions.

Afer, black, phlegmatic, relaxed

1. Stearn, "The Background of Linnaeus's Contributions."
2. Linnaeus, *Systema naturae*, 1735; Baum, *The Rise and Fall*, 65.

hair black kinked, skin silky, nose flat, lips enlarged, women without shame, breasts lactate profusely, crafty, slow, negligent, anoints himself with grease, ruled by whims.[3]

Linnaeus was a man of science. He neither owned slaves nor participated in the slave trade. His interest was in classifying plants and animals as accurately as possible. But classifications are based on differences. And in his attempt to classify humans, whose only truly objective differences were skin color and geographic distribution, Linnaeus made the mistake of assigning appearance and behavioral characteristics to each group, not based on objective observation or testing, but on the stereotypes that had been created solely to justify slavery. This was not a simple mistake. He had never traveled farther than England and France,[4] and had no opportunity to observe or interact with people from other parts of the world. Yet he published in a scientific text—as objective fact—differences among humans that he surely knew he had no personal knowledge of.

The Origin of "Races"

Another man who made a small but unique contribution was Georges-Louis Leclerc, Comte de Buffon, a French naturalist whose book, *Natural History, General and Particular*, was published in 1749. He describes several groups of humans that he refers to as races. This is the first use of the term "race" in a scientific publication, though it appears he intended it in a general sense rather than as specific classifications.[5] Nonetheless, Ashley Montagu, in his book, *Man's Most Dangerous Myth: The Fallacy of Race*, describes Buffon's contribution in this way:

> Since Buffon's works were widely read and were translated into many European languages, he must be held at least partially responsible for the diffusion of the idea of a natural separation of the 'races' of man, though he himself does not appear to have had such an idea in mind.[6]

3. Linnaeus, *Systema naturae*, 1766; Gould, *The Mismeasure*, 404–5; Slotkin, *Readings*, 177–78; Baum, *The Rise and Fall*, 65–66; Bendyshe, *History of Anthropology*, 424–26; Jordan, *White Over Black*, 220–21; slight variations in translations due entirely to English synonyms chosen.

4. Linnean Society, "Who Was Linneaus?"; Smedley, *Race in North America*, 221–23.

5. Montagu, *Man's Most Dangerous Myth*, 46–47.

6. Ibid. 47.

One other man worthy of special note at this point is Johann Fried-rich Blumenbach, a German anthropologist who provided the classifications that have been carried forward to the present time. The terminology has been modified somewhat over time, but the classifications are generally unchanged. In the third edition of his book, *On the Natural Variety of Mankind*, published in 1795, Blumenbach divided man into five groups: the Caucasian variety, the Mongolian variety, the Ethiopian variety, the American variety, and the Malay variety.[7] These were essentially the same groups used by Linnaeus except that instead of the single Asiaticus group, Blumenbach had two—the Mongolian and the Malay varieties.

In the naming and explaining of the five groups Blumenbach also introduced some new ideas concerning mankind. Most telling is his explanation of the Caucasian variety:

> I have taken the name of this variety from Mount Caucasus, both because its neighbourhood, and especially its southern slope, produces the most beautiful race of men, I mean the Georgian; and because all physiological reasons converge to this, that in that region, if anywhere, it seems we ought with the greatest probability to place the autochthones of mankind. For in the first place, that stock displays, as we have seen . . . the most beautiful form of the skull, from which, as from a mean and primeval type, the others diverge by most easy gradations on both sides to the two ultimate extremes (that is, on the one side the Mongolian, on the other the Ethiopian). Besides, it is white in colour, which we may fairly assume to have been the primitive colour of mankind, since, as we have shown above . . . it is very easy for that to degenerate into brown, but very much more difficult for dark to become white, when the secretion and precipitation of this carbonaceous pigment has once deeply struck root.[8]

While scholars agree that his use of the word "degenerate" did not at that time carry the negative connotation that it does now, but rather simply refers to a change from the original form,[9] there is no doubt that he does not see the changes as being for the better. An earlier passage is equally indicative of his perspective:

> I have allotted the first place to the Caucasian, for the reasons given below, which make me esteem it the primeval one. This

7. Gould, *The Mismeasure of Man*, 402.
8. Bendyshe, *Anthropological Treatises*, 269.
9. Gould, *The Mismeasure of Man*, 407.

diverges in both directions into two, most remote and very different from each other; on the one side, namely, into the Ethiopian, and on the other into the Mongolian. The remaining two
occupy the intermediate positions between that primeval one
and these two extreme varieties; that is, the American between
the Caucasian and Mongolian; the Malay between the same
Caucasian and Ethiopian.[10]

Blumenbach was not a racist. He knew that his categories were arbitrary and simply argued that they were the best for the purpose of the study
of man. He was an abolitionist who collected and admired the literary works
of black authors. In his words, "It would not be difficult to mention entire
well-known provinces of Europe, from out of which you would not easily
expect to obtain off-hand such good authors, poets, philosophers, and cor-
respondents of the Paris Academy."[11]

And yet, his acknowledgement of the arbitrariness of his own classifications of human varieties notwithstanding, he chose to use his obviously
subjective opinion regarding beauty to draw a scientific conclusion regarding the original perfect form of humanity and the degree of subsequent
divergence from that original perfection. This certainly gave license to later
hierarchical ranking of human groups, even if there is some question regarding his true feelings about the subject. The terminology he originated
proved to be totally meaningless from a scientific standpoint. Yet it survives
today, and continues to give "scientific" support to the erroneous idea of
separate races that can be ranked by character and intelligence.

10. Bendyshe, *Anthropological Treatises*, 264–65.

11. Bendyshe, *Anthropological Treatises*, 310–12; Gould, *The Mismeasure of Man*,
408–10.

5

1776

On July 4, 1776, fifty-six prominent leaders from all of the thirteen original colonies adopted the Declaration of Independence, establishing the United States of America as an independent nation. The second sentence of the declaration stated unequivocally: "We hold these truths to be self evident, that all men are created equal, that they are endowed by their Creator with certain unalienable rights, that among these are life, liberty and the pursuit of happiness." We look to those words as proof of the true ideal and character of this country and the leaders who were there at its inception. But looking to the words alone, and not the reality that was taking place, allows us to delude ourselves about where we now stand regarding equality and how we got here.

Thomas Jefferson of Virginia was the person who wrote the initial draft of that founding document, including that second sentence. Yet at the time he owned over one hundred slaves.[1] A significant number of the others who signed on to those words owned slaves as well.[2] Our Constitution, as adopted eleven years later, counted slaves as three-fifths of a person for allocating taxes and representation. Four of our first five presidents, including George Washington, owned slaves while they were in office.[3]

This information is not new, and recent decades have seen an emphasis on presenting a more complete and accurate picture of our founding. But

---

1. Jordan, *White Over Black*, 431.
2. "The Founding Fathers"; "How many of the signers."
3. Lopresti, "Which U.S. Presidents."

information alone is not enough. Andrew Levy summarizes the problem in his book, *The First Emancipator*:

> In the interest of promoting a multicultural (or at least bicultural) vision of American history, teachers, scholars, writers, politicians, and students alike have accepted what amounts to a schizophrenic version of our nation's founding. It is only a radical tenth on one edge of the political spectrum that refuses to acknowledge that Thomas Jefferson was a significant defender of the principles of freedom, and it is only another radical tenth on the other edge that refuses to acknowledge that his practice of keeping slaves was a stunning contradiction to his articulation of those principles. The rest of us inhabit a murky middle of the road where Jefferson and Washington, the signers of the Declaration of Independence and the writers of the Constitution, seem to have given us a riddle instead of a country: were they the best of men, or the best of hypocrites?
>
> Because this perspective seems evenhanded, even sophisticated, we forget that it has been out in the open for four or five decades, and we have grown complacent with it. In this new mythos of American history, we *accept* that we are a people badly divided about race.[4]

The problem for us is knowing what to do with this information. Debating the correct balance between honor and blame for these men serves no purpose, but neither does simply accepting the contradictions we see. Those contradictions are not irreconcilable, and they are not irrelevant to our present situation. It is important that we understand the founders and their time so that we can better understand our time and our division about race.

Attitudes and conditions existed at that time that allowed highly educated men to build a nation on the principles of equality and liberty for all and at the same time continue to hold other men, women, and children in lifetime bondage. We must not disregard that reality when we look back at these men and what they built. The reality does not in any way diminish what they accomplished, but it did affect what was left undone. They accomplished what they intended to—the formation of a new independent nation out of thirteen separate colonies. They used the words they needed to accomplish that end, not hypocritically, but also not as we would use them today.

4. Levy, *The First Emancipator*, 193.

All of the founding fathers were leaders in their respective colonies: landowners, businessmen, and lawyers. Most came from prominent families that had been here for generations. They had grown up with slavery, and for many of them slavery was an integral part of their daily lives.[5] It is unlikely that men who had spent their entire lives on plantations where slaves were bought and sold and regarded as property would have considered them as equals. It is their words, rather than their actions, that seem inconsistent with their era.

But viewed in a different light, their words were entirely consistent. There is a subtle, but significant, difference between equality of rights to life, liberty, and the pursuit of happiness, and equality of mental and physical aptitudes. There's no question that many people, including many of the founding fathers, were conflicted by the slaves' lack of liberty while the nation fought a war to secure its own liberty from England. But birth with equal rights and birth with equal capabilities were two very different things, and the truth of the former did not depend on the truth of the latter.

Though Thomas Jefferson never actually freed his own slaves, his writings show that he favored a gradual ending of slavery nationwide. In his *Notes on the State of Virginia*, he gave a summary of proposed legislation: "To emancipate all slaves born after passing the act."[6] The proposed legislation would have replaced the slaves with additional white immigrants while sending the emancipated slaves "to such place as the circumstances of the time should render most proper."[7] Jefferson explained that provision in this way:

> It will probably be asked, Why not retain and incorporate the blacks into the State, and thus save the expense of supplying, by importation of white settlers, the vacancies they will leave? Deep-rooted prejudices entertained by the whites; ten thousand recollections by the blacks of the injuries they have sustained; new provocations; the real distinctions which Nature has made; and many other circumstances, will divide us into parties, and produce convulsions, which will probably never end but in the extermination of the one or the other race. To these objections, which are political, may be added others, which are physical and moral.[8]

5. National Archives, *Signers of the Declaration of Independence*.

6. Jefferson, *Notes*, 148.

7. Ibid., 149.

8. Ibid.

That was followed by six pages describing differences, always reflecting negatively on Blacks and ending with the following conclusion:

> I advance it therefore as a suspicion only, that the blacks, whether originally a distinct race, or made distinct by time and circumstances, are inferior to the whites in the endowments both of body and mind. It is not against experience to suppose that different species of the same genus, or varieties of the same species, may possess different qualifications.[9]

His words speak for themselves and represent the views commonly held at the time. An illuminating contrast is provided by one of Jefferson's friends, Robert Carter III, the subject of Levy's book, *The First Emancipator.* Carter was one of the wealthiest men in Virginia, and he freed all of his slaves, over four hundred and fifty of them, before he died.[10] The thing that set Carter apart was the way he related to his slaves. From the extensive journals, plantation record books, and correspondence left from that time, Levy was able to describe in detail Carter's life and the attitudes and activities of the era he lived in.

He found, for example, that at the balls regularly held by the plantation owners, some slaveholders "thought that their recipes for the torture and domination of African servants were topics for polite conversation."[11] Carter would leave early rather than participate in those conversations.[12] In an era when slaves were never allowed to testify against a white person,[13] Carter regularly accepted the word of his slaves against his white tenants and overseers.[14] When most slaveholders considered it dangerous to educate slaves, Carter had them trained as brick masons, barbers, blacksmiths, butchers, etc. Many had multiple skills.[15] When they were ultimately freed by Carter, they had skills that enabled them to find employment to support themselves. Carter allowed slaves to choose their own spouses[16] and kept families together when he moved them from one plantation to another.[17] Like many plantation owners, Carter was a religious man; unlike the others,

---

9. Ibid., 155.

10. Levy, *The First Emancipator, xi.*

11. Ibid., 35.

12. Ibid., 63.

13. Higginbotham, *In the Matter of Color,* 58.

14. Levy, *The First Emancipator,* 53, 109.

15. Ibid., 52–53, 111.

16. Ibid., 54.

17. Ibid., 9, 62, 111, 121, 147.

he sought out churches that welcomed Blacks, free and slave, as well as Whites.[18]

Levy's book is full of the contrasts between the way Carter considered and treated his slaves as equals in their humanity and the way typical plantation owners considered and treated their slaves strictly as property, despite the fact that some could be shown to be more humane than others. Carter was clearly the exception that proved the rule that almost no plantation owner or politician of the time would have considered that Blacks were equal, as we currently use the term.

It serves no purpose to deceive ourselves about the founding of our country. The words in the Declaration of Independence notwithstanding, our country was not founded on the principle of everyone being created equal. The men we call the founding fathers did a remarkable thing, creating a nation out of thirteen separate and unique colonies. They left us a governing document, our Constitution, which has served us amazingly well for over two hundred years with only twenty-seven amendments. The first ten amendments, the Bill of Rights, were anticipated at the beginning and were ratified simultaneously less than three years after the Constitution was adopted. Two subsequent amendments related to the adoption (and later repeal) of prohibition, leaving only fifteen actual changes. The provision for change written into the original document is a testament to the foresight of the founders and has allowed it to accommodate massive changes since the union of the original thirteen states.

But they did not give us equality. They permitted the continuation of lifetime bondage of some human beings, while promoting liberty and a Bill of Rights for everyone else. This is the reality. Being honest about the reality does not diminish what they did give us. In fact, understanding the times they lived in leads to the inevitable conclusion that the United States could not have been formed except by permitting slavery to continue.

Slavery was much more than just a side story to the founding of the United States. Slavery made colonization possible because the forced importation of massive numbers of free laborers made the colonies economically viable. Though some colonies were prepared to end slavery following the break from England, the economies of others were still very dependent on slave labor. Insisting on an end to slavery at that time would have resulted in a very different country than we now have. It really was an either/or situation, and the choice was made to accept the compromises needed to gain the participation of all thirteen colonies in forming the Union. The founding fathers succeeded in forming a new nation. They were not able to

18. Ibid., 65–93.

end slavery or the effects of one hundred and fifty years of justifying it. That was left to later generations.

That the country we now have could not have been formed without retaining slavery becomes obvious when looking at the intensity of the debate about slavery that followed the founding. It took a civil war to resolve the issue, a war that almost destroyed the country that had been formed eighty-five years earlier. The following chapter looks at that period and how the debate about slavery divided the country. It also explores how the color divide that had been created to support slavery was developing into the racism that took on a life of its own.

6

Racism

The Declaration of Independence and the subsequent war for independence from England resulted in significant traction for the abolitionist movement. In 1787, the drafters of the Constitution included a clause allowing for a national prohibition against the importation of slaves after January 1, 1808. The twenty-year delay was to gain the support of the southern states, not because of any hesitancy by the drafters.[1] On March 2, 1807, Congress passed the law making the importation of slaves illegal, effective January 1 of the following year, the first date allowed by the Constitution. Many saw this as a necessary first step in outlawing slavery altogether.

But as the movement to end slavery was gaining momentum in the North, conditions in the South were having the opposite effect. The common cause against British rule had made compromise between the colonies beneficial. But after the Union was formed, the significant differences in the economic structures of the agricultural South and the industrial North made compromises increasingly difficult. The exponential growth of cotton production and profitability in the South, the struggles with the societal effects of freeing the slaves in the North, and the political battles involved in adding eleven new states to the Union in the first half century, all contributed to the rising tensions between the two regions.

The complex issue of slavery, which had been set aside when the country was formed, became the center of debate in the succeeding decades. A civil war finally resolved the issue and ended slavery in this country. But the racism that had served to justify and support slavery had been reinforced

---

1 Zinn, *A People's History*, 97.

by the bitter power struggle and a devastating war. Racism was taking on a life of its own, ensuring that it would live on long after the slavery that gave it birth had ended.

When Whiteness Became a Part of Federal Law

The first congress under the new Constitution met immediately after the effective date. Along with passing laws to set up the new government, the first congress also passed the Bill of Rights, the first ten amendments to the Constitution, which were then submitted to the states for ratification. The Bill of Rights was seen by many as an essential part of the Constitution in order to guarantee that the rights of all citizens were protected.

The first congress also passed the first naturalization act in 1790. The first line of that act stated that "any alien, being a free white person, who shall have resided within the limits and under the jurisdiction of the United States for the term of two years, may be admitted to become a citizen thereof . . . ."[2] One of the first acts by the first congress of the United States was to establish whiteness as a condition for becoming a naturalized citizen. The naturalization law was modified many times over the years, but the limitation to white persons was not eliminated until 1952.[3]

Slavery And Racism in the North

In the North, where the economy was not dependent on free labor, the need for rationalizations to justify slavery was gone. The humanity of the slaves could not be denied and slavery was now seen as inhumane and immoral. But the effects of slavery would linger. The acceptance of Blacks as human beings entitled to freedom did not change the general view that Blacks were inferior to Whites. And the debates about ending slavery and assimilating the freed slaves served to reinforce those views rather than overcome them.

Immediately after the country was formed, many northern states began considering and adopting emancipation legislation,[4] often compensating slave owners out of public funds for freeing their slaves.[5] In May 1782, Virginia's House of Delegates passed "An Act to Authorize the Manumission

---

2. "Federal naturalization laws."
3. Smith, "Race, Nationality, and Reality."
4. Franklin and Moss, *From Slavery to Freedom,* 92–93.
5. Levy, *The First Emancipator,* 183.

of Slaves"[6] and between the years 1782 and 1861, slave owners in that state freed over one hundred thousand slaves without any compensation.[7]

As the state legislatures debated ending slavery, the big question was how to do it. Many abolitionists wanted an immediate end, but that approach could not get broad support, so a gradual emancipation became the norm; slaves born after a certain date would be free after a certain number of years.[8] Slave owners were concerned about the financial impact, and white laborers were concerned about new competition for jobs. But the biggest factor was that Whites in general were not prepared to begin treating freed slaves as equals.[9]

The debate about Emancipation always involved the issue of assimilating the freed slaves. There were some who argued for total equality for free Blacks. Like most people of the time, they generally considered Blacks deficient; but many believed it was due to having been enslaved and would be overcome in time. Yet, there were many others who felt there were intrinsic differences between races and that Blacks were inferior by nature. Even among those most adamantly opposed to slavery, there were many who felt, like Jefferson, that free Whites and free Blacks could not live together.[10] They supported Emancipation, but felt that some form of separation was necessary. For them, voluntary relocation of the freed slaves offered the best solution.

The American Colonization Society was formed in 1816 to encourage and implement the relocation of freed Blacks to Africa. A number of northern states formed their own colonization societies, as well. Despite the organized efforts of the colonization societies and promotion by White policy makers, very few Blacks chose to relocate. Most had been born in America and had no interest in moving to a continent to which they had no connection. Also, it became obvious fairly quickly that the logistics and costs involved made the idea totally impractical. Yet the idea persisted for decades. In historian Winthrop D. Jordan's words, "That the notion of colonizing America's Negro population in some remote region was so persistent while so preposterously utopian suggests that it was less a quirk of fancy than a compelling fantasy."[11]

6. Ibid., 101.

7. Ibid., 183.

8. Jordan, *White Over Black*, 345, 354.

9. Franklin and Moss, *From Slavery to Freedom*, 184–91; Wilder, *Ebony & Ivy*, 243–73; Jordan, *White Over Black*, 415–18, 566–69; Fredrickson, *The Black Image*, 35–42.

10. Jordan, *White Over Black*, 549.

11. Ibid., 567.

When the removal of Blacks proved impractical, a level of separation was achieved by discriminatory laws. Discrimination against free Blacks that existed during slavery continued, and in many cases increased, after Emancipation.[12] Many of the state constitutions of the northern states adopted language similar to the Declaration of Independence stating that all men had equal rights. Equal rights were rarely granted though.[13] Higginbotham notes that in Pennsylvania, "It was to be decades before blacks had access to some of the most fundamental concomitants of citizenship, such as the ballot box, and more than a century and a half before the nondiscrimination legislation in housing, employment, and public accommodations was enacted."[14]

In New York, following the passage of their emancipation act, the state constitution was amended, removing the requirement of property ownership for white men to vote, while at the same time more than doubling the amount of property ownership required for black men to vote from $100 to $250.[15]

Particularly indicative of attitudes in the North at this time regarding people of African descent was the more direct approach taken by the new states admitted to the Union after the initial thirteen. The addition of new states to the Union, as provided for by the Constitution, began immediately after its adoption and created a struggle within the balance of power. As new states were added, the question of whether they would be free states or slave states was the primary concern as each side attempted to shift federal power their way. Eleven new states were added by 1821, and ten more were added by 1861.

In order to maintain the balance of power, northern and southern states were admitted alternately (approximately). Vermont (1791), Ohio (1803), Indiana (1816) and Illinois (1818) were the first new northern states, as the fourteenth, seventeenth, nineteenth and twenty-first states, respectively. The constitutions of Ohio, Indiana, and Illinois all prohibited slavery. They also all specifically limited voting to white men.[16] In less than forty years, Illinois and Indiana adopted new constitutions, this time prohibiting Blacks from moving into the state.

12. Fredrickson, *The Black Image*, 20–21.

13. Kendi, *Stamped from the Beginning*, 120.

14. Higginbotham, *In the Matter of Color*, 302.

15. Ibid., 148.

16. "Ohio Constitution," *Ohio History Central*; "Constitution of 1816," *Indiana Historical Bureau*; "Constitution of the State of Illinois," *Illinois Digital Archives*.

The first Illinois constitution was replaced in 1848. Article XIV of the new constitution provided that, "The general assembly shall at its first session under the amended constitution pass such laws as will effectually prohibit free persons of color from immigrating to and settling in this state, and to effectually prevent the owners of slaves from bringing them into this state for the purpose of setting them free."[17] In compliance with this provision the General Assembly passed a law in 1853 prohibiting free Blacks from another state from remaining in Illinois more than ten days.[18]

The new constitution adopted by Indiana in 1851 was more direct. Article 13, Section 1 of that new constitution stated: "No negro or mulatto shall come into or settle in the State, after the adoption of this constitution."[19] Even the far western free state of Oregon, which was admitted as the thirty-third state in 1859, included an exclusion clause in its initial constitution: "No free negro or mulatto not residing in this state at the time of the adoption of this constitution, shall come, reside or be within this state . . . ."[20]

Slavery and North-South Strife

The invention of the cotton gin in 1793 made the growing of cotton very profitable, and set the South on a very different path than the North. Since cotton would only grow in southern climates, the South had a monopoly, and cotton became the driving economic force in the region. The proliferation of cotton plantations created a new demand for large numbers of slaves. According to census records, the number of slaves in the United States increased from about 700,000 in 1790 to over 3.9 million just before the Civil War.[21] Much of the increase was due to the addition of new slave holding states, including the primary cotton producing states.

The lucrative cotton plantations also drove the demand for more land and for statehood for those areas of expansion. The purchase of the Louisiana Territory from France in 1803 led to the addition of the state of Louisiana in 1812, with Mississippi and Alabama following in 1817 and 1819, respectively. With the addition of each new state, the tensions between the North and the South increased. Each new state added two senators to Congress,

17. Verlie, *Illinois Constitutions*, 98.
18. Bridges, "The Illinois Black Codes."
19. "Constitution of 1851," Indiana Historical Bureau.
20. Oregon Blue Book, "Original 1857 Constitution of Oregon"; Nokes, *Black Exclusion Laws*.
21. Franklin and Moss, *From Slavery to Freedom*, 139.

shifting the power balance toward the North or the South, depending on where the new state was located.

The slave states were able to maintain the balance of power in Congress as states were added, but the process required intense debates and compromises. As the debates became more heated and the compromises more difficult to reach, it began to appear that more than political power was at risk: slavery itself seemed to be in jeopardy. Breaking away from the United States was seen as the only solution to preserving the southern way of life. The resulting Civil War will be discussed in the next chapter.

Because slavery was such an integral part of the economy of the South, any argument for ending it was vigorously opposed. The Curse of Ham was used to justify slavery from a moral standpoint, while the evolving scientific study of human differences was used to defend it from a humanitarian position. For the people in the North, those arguments were not persuasive enough to justify slavery, but they did reinforce the idea of the inferiority of people of African descent.

In turn, people in the South became enthusiastic supporters of the northern idea of colonization. In the South, the presence of free Blacks was seen as a threat to the system of slavery;[22] this colonization of free Blacks was seen as a way to remove that threat. In the North, the idea of colonization had been born out of the desire to remove all Blacks and create an all White nation. The opposition of many northerners to southern expansion of slavery into new states was not because of the evils of slavery, but because they saw the increase in the number and distribution of Blacks as counter to their hope for an all White country.

In that way, the regional disagreements about slavery served to ultimately reinforce attitudes on both sides that all Blacks, whether enslaved or free, were inferior. As outsiders and pawns, rather than as affected participants in the disputes and compromises, the needs and concerns of Blacks were naturally discounted and frequently ignored altogether.

Racism Toward Native Americans

The situation was exactly the same regarding Native Americans, whose needs and rights were totally disregarded as policy debates centered on the political and economic interests of the White citizens. During the entire colonial period, attitudes toward Native Americans, and relations with them, were mixed. Early settlers lacked the numbers to engage in major warfare against the original inhabitants. They were also poorly equipped to survive

22. Ibid., 188–90; Jordan, *White Over Black*, 408–11.

independently, and often depended on the Native nations for assistance, sometimes through trade and other times through direct aid. They formed alliances with friendly Native nations for defense against unfriendly Native nations and against other European nations.

Throughout this period there was often a respect for the native peoples and an expectation by some that they would one day be assimilated, or at least a means of peaceful coexistence would be found. In a 1751 essay titled, "Observations Concerning the Increase of Mankind, Peopling of Countries, etc.," Benjamin Franklin decried the increase in German immigrants in his home state of Pennsylvania and of African slaves in other parts of the country, while he included Native Americans in his ideal America:

> The number of purely white people in the world is proportionably very small. . . . And while we are, as I may call it, scouring our planet, by clearing America of woods, and so making this side of our globe reflect a brighter light to the eyes of inhabitants in Mars or Venus, why should we in the sight of superior beings, darken its people? why increase the sons of Africa, by planting them in America, where we have so fair an opportunity, by excluding all blacks and tawneys, of increasing the lovely white and red?[23]

While there are many indications of a level of respect for Native Americans by the colonists, it is also clear they considered them inferior and uncivilized. In our founding document, the Declaration of Independence, Native Americans are referred to as "merciless Indian Savages." Some early conflicts were resolved through treaties and purchases of the land and, though a few were done honestly and were honored, many were not.[24] Where armed conflicts did occur, some captured Native Americans were enslaved and sold to plantations in the West Indies. As expansion accelerated, armed conflicts became more frequent and more brutal. There were rarely any survivors to be sold into slavery. Even non-combatant women and children were killed; villages and crops were destroyed.[25]

The westward expansion at that time also put the colonies in conflict with the French, who had been trying to lay claim to the central part of what is now the United States. Some Natives formed alliances with the French in an attempt to slow the expansion of the British colonies. That conflict, which lasted from 1754–1763, is known as the French and Indian War. When the French were defeated, the Natives were seen as an impediment to

23. Franklin, *Observations*, 10.

24. Zinn, *A People's History*, 125–145.

25. Dunbar-Ortiz, *An Indigenous Peoples' History*, 56–94.

expansion and as enemies of war; thus, the military aggression against them continued unabated.[26]

Similarly, when the colonies began their war for independence from England in 1775, several Native nations allied themselves with the English, again in the hope that this would help stop the expansion. When the English withdrew, the Natives were again left to resist expansion alone.[27] Having defeated both the French and the English, the United States army was organized and seasoned by war. Policy makers in the new United States had a new sense of their power and began to see the Native Americans as simply another impediment to the growth of the nation.

The demand for land for cotton production that led to the addition of the states of Louisiana, Mississippi, and Alabama also led to a demand for total removal of the Native American population from those areas. The purchase of the Louisiana Territory from France in 1803 was initially seen as a way to solve that "problem." From that huge expanse of new land west of the Mississippi River, portions would be set aside for the various Native tribes to relocate, leaving all of the land east of the river for white expansion.[28]

In 1830, President Andrew Jackson signed the Indian Removal Act, which documented and authorized that exchange. The exchange was to be voluntary, but few Native tribes agreed to be relocated, and most had to be relocated by force. Though the Supreme Court ruled that the Cherokee nation was a sovereign nation and entitled to the lands they occupied, President Jackson simply defied their ruling.[29] In the winter of 1838, the United States army forced the Cherokee nation to move west of the Mississippi in a forced march that resulted in the death of approximately four thousand people.[30]

The admission of Texas to the Union in 1845, the Oregon Treaty with England in 1846, and the Treaty of Guadalupe Hidalgo with Mexico in 1848 defined all of the current borders of the continental United States. In support of the acquisition of Texas and the Oregon Territory, a journalist, John L. O'Sullivan, coined the term, *manifest destiny*:

> And that claim is by the right of our manifest destiny to
> overspread and to possess the whole of the continent which

26. Wilder, *Ebony & Ivy*, 160–64; Dunbar-Ortiz, *An Indigenous Peoples' History*, 67–71.

27. Wilder, *Ebony & Ivy*, 170–79; Dunbar-Ortiz, *An Indigenous Peoples' History*, 71–94.

28. Zinn, *A People's History*, 125, 131.

29. Dunbar-Ortiz, *An Indigenous Peoples' History*, 110.

30. Zinn, *A People's History*, 146.

Providence has given us for the development of the great experiment of liberty and federated self-government entrusted to
us.[31]

The idea that God had provided the land to the people of the United
States and that it was the duty and responsibility of those people to inhabit
and "civilize" that land provided a moral justification for whatever measures
were taken in the process. The availability of cheap land and plentiful natural resources, the California gold rush of 1848, and conditions in Europe
that resulted in massive numbers of new immigrants, all fueled a rapid westward expansion. The Louisiana Territory, which only a few decades earlier
had seemed so limitless that it could be freely assigned to the eastern Native
tribes under the Indian Removal Act, was soon divided up into states and
occupied by white settlers. The pattern of fraud, broken treaties, and military intervention against the Native peoples throughout the area during this
period of expansion has been well documented.

Unlike the Blacks who could be excluded from the new areas of expansion, the Native people were already on the land and had to be driven off.
The term "genocide" did not exist until 1944 when it was coined to describe
the Nazis' actions against the Jews. Whether it is appropriate to apply that
term to the actions against the Native people within the United States during
the western expansion is a matter of scholarly debate about what the precise
definition of the word should be. The massive numbers of Natives killed or
displaced—millions killed; dozens of tribes relocated, often to places with
limited resources to maintain life; and the prevailing attitude that Whites
were entitled to possess the land by any means necessary—demonstrate that
any definition of genocide should encompass that period in our history.[32]

It was arrogance and greed that were the driving force behind those
actions, but it was racism that provided the justification. The racism that
had been created to justify the enslavement of Africans was now, as slavery
was ending, being used to justify the annihilation of Native Americans.

31. O'Sullivan, "The True Title," as quoted in Pratt, "The Origin of 'Manifest
Destiny.'"

32. "What is Genocide?" United States Holocaust Memorial Museum; Brown,
Bury My Heart at Wounded Knee.

7

Civil War

Abraham Lincoln is one of our most esteemed presidents, credited with ending slavery. There is no question that he served during one of the most difficult periods in our history, and with skill and honor led the country through those difficult times, preserving the Union. The honor and respect he receives is clearly warranted.

But, like the founding fathers, he left some tasks unfinished. If we are to truly understand racism, it is important that we not allow our celebration of the accomplishments to distract from the reality of everything that was going on at the time. Lincoln, like the others around him, was a product of his time. As noted earlier, his home state of Illinois had changed its constitution in 1848 to prevent free Blacks from moving into the state. Lincoln stated his attitude regarding race in an 1858 debate against Stephen A. Douglas during his campaign for the U.S. Senate:

> There is a physical difference between the white and black races which I believe will forever forbid the two races living together on terms of social and political equality. And inasmuch as they cannot so live, while they do remain together there must be the position of superior and inferior, and I as much as any other man am in favor of having the superior position assigned to the white race.[1]

Lincoln opposed slavery, but did not consider himself an abolitionist. He favored voluntary emancipation with compensation to the slave owners and, because he didn't think Blacks and Whites could live together, he was

1. "Fourth Debate," *National Park Service.*

a strong proponent of colonization of freed slaves.[2] In his first inaugural address in 1861 he made it clear that he did not enter the presidency with the intent to end slavery: "I have no purpose, directly or indirectly, to interfere with the institution of slavery in the States where it exists. I believe I have no lawful right to do so, and I have no inclination to do so."[3]

He felt the fugitive slave provision written into the Constitution (Article IV, Section 2, Clause 3) prevented him from ending slavery.[4] Civil war was imminent at the time of the address, seven states having already declared their secession from the United States; much of his address was an appeal to avoid war. The issue of slavery, particularly the future of slavery, was unquestionably the force that ultimately led to war. But the actual battle was about preserving the Union, not ending slavery, even though abolitionists were hopeful that would be the outcome. In fact, many northern soldiers who were willing to fight to preserve the Union were not willing to fight just to free the slaves.[5]

Many people refer to Lincoln's Emancipation Proclamation, which was effective on January 1, 1863, as the end of slavery. And though it did free most of the slaves in the United States at the time, it is important to recognize that the actual ending of slavery was more complicated than a presidential proclamation. The Emancipation Proclamation only freed the slaves in those states and parts of states that were in rebellion, and was intended as a war maneuver meant to weaken the Confederacy. Lincoln felt that as Commander in Chief in time of war he could use that action against the enemy,[6] even though he felt the Constitution prevented him from ending slavery everywhere. It took an amendment to the Constitution, the thirteenth, adopted almost three years after the Emancipation Proclamation, to actually end slavery everywhere in the United States.

There is significance in the fact that it took an amendment to the Constitution to abolish slavery. As will be discussed in the next chapter, it also took two additional amendments to ensure that the Constitution applies equally to everyone. Yet these amendments are subject to Supreme Court interpretation, so the rights of People of Color are always dependent on favorable interpretation by judges. Though many of the ramifications of this

2. Zinn, *A People's History*, 183; Franklin and Moss, *From Slavery to Freedom*, 229–30.

3. "Abraham Lincoln," Library of Congress.

4. Ibid.

5. Zinn, *A People's History*, 187; Franklin and Moss, *From Slavery to Freedom*, 231.

6. Franklin and Moss, *From Slavery to Freedom*, 230–32.

are too technical for the broad overview intended by this book, a few of the effects will be discussed in the chapter on the Supreme Court.

The ending of more than two hundred years of government sanctioned and enforced chattel slavery, the ownership of human beings by other human beings, was unquestionably an important event in our history. But equally important is the fact that ending slavery did nothing to slow the racism that was its legacy. Slavery has been gone for over one hundred and fifty years, but its effects remain and continue to divide us.

PART II

Racism from the Civil War
to the Present

8

Post Slavery Racism

The Civil War and the assassination of Lincoln five days after its end were significant events; thus, there is a tendency to focus on the events and to neglect a deeper consideration of the underlying conditions and attitudes. The North had prevailed, so the Union was intact. Slavery had been abolished. There remained, though, many tasks to ensure the peace, ensure the loyalty of states returning to participation in the federal government, and ensure no return to the conditions that led to the conflict.

In the South, the plantation owners would not easily adapt to the loss of the free labor that had been a major part of their operations. The implementation of a massive new system of labor would have been difficult in the best of conditions, but the obstinate resistance by the employers of the South presented significant additional challenges. Immediately after the war, the southern states turned to "Black Codes" to maintain Whites' control over Blacks. The "Black Codes" were laws, such as vagrancy and failure to pay debts, which were selectively and fraudulently enforced against Blacks.

Most people in the North knew that the freed slaves would need physical and legal protection from the former slave owners who would do everything they could to re-create the conditions of the past as nearly as possible. They also recognized that four million freed slaves, who were starting with nothing—no homes, money, or possessions—would need some initial public support. But the amount of time and resources the North was willing to commit to that process was limited. The Union army was withdrawn from the South within twelve years.

The hard feelings between the North and South that led to war had been compounded by four years of battles that resulted in the death of over

600,000 young men.[1] The post war changes being imposed on the South, and enforced by the Union army of the North, continued the animosity after the war ended. Yet, there were political and economic reasons for both sides to find a way to return to normal. The anger was soon redirected at the freed Blacks, who many in both the North and the South began to see as the only beneficiaries of the war.

Two hundred years of slavery had created the stereotype of slaves as stupid, lazy, and irresponsible. The disproportional arrest and conviction of Blacks under the "Black Codes" was then used to argue that without the control of slavery they were also prone to criminality. With the end of slavery, there was no longer a distinction between enslaved and free Blacks. As a consequence, the stereotypes that had been created under slavery, and the new stereotypes being created by the actions of the South, were applied to all people of African descent. That was true in the North as well as in the South. Those stereotypes were then reinforced by the faulty science of the time, as will be discussed in the next chapter. By the end of the nineteenth century, when slavery was long past, racism was firmly entrenched and gaining momentum.

Lincoln and His Successor

Lincoln had viewed the attempts to secede from the Union to be the actions of men, not the states themselves, and hoped that after the war ended the states could be returned to the Union quickly, with only the leadership of the rebellion excluded. He was fully aware of the challenges of ensuring loyalty from the mass of citizens in the returning states, the need to implement an entirely changed system of labor within those states, and the needs of four million freed slaves who had no homes or money. Prior to the end of the war he attempted to address those issues with the Border States but found them unwilling to accept the compromises needed.[2] So no preliminary work or testing could be done prior to the end of the war, and the actual work of rebuilding the nation fell to his successor, Andrew Johnson.

Lincoln had been elected as a Republican in 1860, but the party temporarily adopted the name National Unity Party when he ran for, and won, reelection in 1864. As a further signal of his desire for national unity, Lincoln selected Andrew Johnson, a Democrat, as his vice presidential running mate for his second term. Andrew Johnson was a senator from Tennessee when that state joined the Confederacy in 1861. Because he opposed

1. Faust, *Death and Dying.*
2. Du Bois, *Black Reconstruction*, 155.

secession, he had kept his Senate seat, despite his state's secession. After the Union army occupied a portion of Tennessee in 1862, President Lincoln rewarded Johnson's loyalty by appointing him military governor of the state. He became vice president on March 4, 1865 and, less than two months later, on April 15,1865 he became president when Lincoln was assassinated. That was less than a week after the end of the Civil War, and the following summary by W. E. B. Du Bois describes the situation:

> Here then was Andrew Johnson in 1865, born at the bottom of society, and during his early life a radical defender of the poor, the landless and the exploited. In the heyday of his early political career, he railed against land monopoly in the South, and after the Civil War, wanted the land of the monopolists divided among peasant proprietors.
>
> Suddenly, by the weird magic of history, he becomes military dictator of a nation. He becomes the man by whom the greatest moral and economic revolution that ever took place in the United States, and perhaps in modern times, was to be put into effect. He becomes the real emancipator of four millions of black slaves, who have suffered more than anything that he had experienced in his earlier days. They not only have no lands; they have not owned even their bodies, nor their clothes, nor their tools. They have been exploited down to the ownership of their own families; they have been poor by law, and ignorant by force. What more splendid opportunity could the champion of labor and the exploited have had to start a nation toward freedom?[3]

Du Bois' characterization of Johnson as "military dictator of a nation" reflects the fact that, during the war, more than normal decision making authority had passed to the President. Following the surrender of the Confederate army, every state in the South was under direct military control with the President as Commander in Chief. Further, Congress had adjourned prior to the surrender and was not scheduled to reconvene until December, eight months later. Johnson could have called a special session, but chose not to.[4] Instead, he assumed sole responsibility for the complex task of reconciliation and reconstruction. He did listen to the views of congressmen, members of the cabinet he inherited from Lincoln, and many private citizens, including representatives of southern landowners and representatives of the freed slaves. But his actions quickly reflected his past as a Democrat,

3. Ibid., 206–7.
4. Ibid., 208.

which was the conservative party at the time, and as a southerner who had owned slaves.

Johnson's guiding principle became the return of power to the states and limiting the power of the federal government as quickly as possible. His idea of power to the states, though, only applied to white men. In a meeting with Black leaders in February 1866, Johnson said, "Do you deny that first great principle of the right of the people to govern themselves?" One of the Black men responded immediately, "Apply what you have said, Mr. President, to South Carolina, for instance, where a majority of the inhabitants are colored." At the time, Blacks were almost 60 percent of the population of South Carolina. Johnson evaded the issue with a feeble attempt to claim that Ohio was a better example. Then ignoring the inconsistency that had just been pointed out, he finished with, "It is a fundamental tenet in my creed that the will of the people must be obeyed. Is there anything wrong or unfair in that?"[5]

Johnson's criteria for the states to regain the right of representation in Congress were the same as those discussed by Lincoln and the Congress before the war ended. The states had to recognize the abolition of slavery, repeal their secession ordinances, repudiate the war debts of the Confederacy, and be subject to provisional governors until new state governments were formed. A Declaration of Amnesty was issued for all citizens of the South except the leaders of the Confederacy and landowners with a net worth of more than $20,000. Those not granted amnesty could not participate in the new state governments, though within nine months Johnson had pardoned fourteen thousand of those not originally granted amnesty.[6]

Before Congress met in December 1865, all of the states had met all of the conditions with only the rare exception.[7] The only real change, though, was the absolute prohibition against slavery, and the states immediately began enacting "Black Codes," designed specifically to keep the freed slaves in a controlled and subordinate status that was virtually unchanged from actual slavery.[8]

5. McPherson, *The Political History*, 52–55.

6. Du Bois, *Black Reconstruction*, 207–9.

7. Ibid., 210.

8. Ibid., 136; Franklin and Moss, *From Slavery to Freedom*, 250–52; Malcomson, *One Drop of Blood*, 208–9; Blackmon, *Slavery by Another Name*, 27.

Regional And Party Politics In Congress

A major indication that the southern states expected that they could control their own destinies was the fact that when Congress met in December 1865, the vice president of the Confederacy, four Confederate generals, five Confederate colonels, six Confederate cabinet officers, and fifty-eight Confederate congressmen had been elected senators and representatives, all intending to take their seats in Congress.[9] They were not allowed to do so.

Partly in response to the actions and arrogance of the southern states, partly out of genuine concern for the welfare of the freed Blacks, but primarily for purely political reasons, Congress was determined to assume control over the reconstruction process. Among their concerns was the appropriate balance of power between the administrative and legislative branches of the government. They felt that the president had clearly overstepped his authority with the actions he had taken unilaterally while Congress was not in session.

Within Congress itself, there was the issue of the balance of power between the North and the South. Prior to Emancipation, in allocating representation in Congress, slaves had been counted as three-fifths of a person. As free persons, after Emancipation, they would be counted as whole persons, accounting for twenty-eight of the representatives from the southern states.[10] The individual states had always determined who could vote and, while that right was restricted in all of the states, in the South voting rights were so restrictive that all of the power rested in the hands of a few landowners.[11] The additional representatives would give them even more power. That was not acceptable to the people in the North, who felt that those who had promoted rebellion should be punished, not rewarded, for the effects of their actions.

There was also the issue of the balance of power between the political parties. Leading up to the war, and in its aftermath, the South was almost exclusively Democratic. The North was strongly Republican, but also included many Democrats, although they had mostly opposed the war. If the Democratic Party could be unified, they would greatly outnumber the Republicans, and would be controlled by their superior numbers in the South. The Republican-dominated Congress was determined to prevent that from occurring.

9. Du Bois, *Black Reconstruction*, 214; Franklin and Moss, *From Slavery to Freedom*, 252.

10. Du Bois, *Black Reconstruction*, 237.

11. Ibid., 25–26.

An obvious first priority for Congress was the situation of four million freed slaves who needed homes, a means to support themselves, and legal protection for their rights. But, other than freedom, the rights they were entitled to were a matter of debate. The reality was that even in the North, ninety years after the Declaration of Independence, nowhere were Blacks given equal rights with Whites. In his book, *The Strange Career of Jim Crow*, C. Van Woodward describes the situation in the north:

> . . . the Northern Negro was made painfully and constantly aware that he lived in a society dedicated to the doctrine of white supremacy and Negro inferiority. The major political parties, whatever their position on slavery, vied with each other in their devotion to this doctrine, and extremely few politicians of importance dared question them. . . . They made sure in numerous ways that the Negro understood his "place" and that he was severely confined to it. One of these ways was segregation, and with the backing of legal and extra-legal codes, the system permeated all aspects of Negro life in the free states by 1860.[12]

Still, the reality of four million freed slaves in need of jobs, food, and housing could not be ignored. As the Union army had moved through the South, thousands of slaves came over to their side, weakening the Confederate forces, but also requiring the Union forces to feed and care for them. Many were put to work building fortifications and a substantial number were given weapons and fought with the Union army. They performed well as workers and soldiers and were recognized as a major force in the Union victory. Gratitude for their contributions to the war effort, and the daily reminders of their most basic needs for survival, led Congress to create a Bureau of Refugees, Freedmen and Abandoned Lands just before the end of the war. After the war, the new Congress extended the scheduled termination of the Bureau, known as the Freedmen's Bureau, and charged it with assisting the freed slaves to achieve self-sufficiency. The Bureau provided temporary food and housing relief, medical care, established schools, oversaw labor contracts with employers, and administered confiscated lands.[13]

But gratitude and sympathy did not change the general feeling of Black inferiority, even in the North. There were eloquent and influential leaders in both the Senate and House of Representatives urging true equality for Blacks, but they could never garner broad support. Each victory was hard-won and required compromises. In early 1866, Congress was able to pass a Civil Rights law granting citizenship to all Blacks and giving them the right

12. Woodward, *The Strange Career*, 18.
13. Franklin and Moss, *From Slavery to Freedom*, 255–57.

to enter into contracts, to own property, and to have access to the courts and equal protection under the law. The right to vote had been debated from the beginning, but was considered too controversial to be included. President Johnson vetoed the bill, but Congress was able to override his veto.[14]

Congress immediately followed with the Fourteenth Amendment to the Constitution, making the citizenship and equal protection provisions of the Civil Rights Act a part of the Constitution. When all of the southern states except Tennessee refused to ratify the Fourteenth Amendment, Congress passed a series of reconstruction acts, the first of which required ratification of the Fourteenth Amendment before any southern state could regain representation in Congress.[15]

The Fourteenth Amendment also contained a provision that a state's representation would be reduced in proportion that male citizens over the age of twenty-one were denied the vote. That provision was inserted to counter the increased representation the South would gain by counting freed slaves without having to guarantee voting rights for those Blacks. Yet, as the debate regarding the status of the freed slaves continued, it became difficult to defend against the view that rights for the freed slaves were meaningless if they lacked the ability to protect those rights with the ballot. Of course, even in the North, not every state allowed Blacks to vote; so legislation mandating universal suffrage met resistance in the North as well as in the South.

The attempts of Congress to set the terms of reconstruction continued to meet with active resistance from President Johnson, who ultimately vetoed 23 bills.[16] Black suffrage was increasingly seen as a necessity to guarantee that rights for Blacks and other critical post war changes would endure. On March 4, 1867, Congress overrode a veto to pass a law mandating Black suffrage in all of the returning states.[17] President Johnson left no doubt regarding his attitude about that law and toward Blacks in general in his third annual address to the nation in December 1867, when he made the following comments:

> Negro suffrage was established by act of Congress, and the military officers were commanded to superintend the process of clothing the Negro race with the political privileges torn from white men. . . . It is not proposed merely that they shall govern

14. Du Bois, *Black Reconstruction*, 233–34; Franklin and Moss, *From Slavery to Freedom*, 252.

15. Du Bois, *Black Reconstruction*, 274; Franklin and Moss, *From Slavery to Freedom*, 253.

16. Du Bois, *Black Reconstruction*, 282.

17. Ibid., 273–74.

themselves, but that they shall rule the white race, make and ad-
minister State laws, elect Presidents and members of Congress,
and shape to a greater or less extent the future destiny of the
whole country. . . . But if anything can be proved by known facts,
if all reasoning upon evidence is not abandoned, it must be acknowledged that in the progress of nations Negroes have shown
less capacity for government than any other race of people. No
independent government of any form has ever been successful
in their hands.[18]

On February 26, 1869, two years after legalizing Black suffrage, Congress passed the Fifteenth Amendment, making universal male suffrage a
part of the Constitution.

Ultimately, Congress had been able to pass the legislation it wanted. In
the absence of representation from the southern states, both houses of Congress had substantial Republican majorities. But not all Republicans were
unified in their views, particularly their views regarding the freed Blacks.
The one unifying issue was the desire to limit the power of the southern
states, though the concerns of northern industry were often seen as a more
important reason than the concerns of southern Blacks. Often the hard-
fought political battles were seen as caused by Blacks and solely for the benefit of Blacks, overshadowing the reality of a country founded on forced free
labor re-creating itself. The victims were resented for the costs of the war
that freed them, the costs of the occupying force that continued to protect
them from their former oppressors, and the costs of the Freedmen's Bureau
that provided for the basic needs that they had been prevented from providing for themselves.

Reconstruction in the South

A broad overview of conditions and attitudes in the South is difficult and
bound to be incomplete because it covers many states with diverse geogra-
phies, economies, and histories. But all had the shared experience of losing
an emotionally and financially costly war, and adapting to dramatic social
and economic changes due to the ending of slavery. During slavery, segregation did not exist in the south. Plantation owners and overseers were in daily
contact with the slave workers. Cooks and maids, and the personal slaves
of the owners' family members, were a constant presence in the owners'
homes.[19] Woodward describes the logical initial effect of the end of slavery:

18. "Andrew Johnson, Third Annual Message."
19. Woodward, *The Strange Career*, 12; Du Bois, *Black Reconstruction*, 27.

The immediate response to the collapse of slavery was often a simultaneous withdrawal of both races from the enforced intimacy and the more burdensome obligations imposed by the old regime on each. Denied the benefits of slavery, whites shook off its responsibilities—excess hands, dependents too old or too ill or too young to work, tenants too poor to pay rent. Freedmen for their part often fled old masters and put behind them old grievances, hatreds, and the scene of old humiliations.[20]

But the sheer numbers of four million freed slaves without homes or income, and an agricultural economy that was dependent on large numbers of workers, meant that segregation was not a practical first step. The war had also led the South to develop its own iron and steel production facilities and the supporting industries such as iron ore and coal mining, timber and lumber production, and railroad building, all of which required large numbers of workers.[21] Despite the significant physical impacts of the war, necessity dictated that a level of normalcy be achieved in reasonable time. Landowners returned to their plantations, business owners repaired war damage and resumed operations, and many freed Blacks remained with, or returned to, former owners as contract laborers.

Some former slave owners graciously accepted the changes and treated their new employees fairly. Blacks and Whites began working together, eating and socializing together and traveling together in unsegregated streetcars and trains.[22] Some former slaves were able to acquire their own farms and others were able to start their own businesses. Some gathered together in their own communities.[23]

But this was not at all the norm. Generally, the process was difficult, and often violent, due to anger, resentment, and firmly held prejudices. In his book, *Black Reconstruction in America*, W. E. B. Du Bois outlines some of the difficulties:

> It is always difficult to stop war, and doubly difficult to stop a civil war. Inevitably, when men have long been trained to violence and murder, the habit projects itself into civil life after peace, and there is crime and disorder and social upheaval . . . But in the case of civil war, where the contending parties must rest face to face after peace, there can be no quick and perfect peace. When to all this you add a servile and disadvantaged

20. Woodward, *The Strange Career*, 22.
21. Blackmon, *Slavery by Another Name*, 19–22, 46–51.
22. Woodward, *The Strange Career*, 25–43.
23. Blackmon, *Slavery by Another Name*, 86.

race, who represent the cause of war and who afterwards are left near naked to their enemies, war may go on more secretly, more spasmodically, and yet as truly as before the peace. This was the case in the South after Lee's surrender.[24]

Yet, the Union army did provide some level of order. And the Freedmen's Bureau provided oversight of labor contracts that allowed workers to return to work and farm and industrial production to resume. Agricultural production had dropped dramatically during the war years but, despite the changes in labor, had improved substantially within five years of the war's end and fully recovered within fifteen years.[25] Blacks were able to register and vote. Blacks were elected to local offices, state legislatures, and even to Congress.[26] Blacks were appointed to judgeships and served on juries. For a while, both political parties courted black voters.[27]

Blacks were the majority in South Carolina and Mississippi, and almost equal in numbers with Whites in four other states. Consequently, they elected significant numbers to state legislatures. As legislators, they directed their attention to the most urgent needs. Since slaves had been denied education by law, legislation was passed establishing tax-supported school systems that were available to everyone. They debated, and often enacted, laws making primary education for all children compulsory. They modified or repealed laws to eliminate discrimination. They formed commissions to document total state debt and provided taxation to reduce the debt and finance new expenditures such as expanded school systems. Their participation in the legislative bodies was measured and respectful, and often drew complimentary comments from White colleagues.[28]

Legislation promoted and enacted by Blacks emphasized equity, including equity for poor Whites. There were five million poor Whites in the South who had also suffered under the economic system based on slavery. In fact, while slavery was in effect, poor Whites resented the system that they saw as limiting their employment opportunities and keeping them poor. Yet they had directed their anger at the slaves, rather than at the landowners who maintained the system. And they consoled themselves that the slaves were of a lower status and lesser worth than themselves. Understandably, after the war, which cost them family members and friends and seemed to

24. Du Bois, *Black Reconstruction,* 549.

25. Ibid., 482.

26. Franklin and Moss, *From Slavery to Freedom,* 266–69; Zinn, *A People's History,* 195; Du Bois, *Black Reconstruction,* 362.

27. Franklin and Moss, *From Slavery to Freedom,* 282.

28. Ibid., 269.

benefit only the slaves, finding themselves now being treated as equals with those freed slaves was not easy to accept. Consequently, though their only benefit was to salve their resentment, poor Whites aligned themselves with landowners to resist any power in the hands of Blacks.

Dozens of secret societies, such as the Knights of the White Camelia and the Knights of the Ku Klux Klan, were formed immediately after the war and quickly grew in membership; terrorist activities became common in a campaign to maintain white supremacy. Broad public support for their intimidation tactics, by Whites who often included local sheriffs and judges, gave the perpetrators cover and effectively countered the limited capability of the Union army.[29] It is important to note that the secret societies did not always operate with total impunity, and their experiences varied by era and locale. Within some states, strict laws prohibiting secret societies, often prohibiting even the possession of society costumes, were enacted and vigorously enforced. In 1870 and 1871 the U.S. Congress passed legislation outlawing such groups.[30]

The fact that the societies survived despite efforts to stop them demonstrates the persistence of the participants, the limited commitment by those trying to stop them, and how things might have been different if the levels of commitment had been reversed. The objective of the secret societies and their intimidation, beatings, and murder was to limit the political participation and power of Blacks. To do this they targeted not only Blacks, but also any Whites who supported them. This included both Northerners administering the provisional governments and the Freedmen's Bureau and southern-born Whites who dared to embrace the new order.[31]

The End of Reconstruction

The presidential election of 1876 was a turning point that had an immediate impact in the South, but also affected the country as a whole although it took many years for the full impact to be felt. The country had been in a major recession for several years, and the natural tendency in those situations is to blame the incumbent party. By then, the people in the North were also getting weary of the commitment of troops and resources in the South, and this too fueled an interest in political change. The Democratic Party in the

29. Ibid., 275.

30. Franklin and Moss, *From Slavery to Freedom*, 276; Du Bois, *Black Reconstruction*, 453, 559–60.

31. Franklin and Moss, *From Slavery to Freedom*, 275–76; Blackmon, *Slavery by Another Name*, 42; Zinn, *A People's History*, 198; Du Bois, *Black Reconstruction*, 389–90.

South had consolidated its power, with all of the southern states restored to representation and, with their increased support in the North, the election was bound to be close. And it was. It was also prone to various forms of electoral abuse that resulted in a very disputed outcome.

Periods following war are subject to corruption and fraud as governments are disrupted, oversight is reduced, and personal rationalizations for actions replace clear legal guidelines. This was unquestionably still the case at the time of the election, and since it occurred in both the North and the South, and in both political parties charges of fraud, bribery, and corruption contributed to the controversy.[32] Masked riders, employing violence and intimidation against Blacks and other Republicans throughout the South, also had a significant impact on the vote.

After Election Day, both parties claimed victory in South Carolina and Louisiana, leaving enough electoral votes in dispute that neither candidate could be declared the winner. Though the Democratic candidate, Samuel Tilden, had a clear majority of the popular vote, a negotiated compromise resulted in all of the disputed electoral votes going to the Republican candidate, Rutherford B. Hayes, who became president by one vote.[33]

In exchange for the presidency, Hayes and the Republicans had agreed to withdraw all federal troops from the southern states. The withdrawal was done promptly and, twelve years after the defeat of the attempted secession, the southern states were again in control of their own affairs.[34] The progress made in the previous twelve years was not immediately undone, and some of the changes had permanent impact. But the predominant attitude toward Blacks was not changed, and the process of establishing White control could now resume without federal interference. The secret societies continued their intimidation tactics for a while but, as Whites regained political control, secrecy was no longer needed and the societies disbanded. Old Black codes could now be enforced and new ones written.

Some laws were directed specifically against Blacks, in clear violation of the Constitution. But usually, to avoid a constitutional challenge, the laws were written in a general form, with an understanding that they would only be enforced against Blacks. Laws against vagrancy, for example, were vaguely defined and could be enforced in such a way that any Black on the street could be arrested and charged for being unemployed. Unless he worked for a white farmer or sharecropped a white farmer's land, and the white

---

32. Franklin and Moss, *From Slavery to Freedom*, 280–81; Du Bois, *Black Reconstruction*, 397, 566.

33. Ibid.

34. Ibid.

farmer was willing to testify on his behalf, he would be found guilty.[35] Laws prevented workers from changing employers without permission, allowing farmers to mistreat or underpay employees at will. If the employee left the farm without permission, he was guilty of a crime.[36] Sharecroppers had no control over the revenues produced or the allocation of costs, leaving them always in debt to the landowner and unable to leave without being charged with the crime of failing to pay a debt. Even those Blacks who had been able to acquire their own farms were prohibited from selling their crops, except to certain buyers who could set the price at whatever level they chose.

Convict Leasing

Convict leasing, adopted by every southern state but Virginia,[37] was then used in conjunction with these questionable laws to supply workers for the farms and mines. In his book, *Slavery by Another Name*, Douglas A. Blackmon describes this process, which lasted well into the twentieth century. The Thirteenth Amendment, which prohibited slavery, provided an exception for punishment for crimes. This exception allowed for convicted individuals who could not pay their fines and costs to be leased to a farmer or mine owner for the amount owed. The costs were often much greater than the fine and included payments to the sheriff, the judge, and any others involved in the arrest and conviction. The fines provided revenue for the state or county, the costs of sheriffs and judges were paid directly, and there were no expenses for incarceration. Blackmon's research showed that by the end of the 1880s there were about ten thousand leased convicts in the south.[38]

The leased convicts were actually slaves, chained and locked up at night, worked from sunup to sundown, given inadequate housing, food and clothing, and beaten if they did not meet production goals. In prewar slavery, the slave owner had a financial investment in his slaves, which provided some incentive for concern about the slave's survival and well being. Under convict leasing, there was no investment and convicts who died could be easily replaced, resulting in a brutality that is almost inconceivable. Blackmon found that "In the first two years that Alabama leased its prisoners, nearly 20 percent of them died. In the following year, mortality rose to 35 percent. In the fourth, nearly 45 percent were killed."[39]

35. Blackmon, *Slavery by Another Name*, 53.
36. Ibid., 54.
37. Ibid., 56.
38. Blackmon, *Slavery by Another Name*, 90.
39. Blackmon, *Slavery by Another Name*, 57.

As early as 1882 state inspectors in Alabama reported that the convict camps they inspected were "totally unfit for use, without ventilation, without adequate water supplies, crowded to excess, filthy beyond description, and infested with vermin." They also reported that prisoners were: "poorly clothed and fed . . . excessively and sometimes cruelly punished; there were no hospitals; the sick were neglected; and they were so much intimidated that it was next to impossible to get from them anything touching on their treatment."[40] The chief inspector found men held beyond their release dates and men for whom there was no record of a conviction or sentence. He wrote to county judges throughout the state and to the governor, but nothing changed.[41]

Convict leasing was lucrative to the states and counties,[42] and also to the sheriffs and judges, often low-level local officials. Costs assessed, and paid from the lease payments, were paid directly to the officials.[43] Since there was a constant demand by the mines and farms, sheriffs and justices could make a lot of money by filling that demand. With the financial incentives involved, and without any protection from abuse, the system quickly evolved into de facto slavery. Because of collusion between local sheriffs and judges, Blacks would be arrested without cause, charged with any crime, and quickly convicted, fined, and sold to a mine owner or farmer. Often, there was no written record of the proceedings.[44]

By 1903, the situation had gotten so bad that the federal government finally undertook some investigations and prosecutions.[45] A grand jury, impaneled early that year, heard testimony from a number of victims. Their testimony regarding their false convictions, and the scars they showed from the beatings they had received, provide much of the historic record of the illegality and brutality of the system. Farmers, mine owners, sheriffs, justices of the peace, and others directly and indirectly involved also testified. Though most of those directly involved insisted that everything had been done in accordance with the law, and that no prisoners were beaten or abused, a few corroborated the testimony of the prisoners.

40. Cobb "History of the Penitentiary," 357; Blackmon, *Slavery by Another Name*, 73.

41. Blackmon, *Slavery by Another Name*, 76.

42. Blackmon, *Slavery by Another Name*, 7–8, 73, 100; "Third Biennial Report," 78–79.

43. Blackmon, *Slavery by Another Name*, 62–66.

44. Ibid., 1, 7, 66, 193.

45. Ibid., 156.

Sometimes mothers, or attorneys who had been hired by them to locate their sons, provided corroborating testimony.[46] In an eight-page report to the Attorney General of the United States, the federal prosecutor in Montgomery, Alabama summarized the results of the investigation and the indictments handed down: "The indictments so far found are based upon some twenty-five negro men and women who have been the subjects of these violations. These are some of the most severe instances, but it has been discovered there are hundreds of other cases."[47]

As the investigation broadened, it became increasingly obvious that these were not isolated cases. The practice extended in several counties of Alabama and throughout the southern states, from the largest operations to the smallest farms. As it became more apparent that the investigation could effectively disrupt the entire southern economy and lead to charges against hundreds of individuals, southern concern turned to anger. The Alabama Secretary of State spoke out in defense of the indicted white men, and even intimated that he might defend them in the courtroom.[48] Almost daily, the local newspaper published editorials such as the following, complaining about the investigation and its effects:

> What do we see? All over the North we find public speakers and newspapers assailing our methods and our people and in every way, as words can do, inciting the colored people to resist, fomenting discord between the races and in many cases maligning and vilifying the Southern people for their course.
>
> Our people do resent the interference of Northern people in a matter with which they have no real concern, and we intend to continue resenting it. What is more, we intend to settle this race question in our own way and if the result is to have the country "rent again into factions hating each other" . . . we shall not feel that we of the South are the offending party. We do not hate the North, but we will settle the race question.[49]

So much local resistance to the investigation had developed that one of the Department of Justice investigators wrote: "In some localities the sentiment has reached such a pitch that it is considered unsafe for anyone known as or suspected as being a government detective to travel."[50] It also

46. Ibid., 181–208.

47. Reese, "Reese to Knox," as quoted in Blackmon, *Slavery by Another Name*, 208.

48. Blackmon, *Slavery by Another Name*, 196.

49. Editorial, *Montgomery Advertiser*, June 13, 1903, 4, as quoted in Blackmon, *Slavery by Another Name*, 215.

50. Finch, "Stanley W. Finch to Frank Strong," as quoted in Blackmon, *Slavery by*

became apparent that finding a jury willing to convict would be virtually impossible.[51] When one case went to trial, the evidence was overwhelming. In his instructions to the jury, the judge carefully described the applicable law and reviewed all of the evidence.[52] When the jury quickly sent word that they were deadlocked, he called them back into the courtroom and practically demanded a guilty verdict: "If you do not return a verdict of guilty you will perjure yourselves in the sight of God and dishonor yourselves in the eyes of men."[53] They deliberated for more than a day, but the jury remained deadlocked, with five jurors refusing to convict. Though a different result would have been unlikely, the prosecutor was determined to try again. However, to avoid a new trial, the defendant chose to plead guilty. He received a nominal fine.[54]

Despite the likelihood of favorable juries, most of those charged preferred to avoid trial and pled guilty. One large plantation owner pled guilty and admitted to the actions charged, but first argued that those actions did not amount to peonage, so he could appeal his conviction to a higher court. He also admitted to having held people in involuntary servitude and argued that there was no federal law prohibiting it.[55] When the Constitution was amended to prohibit slavery, no specific implementing legislation was passed, so there was some question about which laws were being broken.[56] Though these were clearly cases of people held in involuntary servitude—slavery—those were not the specific charges being brought. Prosecutors felt the best cases could be made by focusing on peonage laws, prohibiting forced labor for payment of a debt. Following his guilty plea, the plantation owner was sentenced to five years in prison, but he was released on bond pending his appeal.[57] In the end, his appeal was unsuccessful, but he received a presidential pardon before he served any time.[58]

Only two other men received prison sentences. They each received one-year sentences but, shortly after they entered prison, a petition signed

---

Another Name, 218.

51. Blackmon, *Slavery by Another Name*, 225; Adams, "Edward M. Adams to John E. Wilkie," as quoted in Blackmon, *Slavery by Another Name*, 225.

52. Blackmon, *Slavery by Another Name*, 231.

53. "Judge Scores Alabama Jury," *New York Times*; Blackmon, *Slavery by Another Name*, 231–32.

54. Blackmon, *Slavery by Another Name*, 232.

55. Ibid., 219.

56. Ibid., 226–27.

57. Ibid., 219–20.

58. Daniel, *The Shadow of Slavery*, 63; Blackmon, *Slavery by Another Name*, 277; Almanac of Theodore Roosevelt, "The Complete Presidential Pardons."

by over three thousand people requested a presidential pardon. Even the judge, who had sentenced them, appealed on their behalf. The president quickly issued the pardons.[59] All other convictions resulted in only nominal fines. In the end, the investigations did little more than document the abuses, demonstrate public support for what was taking place, and show the lukewarm commitment of the federal government to defend the rights of Blacks. Most of those found guilty paid their nominal fines and went right back to doing what they had done before.

As widespread and horrific as convict leasing and its abuses were, the 100,000 to 200,000 prisoners[60] and their families who were directly affected were only a small percentage of the freed Blacks and their descendents. But the indirect effects were much broader. The system was justified on the basis that this was punishment for criminal behavior. The large numbers of black convicts then led to the commonly held opinion that the freed slaves, no longer under the control of masters, were inclined toward illegal behavior.[61] This, of course, affected attitudes toward all Blacks. Attitudes in the South also influenced attitudes in the North, and in federal policies and actions.

Another effect of convict leasing was the continued subordination of Blacks to Whites. Since white men held the positions of authority, any Black who offended a white person was at risk of being falsely charged and convicted.[62] This ability of White-controlled institutions, political processes, and law enforcement to sanction legal and extra-legal violence against Blacks was becoming firmly established outside of slavery. It continued through much of the twentieth century.

Westward Expansion And Racism

Following the Civil War, the westward migration of European Americans continued to grow. The discovery of gold in California in 1848, and the resulting gold rush, had changed the process from gradual encroachment to quickly connecting the East to the West. Railroads provided the best opportunity for that connection, and the drive for the completion of the transcontinental railroad was a major component of public policy for several decades. The ease of travel following the completion in 1869 increased the rate of migration, not just to California, but also to all of the areas along the way where the trains stopped.

59. Blackmon, *Slavery by Another Name*, 247–48.
60. Ibid., 7.
61. Ibid., 5–9, 69; Du Bois, *Black Reconstruction*, 582–83.
62. Blackmon, *Slavery by Another Name*, 5–9.

The idea that the settlement of the entire country was both the right and the duty of European Americans continued to relegate Native Americans to ever-smaller reservations. The Indian Appropriations Act enacted in 1851 set up reservations to confine the Native tribes that were seen as an impediment to white settlers.[63] A subsequent Indian Appropriations Act enacted in 1871 established that Native American tribes would no longer be considered as sovereign nations and no further treaties would be negotiated. While the Act committed to honoring previous treaties, this was the first step in limiting the power and influence of the various tribes that were being encountered in the westward advance.[64]

In 1887, the Dawes Act, sometimes referred to as the General Allotment Act, allotted 160 acres of farmland, or 320 acres of grazing land, to each Native family within the various reservations. This act was intended to break up the reservations into individually owned parcels and effectively disband the Native groups. The total allotments used only one half of the reservation lands. The other half was taken back by the government and sold to white settlers.[65]

The Nations who had been forced to relocate from east of the Mississippi River were still considered sovereign nations, so their lands were not considered reservations and could not be broken up under the General Allotment Act. To resolve that issue, Congress simply passed a law in 1898, the Curtis Act, eliminating their sovereignty. Their lands were then allotted as had been done with the reservations, and the excess land was sold to settlers.[66]

Understandably, many Native Americans resisted the removal from their homelands and confinement to assigned reservations or individual allotments. They did this in various ways. Some simply left the reservations and went back to their homelands. Others refused to relocate to the reservations at all. The United States Army, no longer involved in fighting the Civil War, applied its full force to driving the Native Americans to isolated sites designated by the federal government. Those were not a few isolated skirmishes, as it is often portrayed. This was full-scale warfare, often under the command of the same officers who had served in the Civil War. Regardless of natural rights, or treaty rights, or even standard rules of warfare, the end

63. Singletary and Emm, "Working Effectively."

64. Dunbar-Ortiz, *An Indigenous Peoples' History*, 142.

65. Ibid., 157–59; "The Dawes Act 1887," nebraskastudies.org,; Singletary and Emm, "Working Effectively."

66. Dunbar-Ortiz, *An Indigenous Peoples' History*, 158.

always justified the means.[67] And both the means and the ends were justified by, and served to reinforce, the racism that defined the original inhabitants as primitive beings standing in the way of progress and civilization.

The migration into Texas and the lands acquired from Mexico added another element. There were Native American nations living in those lands and they too became the targets of the United States Army. But many of the Mexicans living there were descended from the Spanish, who had colonized Central and South America in the 1500s. The Spanish had never prohibited marriage between people of different ancestries, so after several generations of unions of Africans, Spanish, and Natives in various combinations, there were no clear-cut "races." There was a social hierarchy based loosely on color, though levels of education and wealth were also a factor. Lighter skin generally resulted in higher rank because of being more closely identified with the conquerors.[68] When those in the higher social categories in Mexico found themselves in the lower "racial " categories of the United States, it resulted in different dynamics, some of which continue to this day.[69] But it never led to any reassessment of the myth of race.

As the population in California grew, so did commerce across the Pacific. Political and economic problems in many Asian countries led people there to look to the United States as a land of opportunity, much as Europeans had looked across the Atlantic. Prior to completion of the transcontinental railroad, Chinese men came to California to work in the gold mines, and there are indications that they were initially welcomed.[70] When mining ceased to be profitable, the Chinese were given work laying rail tracks eastward from California to meet those building from the east. The railroad company was happy to hire them because they could be paid significantly less than White workers.[71]

The completion of the line in 1869 immediately left them without jobs, and the entire country was headed for a depression that would further add to unemployment. White workers, who already blamed the Chinese for low wages, had no interest in competing with them for the available jobs. In response to pressure from White workers, Congress passed the Chinese Exclusion Act in 1882, prohibiting the immigration of any more Chinese workers. Ten years later, the law was renewed, this time including the requirement that the Chinese workers already here register themselves

67. Ibid., 117–61.

68. Smedley and Smedley, *Race in North America*, 139–44.

69. Montejano, *Anglos and Mexicans*, 82–99, 156–96, 220–54, 315–16.

70. Takaki, *A Different Mirror*, 178–80.

71. Ibid., 181.

to receive a residence certificate, which they had to carry at all times or risk deportation. In 1902, the law was made permanent and remained in force until 1943.

Large-scale Japanese immigration did not begin until the 1880s. As elsewhere, politics and economics played a role. But family situations also played a role for the Japanese. Because of the small size and mountainous geography of Japan, family farms were very small, less than two and a half acres. Dividing such small tracts among heirs was impractical, so by tradition the first son inherited the farm and assumed responsibility for the care of the aging parents. Younger sons had to find employment in the cities. Emigration to Hawaii or the United States provided an alternative. Unlike the Chinese immigrants, who generally came without their spouses, the Japanese often came as families.

They also came at a time of transition that proved fortuitous to them. The development of irrigation in California made small-scale fruit and vegetable farming possible. Also, the recent completion of the transcontinental railroad and the development of refrigerated rail cars allowed California farmers to supply fresh produce to the growing cities throughout the country. Family farming was extremely hard work, but it did allow husbands and wives to work together for the benefit of their families, and gave them some separation from the racial animus that was becoming more intense and being directed at any and all groups not of European descent.[72]

72. Ibid., 232–36, 252–57.

9

Scientific Racism

The arguments about slavery prior to the Civil War naturally led to debates about those who were enslaved. The idea that Blacks were a distinct race was compelling, and doctors and scientists committed themselves to the study of differences. The search for objective, defining characteristics of separate "races" became intense and sometimes reached such ludicrous extremes that they would be funny had the end results not been so damaging. Reviewing the work of the various scientists, it is obvious that in some cases they were not at all objective, and were clearly attempting to justify discrimination against Blacks. That said, it is also apparent that many others tried to be objective, though they were generally influenced by the biases of their time.

But more important than the mistakes that were made, or the motives of the scientists, is the reality that, just as racism was used to justify and support slavery, science in the nineteenth century was being used to justify and support racism. It is also important to note that, though the science of that era has been disproved, the terminology remains. The continued use of terms carried over from the flawed science of the past adds to our present confusion and misunderstandings about racism.

The Origin of the Myth of Race

Chapter 4 introduced the contributions of Carl Linnaeus and Johann Friedrich Blumenbach to the development of the idea of races and intrinsic differences between the races. Linnaeus developed the scheme of classification of plants and animals that is still used to this day. As the study of the natural sciences developed in Europe, it was entirely logical that the thousands of plants and animals would ultimately require a method of ordering and classifying them. Linnaeus' attempt to apply that scheme to humans was doomed to failure, since there are no scientific differences among men. Unfortunately, his error was compounded rather than corrected.

Blumenbach gave us the terminology of Caucasian, Mongolian, etc. which remains in our vocabulary today, though he understood that there were no distinct categories. He wrote:

> Although there seems to be so great a difference between widely separate nations, that you might easily take the inhabitants of the Cape of Good Hope, the Greenlanders, and the Circassians for so many different species of man, yet when the matter is thoroughly considered, you see that all do so run into one another, and that one variety of mankind does so sensibly pass into the other, that you cannot mark out the limits between them.[1]

Yet significant differences in appearance did exist, and the desire to assume that this was sufficient to demonstrate that other differences also existed seems to have been irresistible. Montagu describes the situation this way:

> The classifiers of the "races" of mankind who have devised the various classificatory schemes of mankind during the past hundred years have mostly agreed in one respect—they have unexceptionally taken for granted the one thing which they were attempting to prove, namely, the existence of human "races."[2]

This was particularly true of scientists during the nineteenth century. The idea that science and scientific inquiry were entirely objective and based on identifiable facts had broad appeal at a time when biblical justifications of current conditions were becoming strained. Of course, people were not prepared to discard the Bible; rather, they were primarily looking for factual confirmation of that which previously had been accepted solely on faith. So in the study of humans, the basic premise of the relation of humans to God and to the other animals found in Genesis had to be accommodated:

> So God created man in his own image, in the image of God created he him; male and female created he them. And God blessed them, and God said unto them, Be fruitful, and multiply, and

1. Bendyshe, *Anthropological Treatises*, 98–99; Gould, *The Mismeasure of Man*, 407.

2. Montagu, *Man's Most Dangerous Myth*, 26.

replenish the earth, and subdue it: and have dominion over the fish of the sea, and over the fowl of the air, and over every living thing that moveth upon the earth.[3]

Though the initial reaction to Linnaeus' classification of humans among the animals, rather than above them, was negative, a way remained to reconcile that with Genesis. The idea of a chain of being extending from God to humans to the other animals, while not entirely new, was now seen as a way to retain the connection of humans to God and above the other animals. Seeing God's plan as an orderly arrangement of all animals from insects to fishes to amphibians to mammals to humans to angels and finally to God was easy to understand and satisfied the need for compatibility between science and the Bible. Humans were seen as part physical and part spiritual, separating them from the strictly physical of other animals, and connecting them to the strictly spiritual found in angels and God. The chain of being was not a perfect fit with the findings of science, but it filled a need. Sadly, this view also allowed for the consideration that humans were not necessarily a single link in the chain, but several, and that some humans were therefore of a lower order than others.[4]

Ranking of Human Groups

As objective as the scientists attempted to be, or pretended to be, we can see that they invariably started with assumptions that they then attempted to prove. As Montagu noted, one of those assumptions was that separate races existed and the search was for the distinguishing characteristics. In retrospect, another assumption that we can see is the general expectation that the distinguishing characteristics would demonstrate an ordering by level of advancement and intelligence.

Classification of plants and animals was based on physical traits, differences in form, and appearance. So the scientific study of humans began with the search for physical differences. John S. Haller, Jr., in his book *Outcasts From Evolution*, notes that facial angle, the angle between a horizontal line from the bottom of the nose to the ear, and a vertical line from the upper jaw bone to the forehead, had been used from the time of Aristotle as an indication of intelligence, but that it now became "the most extensively elaborated and artlessly abused criterion for racial somatology."[5] Petrus

3. Gen. 1:27–28 (King James Version).
4. Jordan, *White Over Black*, 222–23.
5. Haller, *Outcasts from Evolution*, 9.

Camper (1722–1789), a highly educated and respected Dutch physician, professor and researcher, presented the concept of facial angle in the 1770s:

> The two extremities therefore of the facial line are from 70 to 100 degrees, from the negro to the Grecian antique; make it under 70, and you describe an orang or an ape; lessen it still more, and you have the head of a dog.[6]

He also wrote about skulls he had in his collection:

> It is amusing to contemplate an arrangement of these, placed in a regular succession: apes, orangs, negroes, the skull of an Hottentot, Madagascar, Celebese, Chinese, Moguller, Calmuck, and divers Europeans. It was in this manner that I arranged them upon a shelf in my cabinet.[7]

Since the primary focus of his writing was on art and proportion, there is room for debate about his intent. When commenting on the facial angle of the various human skulls, he did choose to include the apes, and in two sections he mentioned the similarity between the Blacks and the apes. He specifically declined to state a connection, though he noted that others had, and invited his readers to refer to their writings.[8] More important than his intent is the subsequent use of this concept over the next one hundred years to reinforce the idea of the chain of being and the different positions of races in the chain.

The measurement of facial angle was just the beginning. A more acute angle suggested a lower forehead, which in turn suggested a smaller brain cavity and a smaller brain. It was simply assumed that larger brain size indicated greater intelligence. Samuel Morton (1799–1851), a physician and professor of anatomy at the University of Pennsylvania, did extensive work collecting and measuring the internal size of skulls and publishing three books that summarized the results of his analysis. At the time of his death, he had collected over 860 skulls.[9] He carefully measured the size of each skull by filling it with lead shot and then calculating the volume of the shot. He then averaged the sizes by racial category and concluded that Caucasians had the largest brains, followed by Mongolians, Native Americans, and finally Negroes.

In his book, *The Mismeasure of Man*, Stephen Jay Gould points out that Morton's careful measurements and accurate data, while absolutely

6. Camper, *The Works of the Late Professor Camper*, 42.
7. Ibid., 50.
8. Ibid., 9, 32.
9. Renschler and Monge, "The Samuel George Morton Cranial Collection."

objective, were used to produce results that were neither objective nor accurate. Gould notes that skull size is related to body size and, since some groups of people tend to be larger and others tend to be smaller, the way those subgroups are used in the analysis will affect the outcome. For instance, within the Native American group, the Iroquois tended to be larger and the Inca Peruvians tended to be smaller. Yet, Iroquois skulls represented only 2 percent of Morton's sample, while Inca Peruvian skulls represented 25 percent of his sample.[10] Conversely, within the Caucasian group, the Hindu subgroup tended to be smaller. Because of this, Morton intentionally reduced the percentage of Hindu skulls in that sample.[11] The numbers of male skulls and female skulls in his samples also had an effect that had not been taken into account. Gould adjusted for all of these variables and found that no truly objective differences between the racial groups could be proven from the data.[12]

Morton was extremely careful in taking his measurements and documenting his analysis, and Gould concludes he was making a sincere attempt to be objective.[13] Yet his work was clearly affected by the social norms of the time. Had the outcomes of his analysis produced results contrary to those he expected, it is doubtful either he or the scientific community would have accepted them as proof of a different order of the races.

An illustration of this is provided by the work of Paul Broca (1824–1880), a French physician and anthropologist. Broca is well-known and respected for some of the pioneering work he did with the study of brains. But he was also a product of his times and much of his anthropological work involved measuring heads and bodies. He invented many instruments for the measuring of heads, including facial angle.[14] At the time of his death, he had accumulated over 185,000 measurements.[15] His measurements were precise and extensive but, as with Morton, the way the data was used is informative. For instance, Broca began to test a theory that the length of the lower arm bone might be a basis for ordering human beings, since a longer forearm would indicate closer affinity to the apes. Measurement by major racial groups seemed to bear that out. But analysis by subgroups produced a different result. Rather than concluding that the new results indicated a different order, Broca decided that the theory was no longer valid:

10. Gould, *The Mismeasure of Man*, 89.

11. Ibid., 92.

12. Ibid., 86–101.

13. Ibid.

14. Fletcher, "Paul Broca and the French School," 129–30.

15. Ibid., 139.

After this, it seems difficult to me to continue to say that elonga-
tion of the forearm is a character of degradation or inferiority,
because, on this account, the European occupies a place between Negroes on the one hand, and Hottentots, Australians,
and Eskimos on the other. [16]

His unusual argument of noting the failure of brain size measurements
to always produce the expected results, while continuing to defend it as
proof of the inferiority of some groups, shows how any data could be, and
was, used to defend preconceived ideas:

A table on which races were arranged by order of their cranial
capacities would not represent the degrees of their superiority
or inferiority, because size represents only one element of the
problem [of ranking races]. On such a table, Eskimos, Lapps,
Malays, Tartars and several other peoples of the Mongolian type
would surpass the most civilized people of Europe. A lowly race
may therefore have a big brain. But this does not destroy the
value of small brain size as a mark of inferiority. The table shows
that West African blacks have a cranial capacity about 100 cc
less than that of European races. To this figure, we may add the
following: Caffirs, Nubians, Tasmanians, Hottentots, Australians. These examples are sufficient to prove that if the volume of
the brain does not play a decisive role in the intellectual ranking
of races, it nevertheless has a very real importance. [17]

Initially, most scientists accepted that all humans came from a single
origin. The idea of creation by God, and the familiar story of Adam and Eve,
could not be discarded lightly. For some, though, the search for explanation for the perceived differences in the races led them to conclude that the
different races had different origins. This theory had its strongest support
among scientists in the United States and became known as the "American
school" of anthropology. Some of the most qualified and respected scientists
held this view, and supporters of slavery embraced it, since it allowed the
argument that some races were not actually human. In the end, though, this
radical departure from scripture was never broadly accepted.

Charles Darwin's book, *On The Origin of Species*, published in 1859,
provided a new way to explain the differences between the races. Blumenbach had argued that human origin began in its most perfect form near the
Caucasus mountains and had degenerated into the darker races. Darwin's

16. Broca, "Sur les proportions," 11, as quoted in Gould, *The Mismeasure of Man,*
118–19.

17. Broca, "Sur les cranes," 38, as quoted in Gould, *The Mismeasure of Man,* 119.

findings now allowed for the argument that humans were evolving and, whether they had split into separate subspecies after creation or just evolved at different rates, the white race had evolved to a higher level of intelligence and civilization than the others.[18] The question of whether God created man, or humans evolved from animals was a debate for another time.

In reality, none of the extensive data collection and analysis had any scientific value. Whether the data was collected correctly or analyzed correctly is irrelevant. It's not a question of whether the ordering of groups of people was done correctly, since there is no correct way of ordering humans. What is relevant is the fact that, at that point in time when racism was taking on a life of its own, separate from slavery, brilliant doctors and scientists were finding ways to reinforce the idea of race and of inferior and superior groups of people. Many warned against using their findings to justify slavery. The connection between racism and slavery was being broken, but the idea of inferior and superior groups of people was considered scientific fact.

Current Use of Flawed Terminology

The terminology these scientists used ensured that their biases would live on. Anthropologist Carolyn Fluehr-Lobban notes that, just before the Nazi takeover in 1931, it was a German scientist, von Eichstedt, who proposed scientific names for the "races." Blumenbach's racial varieties became "oids," such as Caucasoid, Mongoloid, etc.[19] The suffix "oid" means "resembling" and demonstrates the inability to find clear lines of demarcation between "races." Yet, those became the official names of the "races." And, significantly, Blumenbach's original Ethiopian variety became Negroid, the only group identified by color rather than location. Fluehr-Lobban also points out that this was the anthropology she was taught as an undergraduate in the late 1960s.[20] And, while anthropology is no longer taught in that way, the terminology remains in use today, with the confusing result of scientific names for non-existent "races."

Further adding to the confusion is the continued use of the term "race." Anthropologist Audrey Smedley points out:

> During the first half of the twentieth century, certain sectors of the scientific community began to react with skepticism to the concept of race and its ideological themes. Among many

18. Fredrickson, *The Black Image*, 232.
19. Fluehr-Lobban, *Race and Racism*, 85.
20. Ibid.

scholars, race was transformed and limited in its conceptualization to biogenetic features of human groups, and new scientific definitions of *race* were introduced.[21]

She also notes that attempts to transform the meaning of race had limited success because "In the wider society, the folk sense of race and race differences was too deeply ingrained in the American psyche and culture."[22] This is a very important point that cannot be overemphasized. It is the very core of the issue of racism. As Smedley says:

> To argue . . . that science had not proved that the races were unequal in their abilities, intellectual and otherwise, was to argue a contradiction in terms. *The central meaning of race has from its origin historically been that of inherently unequal human groups.*[23]

Understandably, this leaves current scientists in a difficult place. As Fluehr-Lobban notes in her concluding chapter, while discussing the future of race:

> While it is probable that race has little future as a biological concept, it is a great error to dismiss its ever-changing sociological significance. . . . Anthropology has often been left at the periphery of sociological dialogues on racism, its role relegated to serial statements about the unscientific nature of and irrelevance of race. The exclusive concern with the biological aspects of and myths about race has limited its ability to comment on the effects of racism in society . . . .[24]

This will be discussed later in this book, but it is helpful to be reminded that, just as the creation of racism was accomplished through coordination of laws, science, religion, and popular culture, ending it will require the same level of commitment and coordination. That coordination is difficult to manage, and the commitment is difficult to maintain. And popular culture is often the most difficult to change. But as popular opinion was intentionally misguided in the past, experts in every field must coordinate their efforts to correct the errors of the past that remain today in popular culture.

21. Smedley and Smedley, *Race in North America*, 289.

22. Ibid., 295.

23. Ibid.

24. Fluehr-Lobban, *Race and Racism*, 248.

10

Racism in the First Half of the Twentieth Century

Like most centuries, the twentieth century had its share of dramatic events, including two world wars and a period of major social upheaval dealing with the issue of racism. As in previous centuries, the major events become the focal point. The events themselves are of primary interest and the changes that can be ascribed to them become the secondary interest. What is frequently missed is a consideration of those things that have not really changed, but instead have adapted.

The First World War led to the massive movement of Blacks from the South to the cities of the North and West and the resulting segregated inner cities that remain with us a hundred years later. The Second World War led to a major uprising in opposition to segregation and discrimination against African Americans. The dramatic successes of the Civil Rights Movement led to drastic changes in the ways racism was manifested, and consequently, in how it was perceived by those who were not directly affected.

Racism in the twentieth century simply continued on from the previous century, fueled by some events and adapting to others. It is more important to notice how racism responded to the events than to become focused on the events themselves. Also important is a focus on the adaptations, with an awareness of what had not changed. By the end of the century, racism was in many ways much less brutal, but in other ways every bit as devastating.

The Century Begins

By 1889, an organization of southern white farmers, the Southern Farmers' Alliance, had branches in every southern state.[1] An unaffiliated but parallel organization for black farmers, the Colored Farmers' National Alliance and Cooperative Union, had over one million members in twelve states.[2] A major depression in the 1880s led the organized white farmers to split from the Democratic Party, which they felt was disregarding their problems in favor of accommodating the industrial interests of the north. That group of white farmers formed the Populist Party, which saw the organized black farmers as allies who could increase their political strength. They appealed to black voters and fought to ensure that their right to vote was protected.[3]

The Democrats fought to maintain their party's political control. They attempted to woo the black voters away from the Populist Party, and when that failed, they often resorted to bribery, fraud, and intimidation.[4] When the Populist Party was unable to displace the Democratic Party, it was partially due to the fear of placing too much power in the hands of Blacks. Whites in both parties resented the fact that Blacks held the balance of power, and could not be controlled.[5]

Blacks outnumbered Whites in several southern states and, as fear of Black control became the primary concern, Whites set aside their other differences and turned their frustrations against all black voters. They saw the solution as the disfranchisement of all Blacks, ensuring that Whites alone would resolve any future disagreements.[6] Beginning in the 1890s, all of the southern states began replacing their constitutions, virtually eliminating the right to vote for all Blacks. Property ownership requirements, literacy tests, and poll taxes (with loopholes for Whites) were the methods used and were very effective. Franklin and Moss cite two examples:

> In 1896 there were 130,344 blacks registered in Louisiana, constituting a majority in twenty-six parishes. In 1900, two years after the adoption of the new constitution, only 5,320 blacks were on the registration books, and in no parish did they make up a majority of voters. Of 181,471 black males of voting age in

1. Franklin and Moss, *From Slavery to Freedom*, 284.
2. Ibid.
3. Ibid., 283–85.
4. Ibid., 281–86.
5. Ibid., 285–86.
6. Ibid., 286.

Alabama in 1900, only 3,000 registered after the new constitutional provisions went into effect.[7]

The Beginning of Southern Segregation

In 1896, the Supreme Court ruled in *Plessy v. Ferguson* regarding the constitutionality of the State of Louisiana law requiring separate accommodations for Blacks and Whites on all railroads carrying passengers within the state. By a vote of seven to one (the ninth justice did not participate in the ruling), the court ruled the law constitutional. The one dissenting justice had the integrity to state the true purpose of the law and the foresight to anticipate the consequences of the Court's ruling:

> The destinies of the two races, in this country, are indissolubly linked together, and the interests of both require that the common government of all shall not permit the seeds of race hate to be planted under the sanction of law. What can more certainly arouse race hate, what more certainly create and perpetuate a feeling of distrust between these races, than state enactments which, in fact, proceed on the ground that colored citizens are so inferior and degraded that they cannot be allowed to sit in public coaches occupied by white citizens? That, as all will admit, is the real meaning of such legislation as was enacted in Louisiana.[8]

With the benefit of hindsight, we can see the extremes of twentieth century segregation that were a direct result of that ruling. We can see the error of the statement of the majority regarding the question of equality. "We consider the underlying fallacy of the plaintiff's argument to consist in the assumption that the enforced separation of the two races stamps the colored race with a badge of inferiority."[9] This was not a minor error in judgment. Its ramifications were immense and have lasted for more than one hundred years. Segregation did in fact reinforce the idea that there was a ranking of human beings and that People of Color, particularly Blacks, were inferior. It remained in place for more than two generations and the hardened attitudes it fostered have remained for generations to this day.

7. Ibid., 288.
8. *Plessy v. Ferguson*, 163 U.S.537 (1896), Harlan, dissenting.
9. *Plessy v. Ferguson*, 163 U.S.537 (1896).

The White Man's Burden

In 1898, the United States acquired the Philippines as a colony. In that year, the United States' support of Cuba in her fight for independence from Spain expanded to support the Philippines' fight for independence as well. When the United States was victorious in the war with Spain, control of the Philippines was transferred to the United States in the Treaty of Paris of 1898. Instead of granting the Philippines their independence, the United States simply took the place of Spain as the colonial power. As would be expected, the people of the Philippines, who had struggled for their independence from Spain, continued the struggle against the United States. And the United States, which had fought in support of the people of the Philippines, now fought against them. A poem written by Rudyard Kipling regarding the U.S. role in the Philippines, entitled "The White Man's Burden," published in 1899 articulated the views of many:

> "Take up the White Man's burden—
> Send forth the best ye breed—
> Go, bind your sons to exile
> To serve your captives' need;
> To wait, in heavy harness,
> On fluttered folk and wild—
> Your new-caught, sullen peoples,
> Half devil and half child."[10]

The concept of a "White Man's burden" was ridiculed by some, but there were many who agreed, and the phrase was soon broadly applied to any "race" that white men considered inferior and a burden that had to be dealt with. The imperialism of the U.S. was seen by many as our duty to the world. Theodore Roosevelt, who had been sent a copy of the poem, said it made "good sense from the expansionist standpoint."[11] In a speech earlier that year he laid out his views regarding the capabilities of the people being conquered, and of our "manifest duty":

> We now have certain duties in the West and East Indies. We cannot with honor shirk these duties. . . . It is, I am sure, the desire of every American that the people of each island, as rapidly as they show themselves fit for self-government, shall be endowed with a constantly larger measure of self-government. But it would be criminal folly to sacrifice the real welfare of the islands, and to fail to do our manifest duty, under the plea of

10. Kipling, "The White Man's Burden."
11. Zinn, *A People's History*, 292–93.

carrying out some doctrinaire idea which, if it had been lived up to, would have made the entire North American continent, as now found, the happy hunting-ground of savages. It is the idlest of chatter to speak of savages as being fit for self-government. . . . If we refrain from doing our part of the world's work, it will not alter the fact that that work has got to be done, only it will have to be done by some stronger race, because we will have shown ourselves weaklings. I do not speak merely from the standpoint of American interests, but from the standpoint of civilization and humanity.

It is infinitely better for the whole world that Russia should have taken Turkestan, that France should have taken Algiers, and that England should have taken India. The success of an Algerian or of a Sepoy revolt would be a hideous calamity to all mankind, and those who abetted it, directly or indirectly, would be traitors to civilization. And so exactly the same reasoning applies to our own dealings with the Philippines. We must treat them with absolute justice, but we must treat them also with firmness and courage. They must be made to realize that justice does not proceed from a sense of weakness on our part, that we are the masters. Weakness in any form or shape, as you gentlemen, who all your lives have upheld the honor of the flag ashore and afloat, know, is the unpardonable sin in dealing with such a problem as that with which we are confronted in the Philippines. The insurrection must be stamped out as mercifully as possible; but it must be stamped out.[12]

At the turn of the twentieth century, the man who would become president of the United States two years later referred to Native Americans as savages who were unfit for self-government and implied that our failure to control the Philippine people would be "a hideous calamity" and traitorous to civilization. As president, he pardoned the three white men who had received prison sentences for holding black men in involuntary servitude almost forty years after slavery was ended.[13] Those trials, resulting from the abuses of convict leasing, were discussed in chapter 8.

Yet he also took some conciliatory steps toward Blacks as he sought compromise that he hoped would result in greater unity within the country.[14] He spoke in favor of a "square deal" for Blacks[15] and consulted

---

12. Almanac of Theodore Roosevelt, "America's Part of the World's Work."

13. Blackmon, *Slavery by Another Name*, 248, 277.

14. Ibid., 158–59.

15. Ibid., 170.

with Booker T. Washington, the most influential black leader of the time. Washington was a moderate black leader who emphasized self-reliance and humility for Blacks and was careful not to offend Whites. But when Roosevelt invited him to dinner at the White House in 1901, the people in the South immediately expressed their outrage. The governor of Georgia said: "No southerner can respect any white man who would eat with a Negro."[16] A U.S. senator from South Carolina, Ben Tillman, was more blunt: "Now that Roosevelt has eaten with that nigger Washington, we shall have to kill a thousand niggers to get them back to their places."[17]

Lynchings And Race Riots

Tillman was more outspoken and crude than most men in his position, but the idea of killing Blacks to keep them "in their places" was accepted by most in the South and by many in the North, as well. Between 1889 and 1922, there were 3,436 lynchings, many of them in the northern states.[18] According to Franklin and Moss, in the first two years of the twentieth century there were 214 lynchings, an average of more than two per week.[19] Yet, numerous attempts to pass a federal anti-lynching law failed. A bill introduced in 1921 passed in the House of Representatives, but was stopped in the Senate by a filibuster by southern Senators.[20] The years following the First World War brought new expectations from Blacks and new push back from Whites. Over 360,000 Blacks served in the military during the war and felt that earned them equal rights as citizens and as veterans.[21] Instead, as Woodward points out, "During the first year following the war more than seventy Negroes were lynched, several of them veterans still in uniform."[22]

Franklin and Moss note that within a year following the end of the First World War the Ku Klux Klan grew from a few thousand members to more than a hundred thousand.[23] By 1924, the membership was four and a half million.[24] During the last seven months of 1919 there were ap-

16. Ibid., 167.

17. Ibid., 166.

18. NAACP advertisement, *The New York Times*, November 23, 1922; Franklin and Moss, *From Slavery to Freedom,* 393.

19. Franklin and Moss, *From Slavery to Freedom,* 291.

20. "Documented History of the Incident."

21. Woodward, *The Strange Career,* 114.

22. Ibid., 114–15.

23. Franklin and Moss, *From Slavery to Freedom,* 384.

24. Zinn, *A People's History,* 373.

proximately twenty-five race riots.[25] Two notable riots, which occurred in Tulsa, Oklahoma in 1921 and Rosewood, Florida in 1923, received some public attention in the 1990s when official commissions were finally formed to provide accurate accounts of the events.

At the time of the riot in Tulsa, the Greenwood district of that city was one of the wealthiest black communities in the United States, having benefited from the oil boom that was taking place in the area. It was so prosperous that it was sometimes referred to as the Black Wall Street. The riot lasted less than twenty-four hours, but resulted in 1,256 residences and the entire business district, including four hotels, two newspapers, several restaurants, theaters, retail stores and professional offices, destroyed by fire.[26] Approximately ten thousand Blacks, almost the entire population of Greenwood, were left homeless.[27] The official count was nine Whites and twenty-six Blacks killed. The commission found death certificates for thirteen Whites and twenty-six Blacks.[28] However, Salvation Army and Red Cross records show that the death toll for Blacks was in the range of one hundred and fifty to three hundred.[29] The disparity speaks to the casual treatment of the black bodies that were buried in unmarked graves before family members were given the opportunity to identify them.

While this is referred to as a "race riot," it was really the action of a white mob, estimated at the time to exceed five thousand men[30] armed with rifles and ammunition taken from local sporting goods stores and pawnshops.[31] The local police had deputized approximately five hundred men and the local National Guard was called up, but rather than controlling the mob they joined in.[32] All Blacks who were not killed, or who did not escape from town, were arrested and placed in detention facilities. The mob then systematically looted and burned the unprotected houses and businesses. White eyewitness accounts reported that uniformed police, as well as deputized civilians and National Guard members, participated in the looting and burning.[33]

---

25. Franklin and Moss, *From Slavery to Freedom*, 385.
26. "Tulsa Race Riot," Oklahoma Historical Society, 12, 22–23, 87.
27. Ibid., 87–88.
28. Ibid., 23, 114.
29. Ibid., 12–13, 86–87, 121, 124.
30. Ibid., 71.
31. Ibid., 64.
32. Ibid., 64, 66–68, 74–76, 78–79, 84.
33. Ibid.

Rosewood, Florida was a much smaller Black community of 344 residents.[34] That incident began on a Monday when a young woman claimed that a black man assaulted her while her husband was at work. Though subsequent research suggests that it could have been a white lover who assaulted the woman, a black escapee from a convict labor camp was soon identified as the primary suspect. On Thursday, a gunfight took place at one of the Black residences where a number of black families had gathered to defend themselves and their property, while the Whites believed they were sheltering the suspect. During the night, the Blacks abandoned the house and hid out in the swamp. The next day the White mob burned the house and a number of other homes in town. On Sunday a group of one hundred to one hundred and fifity Whites participated in burning the remaining twelve houses.[35] None of the former residents ever returned. The town was abandoned. Over the seven days, six Blacks and two Whites had been killed.[36]

No one was ever held to account for the killings or the arsons in either case. The events received substantial local and national press coverage at the time, though the reports reflected the biases of the times. As the years passed and the mob mentality faded, it became easier to bury the past than to address the injustice of what had happened. The 1990s official commissions, more than seventy years after the events, when most of the victims were no longer alive, finally produced accurate accounts and brought the facts to the attention of the public. Yet few Whites are aware of those events.

In the 2007 documentary, *Banished*, Marco Williams tells the stories of towns in Arkansas and Missouri and a county in Georgia that drove out all black residents early in the century and remain virtually all white to this day. In 1901, the white residents of Pierce City, Missouri forced the approximately three hundred black residents to leave town. In 1909, over one hundred Blacks were driven out of Harrison, Arkansas, and in 1912 over one thousand Blacks were driven out of Forsyth County, Georgia. In addition to the stories of the beatings, lynchings, and burning of homes used to force the people out, the documentary also describes the properties lost by those forced to leave their homes and the insurmountable challenges for their heirs attempting to regain the stolen properties or to receive reasonable compensation for them.[37]

34. "Documented History of the Incident."

35. Ibid.

36. Ibid.

37. *Banished*, Directed by Marco Williams.

Those three incidents were not unique, nor were they rare occurrences. In his book, *Sundown Towns,* historian James W. Loewen makes this statement regarding the period after 1890:

> Across America, at least 50 towns, and probably many more than
> that, drove out their African American populations violently. At
> least 16 did so in Illinois alone. In the West, another 50 or more
> towns drove out their Chinese American populations.[38]

Loewen's book documents his research into towns that had an explicit policy prohibiting African Americans from living there. The term "sundown town" comes from the signs posted by many towns at their city limits warning African Americans: *N——, Don't Let the Sun Go Down on You In ____.* Some of those signs remained as recently as the 1970s.[39] In his introductory chapter, Loewen notes how little is known about this history, even by historians. When he began his research, he expected to find about fifty sundown towns nationwide; yet through his research he found that in Illinois alone there were four hundred and seventy-five towns and cities that had no non-white residents in census after census. He determined that almost all of those were sundown towns.[40] He also concluded that:

> There is reason to believe that more than half of all towns in Or-
> egon, Indiana, Ohio, the Cumberlands, the Ozarks, and diverse
> other areas were also all-white on purpose. Sundown suburbs
> are found from Darien, Connecticut, to LaJolla, California, and
> are even more prevalent; indeed, most suburbs began life as
> sundown towns.[41]

Status as a sundown town was not hidden or done surreptitiously. It was proudly proclaimed on signs leading into town and local newspapers and chambers of commerce found it to be useful as a promotional tool. Residents knew and supported the policy. Much of Loewen's information came from residents, long after the signs were gone and the history had been buried. In fact, he found that frequently the policy, though no longer official, continued to be enforced unofficially even at the time of his research.[42]

38. Loewen, *Sundown Towns,* 12.
39. Ibid., 3.
40. Ibid., 4, 7.
41. Ibid., 4–5.
42. Ibid., 6, 12, 21–23, 379–420.

The Beginning of Northern and Western Segregation

In 1910, 90 percent of Blacks still lived in the former Confederate states in the South.[43] Despite harsh working conditions, dishonest and abusive bosses and landowners, laws and law enforcement specifically designed to subjugate Blacks, mob rule, and lynching, few of the former slaves or their descendents had been able to leave. The First World War, which began in 1914, provided a window of opportunity. The war resulted in a significant drop in European immigrants, from 1,218,000 in 1914 to 110,000 in 1918, creating a labor shortage in the North, particularly in the factories.[44]

Representatives from the factories traveled throughout the South promising jobs to anyone willing to relocate. Blacks employed as farm laborers and domestics or doing other menial jobs had minimal resources to finance such a move. They had no experience with big-city living conditions or the availability of housing in the North. Few had any family or friends there to help them get established. Yet in the decade of the war, over 550,000 Blacks moved from the South to the cities of the North, almost three times the number of the previous decade.[45]

That marked the beginning of a massive shift in population that had, and continues to have, significant impacts. In her book, *The Warmth of Other Suns,* Isabel Wilkerson discusses that process and the many reasons why people moved. As many and varied as those reasons were, escape from the brutal and demeaning conditions in the South was the most compelling. When the labor shortage of the World War I years ended, the Blacks who had moved to the North in those years were a resource for family and friends who had remained in the South. A total of 903,000 moved during the following decade, and another 480,000 followed in the depression decade ending in 1940. The labor demands of the Second World War drew another 1.6 million. By 1970, when the trend stopped, almost six million Blacks had moved out of the South,[46] and only 50 percent of the total population of Blacks still lived there.[47]

Though people relocated throughout the North and West, most moved to the industrial centers in the major cities. In sixty years, the Black population in Chicago increased from 44,000 to 1.1 million. In Detroit, the Black

---

43. Wilkerson, *The Warmth of Other Suns,* 10.
44. Ibid., 161.
45. Ibid.
46. Ibid., 217–18.
47. Ibid., 10; Woodward, *The Strange Career,* 128.

population grew from less than 6,000 to more than 660,000.[48] Milwaukee, Cleveland, Pittsburgh, Philadelphia, New York, and Boston all experienced comparable growth. Los Angeles and Oakland became the destination of choice for thousands of Blacks in the decades during and following the Second World War.

Blacks in the North had always been discriminated against, but prior to the twentieth century there was not much segregation. Most Blacks in the North lived in integrated neighborhoods that were predominantly White.[49] In the initial stages of the migration from the South to the North, the new arrivals followed living patterns not unlike those of the European immigrants, finding housing and living near family and friends who had arrived before them. The initial segregation was logical and created by choice. From that point, though, the experience of the Blacks from the South and the immigrants from Europe diverged dramatically.

As the European immigrants became established and their income levels increased, they were able to move to less crowded neighborhoods and into better quality housing. That option was never available to the Blacks. As more Blacks moved to the cities, the areas they were permitted to live in became more rigidly defined. Any Blacks attempting to move from their designated area were met with threats and violence and their houses were vandalized. If the homeowners could not be harassed into leaving, their homes were bombed. In Chicago, fifty-eight houses were bombed between 1917 and 1921.[50]

As the population grew, the available housing became increasingly more crowded. As recently as 1951, a family of five had to share a two-room apartment with a family of four. They eventually found a five-room apartment in the town of Cicero, just outside of Chicago, where the rent of sixty dollars a month was only four dollars more than they were paying for half of the two-room apartment in Chicago. When they attempted to move in, white protesters, supported by the police, prevented them from doing so. They took the case to court and won the right to occupy the apartment. The day they moved in, a mob formed, drove them out, destroyed their furniture and possessions, and ultimately firebombed the twenty-unit apartment building. Though 118 men were arrested during the riot, none of them were charged. Instead, the rental agent and the owner of the apartment building

---

48. Lynch, *The Black Urban Condition*, 426–32; Wilkerson, *The Warmth of Other Suns*, 190, 570.

49. Massey and Denton, *American Apartheid*, 23–24.

50. Ibid., 35.

were charged with inciting a riot. At the time, many of the residents of Cicero were first and second-generation European immigrants.[51]

The unrestrained violence and vandalism spread to also target Blacks who had owned homes in more integrated areas for years. As those people were forced to seek safety by moving out of their integrated neighborhoods, the cities became more segregated, and the areas set aside for Blacks became more crowded. Eventually, those boundaries had to be expanded to accommodate the new arrivals. This led to a cycle of Blacks moving into adjacent areas, Whites resisting for a while, and ultimately moving out. The housing segregation that exists today began with that process of preventing Blacks from integrating White neighborhoods and Whites abandoning neighborhoods as soon as Blacks were allowed in.

As suburban areas were developed to absorb the fleeing Whites, less violent means were developed to keep Blacks out. Restrictive covenants came into use as an effective tool to prevent integration. Restrictive covenants are legal restrictions on how a property may be used, not set by a governmental body, but by the seller of the property. They are established to maintain certain standards for the neighborhood, such as quality of construction, maintenance of yards and buildings, and disposal of garbage. They are generally legally enforceable. Until 1948, restrictive covenants preventing the sale of a property to certain groups of people were legal and enforceable by law.[52] In the North, as in the South, the law and the courts were used to enforce segregation.

In 1948, the Supreme Court ruled that racial restrictive covenants could not be legally enforced. But the ruling did not make the covenants illegal.[53] Sellers, landlords, homeowners associations, and real estate agents were still expected to abide by the covenants. Though the police and the courts were no longer available for enforcement, threats and harassment against sellers and buyers, and especially threats of boycotts against real estate agents, were effective alternatives.

It was not until the Housing Rights Act was passed in 1968 that all racial restrictive covenants became illegal.[54] Though illegal, many still remain in deeds and homeowners association by-laws because of the complicated legal process required to remove them. A review by the Seattle Civil Rights and Labor History Project based at the University of Washington found that over four hundred racial restrictive covenants and deed restrictions

51. Wilkerson, *The Warmth of Other Suns*, 372–74.
52. Massey and Denton, *American Apartheid*, 36.
53. Seattle Civil Rights Project, *Racial Restrictive Covenants*.
54. Ibid.

remained in the Seattle area in 2005. Those covenants and deed restrictions covered thousands of homes in dozens of neighborhoods because major real estate developers had written them to cover entire subdivisions when the plats were recorded in the 1920s, 1930s, and 1940s.[55]

Concern about Enemy Propaganda

The potential for the United States to become involved in the Second World War became apparent with Hitler's invasion of a number of European countries in 1939 and 1940; preparations for the possibility of war began immediately.[56] The Aryan supremacy that Hitler espoused forced the people of the United States to confront the racism at home, and that became a regular consideration as war preparations were taking place. In 1939 the country was still in a depression, with unemployment over 17 percent[57] and factories at less than full capacity,[58] so the preparations for war were economically beneficial for both workers and factory owners.

In the drafting of troops and the hiring at defense plants, preference was initially given to Whites.[59] Since all of the new jobs were being financed by federal spending, Blacks expected and demanded equal access to those jobs. In early 1941, a group of Blacks began planning a march in Washington to highlight those demands.[60] Recognizing the need for national unity and the potential for enemy propaganda, President Franklin Roosevelt averted the march by issuing an executive order prohibiting discrimination "in the employment of workers in defense industries or Government because of race, creed, color, or national origin."[61] As a result, all subsequent defense contracts contained a clause prohibiting discrimination.[62]

In December 1941, the Japanese attack on Pearl Harbor made United States involvement in the war a reality. In addition to the mobilization of military units, potential enemy propaganda continued to be a major concern. Only two months earlier, in October 1941, the last peonage case had been settled when an Alabama man pled guilty to holding a black man in involuntary servitude. His penalty was a $100 fine and six months of

55. Seattle Civil Rights Project, *Racial Restrictive Covenants: Enforcing.*

56. Franklin and Moss, *From Slavery to Freedom*, 477.

57. Galbraith, *A Journey Through Economic Time*, 116.

58. Ibid., 114–15.

59. Franklin and Moss, *From Slavery to Freedom*, 477–78.

60. Ibid., 479.

61. Ibid., 480.

62. Ibid.

probation.[63] Suddenly, this discrimination and violence against black Americans, which had been denied and discounted for decades, became a threat to national security as potential propaganda for the enemy. Blackmon described the response by Attorney General Francis Biddle:

> Five days after the Japanese attack, on December 12, 1941, Biddle issued a directive—Circular No. 3591—to all federal prosecutors acknowledging the long history of the unwritten federal law enforcement policy to ignore most reports of involuntary servitude. 'A survey of the Department files on alleged peonage violations discloses numerous instances of 'prosecution declined.' It is the purpose of these instructions to direct the attention of the United States Attorneys to the possibilities of successful prosecutions stemming from alleged peonage complaints which have heretofore been considered inadequate to invoke federal prosecution.' Biddle proceeded to lay out a series of federal criminal statutes that could be used to prosecute slavery—all of which had long been available to federal officials.
>
> He ordered that instead of relying on the quirks of the old anti-peonage statute as an excuse for not attacking instances of forced labor, prosecutors and investigators should embrace 'building the cases around the issue of involuntary servitude and slavery.'[64]

A few black military units remained after the peacetime reductions following the First World War. The buildup for the Second World War increased that number substantially, primarily in the army. As the scope of the conflict grew, the demands on the military forced movement away from segregation. Maintaining separate facilities for white and black units was inefficient, and coordinating the actions of what were essentially two separate armies reduced effectiveness. In the other military branches, particularly the navy, separate units and accommodations were impractical and the policy of admitting more Blacks had the immediate effect of increasing integration.

By 1944, the unemployment rate had dropped to 1.2 percent.[65] The labor shortage made the executive order prohibiting discrimination in defense plant hiring unnecessary, as the urgent need for workers overcame any inclination to discriminate. The resulting integration of work places combined with the increased integration in military units created the potential

63. Blackmon, *Slavery by Another Name*, 377.

64. Ibid., 377–78.

65. Galbraith, *A Journey Through Economic Time*, 116.

for breakthroughs in residential and social integration. Unfortunately, that did not happen.

Other Effects of the War

The war also led to the repeal of the Chinese Exclusion Act in 1943, more than 60 years after its enactment. In an effort to strengthen ties with China during the war, the exclusion was repealed and a new law allowed an annual immigration of 105 "persons of the Chinese race."[66] As has happened throughout our past, military expediency could be accommodated with the stroke of a pen, while securing basic human rights and dignity for People of Color seemed always out of reach.

The internment of Japanese Americans during the war is an embarrassing example of how easily public policy can diminish the humanity of groups of people. People of Japanese descent whose families had lived here for decades, who had homes and businesses and were active in their communities, were not seen as equals. They were seen as a threat because of their ancestral ties to an Asian nation with whom we were at war.[67] People with ancestral ties to Germany, the European nation with whom we were also at war, were not seen the same way.

At the end of the war, the disclosure of the extremes of Hitler's horrific actions in the interests of racial purity led to a degree of introspection in this country not unlike that which had taken place after the signing of the Declaration of Independence. Jim Crow segregation in the South and housing segregation in the North and West were increasingly viewed as blatantly discriminatory and wrong. Continued racial tensions and violence, in the North as well as in the South, showed that some changes in actions and policy were needed.

Unfortunately, as at other turning points in our history, the question of superiority or inferiority of different groups of people was not dealt with. The underlying attitudes of Whites regarding the inferiority of People of Color were little changed. Blacks expected that the greater recognition that discrimination was wrong would lead to equality. Instead, those expectations were regularly met with Whites' resistance to any policy changes reducing the advantages they saw as their inherent right.

66. Cao and Novas, *Everything You Need to Know*, 43–44.

67. Ibid., 102–12.

11

Racism in the Second Half of the Twentieth Century

The second half of the twentieth century began with great promise, and initially it appeared that it could deliver on that promise. Instead, it stands as an example of the adaptability and endurance of racism. The horrors of Hitler's actions against the Jews in Germany forced an honest look at the segregation and discrimination against Blacks in this country. Over 1.2 million Blacks had served in the U.S. military during the war to stop aggression around the world.[1] The aggression they faced at home because of Jim Crow laws in the South and blatant discrimination in the North could no longer be tolerated by Blacks, or ignored by Whites.

Legal challenges and public protests against discrimination produced some results. Both the legal cases and the actions of protesters were vigorously opposed, but neither the courts nor the general public were willing to accept the status quo. As the campaign for civil rights expanded from the obvious segregation of Jim Crow in the South to the less publicized housing, employment, and criminal justice discrimination in the North, suburban Whites were made painfully aware of the level of injustice that their sheltered lives had hidden from them. Unfortunately, that increased awareness of discrimination was not given enough time to develop into a better understanding of the racism that supported the discrimination.

Despite the early successes at raising the awareness of racism and implementing policies to address it, the politicians wasted no time in exploiting the divisions that remained. The South still carried the scars of the

1. "African Americans," The National WWII Museum.

loss of the Civil War, so the divisions there were more conscious and emotional—and easier to exploit. The rest of the country, though less emotionally invested in racism, also remained under the influence of four hundred years of misinformation, though on a much less conscious level. The appeals to the emotions and to the stereotypes had to be disguised and subtle, but the outcome was the same.

Legally sanctioned and enforced segregation were gone. Derogatory slurs and racist rhetoric were no longer acceptable in public spaces. The obvious manifestations of racism were gone, but the underlying ranking of human beings remained. Racism adapted and remained as strong as ever. Those adaptations are still with us in the form of "law and order" rhetoric, "tough on crime" legislation, selective enforcement of supposedly neutral laws, and mass incarceration of People of Color. The language of racism changed, but it continued to operate as it always had.

Brown v. Board of Education

In 1954, the Supreme Court ruled, in *Brown v. Board of Education*, that segregation in schools was inherently discriminatory and violated the Fourteenth Amendment.[2] This was not the first narrow ruling overturning some of the effects of *Plessy*,[3] and it was not totally unexpected. The new national focus on segregation had forced the South to admit that separate had not been equal, and some efforts were being made to increase equality of facilities and services in order to avoid forced integration.[4] As with previous milestones, the *Brown* ruling is often viewed as a dramatic event that changed history, which in turn distracts from a consideration of what had *not* changed. This beginning of the end of government-mandated segregation did not end all segregation and clearly did not end racism. The implementation of integration of schools in the South took years and the process became the proving ground for alternative tools for the perpetuation of racism.

The Curse of Ham to Justify Segregation

The curse of Ham was covered in chapter 3, in the discussion of biblical justifications for slavery. While the curse did not have its same importance

2. *Brown v. Board of Education of Topeka*, 347 U.S. 483 (1954).

3. Alexander, *The New Jim Crow*, 36.

4. Franklin and Moss, *From Slavery to Freedom*, 452.

after slavery ended, its effects both in the public consciousness and in the treatment of people of African descent remained. Immediately after the *Brown* ruling, writings began to appear invoking the curse as a defense of segregation.[5] Many people continued to view the Bible as the revelation of God's will regarding human relations, to be applied whenever it seemed to fit. According to chapter 10 of Genesis, Ham had three sons in addition to Canaan, all of whom were presumed to be included in the curse since it was to cover all of his descendants. Ham's son Cush had a son named Nimrod, who became the center of the argument for segregation because of his connection to the story of the tower of Babel.

That story, which appears in chapter 11 of Genesis, isn't specific about who exactly was involved, but since in chapter 10 the Bible says about Nimrod "the beginning of his kingdom was Babel,"[6] assigning responsibility to him was not difficult. The tower was to reach to heaven presumably to make the builders equal to God and invincible to any future floods. To prevent the completion of the tower, God separated the people into groups and gave them different languages so they could not communicate with each other. "Therefore is the name of it called Babel; because the Lord did there confound the language of all the earth: and from thence did the Lord scatter them abroad upon the face of all the earth."[7]

The Bible was clear that God had scattered the people, and this was taken as proof that God intended people, especially the descendants of Ham, to remain separated. Separation was seen as a necessity for maintaining order. Nimrod's name was supposedly derived from a Hebrew word meaning "to rebel,"[8] and Nimrod was portrayed as disrupting the order that was God's plan. Order, and God's plan for it, was the key issue. The fact that the slave trade had brought the Africans to this country was disregarded. It was the Black's demand for equal rights that was seen as causing disorder.

But generally a reference to the curse, without any details, was all that was needed. In 1964, during a Senate filibuster against the Civil Rights Act, the Genesis verses regarding the Curse of Ham were read into the Congressional Record, with the remark "Noah apparently saw fit to discriminate against Ham's descendants in that he placed a curse upon Canaan."[9]

---

5. Haynes, *Noah's Curse*, 116.

6. Gen. 10:10 (King James Version).

7. Gen. 11:9 (King James Version).

8. Haynes, *Noah's Curse*, 57–58, 118.

9. *Congressional Record*, 88th Cong. , 2d sess., 1964, 110, pt. 10:13207, as cited in Haynes, *Noah's Curse.*, 116.

States' Rights

During the first two years following the *Brown* ruling, the southern states held out hope that implementation could be put off indefinitely.[10] When the local courts, which had responsibility for overseeing implementation, demanded prompt compliance with the Supreme Court ruling, state legislatures began asserting the priority of the rights of states over the rights of the federal government. Six states adopted resolutions declaring the Supreme Court ruling to be void and of no legal effect. Mississippi and Louisiana amended their constitutions to require segregated schools. This naturally led to a number of confrontations between federal and state authorities.[11]

Alabama schools had still not been integrated in 1963 when the federal courts ordered the integration of the University of Alabama. That resulted in a nationally televised confrontation between Governor George Wallace and U.S. Deputy Attorney General Nicholas Katzenbach at the front door of the university. In a seven-minute speech, Wallace avoided the issue of race and segregation and spoke instead about "the illegal usurpation of power by the Central Government."[12] Within a week, Wallace had received over one hundred thousand letters and telegrams, 95 percent of which agreed with him. More than half were from states outside the South.[13]

From that point on, "states' rights" became synonymous with the right of individual states to determine acceptable distinctions among individuals based on the color of their skin. The issue of the rights of states in their relations with the federal government is a logical and necessary subject of debate on any and all areas where interests intersect. But absent a specific alternate context, and despite the denials by those using the term, "states' rights" has become automatically associated with "race."

Brown v. Board of Education, and a few other rulings, overruled only a few limited areas of segregation. Resistance by Blacks to other areas of segregation occurred regularly in the following years, sometimes with modest success. Then in early 1960, four young college men staged a sit-in at a segregated lunch counter in Greensboro, North Carolina. Within a month, the tactic was used by students in seven southern states, and in subsequent months was expanded to all sorts of commercial and recreational facilities.[14] Non-violent civil disobedience tactics had been used and reported

10. Woodward, *The Strange Career*, 151–54.

11. Ibid., 156–58.

12. Haney Lopez, *Dog Whistle Politics*, 15.

13. Ibid., 16.

14. Woodward, *The Strange Career*, 169–71.

on in the past, but the rapidly expanded use of the sit-in caught the attention of the nation.

The "Freedom Riders," Blacks and Whites riding together on buses traveling throughout the South in protest of the lack of enforcement of the Supreme Court prohibition of segregation on interstate buses, followed in 1961. Some of those protests were met with organized and violent responses and many freedom riders were severely beaten. While these attacks were condoned, if not actively abetted by the police, they were basically mob actions.[15]

In May 1963 though, it was the direct action by the police that drove home to the nation the extremes that would be tolerated to deny equal rights to Blacks. Thousands of high school and college students marched from a central gathering place to downtown Birmingham, Alabama to integrate selected businesses. Hundreds were arrested. The following day, because the local jail was full, instead of arresting marchers the police met them with German Shepard police dogs and high-pressure fire hoses, which they used in full force without any hesitation.[16] The television and newspaper images shocked the nation.

In response to the national outrage, President Kennedy called for immediate civil rights legislation.[17] After Kennedy's assassination, President Lynden Johnson made civil rights legislation his own priority.[18] Through his skill as a politician, and the support of an embarrassed nation, the civil rights law was passed on July 2, 1964. In order to pass, the bill had to overcome the introduction of over five hundred amendments and a lengthy filibuster by southern senators.[19] The law finally ended all legally required and enforced segregation. Unforced segregation and the racism nurtured by decades of forced segregation remained.

Law and Order

Racism had lost the tool of Jim Crow segregation, but it acquired a new tool in the process. In justifying the resistance to the protesters' actions, state officials had stopped talking about segregation and began talking about "law and order."[20] Of course, they were talking about the unlawfulness of the

15. Ibid., 171.

16 " Birmingham Campaign." Encyclopedia of Alabama.

17. Ibid.

18. Woodward, *The Strange Career*, 182.

19. Ibid.

20. Haney Lopez, *Dog Whistle Politics*, 23–24.

civil disobedience of the protesters. The unlawfulness of the mob violence against peaceful protesters, the bombing and burning of black churches, which in one case resulted in the deaths of four young girls, the killings of civil rights workers and the defiance of federal law by state officials, was never considered.

Two other factors crystallized the "law and order" theme into a tool for racism. In 1965, one year after the passage of the civil rights law, a riot broke out in Watts, a predominantly black district in Los Angeles. The riot lasted seven days and left over six hundred buildings damaged, approximately two hundred of them completely destroyed by fire.[21] C. Van Woodward described what followed:

> For four summers, 1965 through 1968, pictures of flaming cars, looting and embattled mobs, and smoking ruins were regular features of newspapers and television. In that period more than 150 major riots and hundreds of minor disturbances occurred in cities as diverse and scattered as Los Angeles, New York, Cincinnati, Des Moines, Tampa, Chicago, Atlanta, Milwaukee, Erie, Buffalo, New Haven, Washington, Newark, and Detroit.[22]

In 1967, President Johnson appointed a commission to study the causes of, and possible solutions to, the widespread unrest. In February 1968, after seven months of study, the Report of the National Advisory Commission On Civil Disorders was issued. The report noted that there was no "typical" riot, and that, "The disorders of 1967 were unusual, irregular, complex and unpredictable social processes."[23] But it also noted that, "Although specific grievances varied from city to city, at least 12 deeply held grievances can be identified and ranked into three levels of relative intensity." The top three grievances were: police practices, unemployment and underemployment, and inadequate housing.[24] The report also included the following comments:

> White racism is essentially responsible for the explosive mixture which has been accumulating in our cities since the end of World War II. Among the ingredients of this mixture are:
>
> - Pervasive discrimination and segregation in employment, education and housing, which have resulted in the continuing exclusion of great numbers of Negroes from the benefits of economic progress.

21. Woodward, *The Strange Career*, 189.
22. Ibid., 190.
23. Report of the National Advisory Commission, 5.
24. Ibid., 7.

. . .

Recently, other powerful ingredients have begun to catalyze the mixture:

- Frustrated hopes are the residue of the unfulfilled expectations aroused by the great judicial and legislative victories of the Civil Rights Movement and the dramatic struggle for equal rights in the South.

- A climate that tends toward approval and encouragement of violence as a form of protest has been created by white terrorism directed against nonviolent protest; by the open defiance of law and federal authority by state and local officials resisting desegregation; and by some protest groups engaging in civil disobedience who turn their backs on nonviolence, go beyond the constitutionally protected rights of petition and free assembly, and resort to violence to attempt to compel alteration of laws and policies with which they disagree.

- The frustrations of powerlessness have led some Negroes to the conviction that there is no effective alternative to violence as a means of achieving redress of grievances, and of "moving the system." These frustrations are reflected in alienation and hostility toward the institutions of law and government and the white society which controls them, and in the reach toward racial consciousness and solidarity reflected in the slogan 'Black Power.'"[25]

While the disturbances rarely extended beyond the inner city communities, their magnitude and intensity frightened Whites throughout the United States, and a longing for "order" overshadowed concern about the injustices underlying the frustrations. As comprehensive as the study was, it was easier for politicians to exploit the fears of Whites than to address the injustices that had been identified and documented. "Order" became more important than justice, and the findings and recommendations of the commission were generally disregarded.

The 1968 presidential campaign marked a dramatic turning point in the use of racism in politics. The Democratic Party had dominated politics in the south since Republicans had forced Emancipation. It was the Democratic politicians of the south who enacted and defended Jim Crow segregation. Outside of the south, politicians of both parties generally ignored the subject of racism except in response to a current crisis. When the Civil Rights Act of 1964 was enacted, only one southern Democratic senator, out

25. Ibid., 10–11.

of twenty-one, voted in favor. The lone southern Republican senator voted against. In the north, forty-five out of forty-six Democratic senators, and twenty-seven out of thirty-two Republican senators, voted in favor.[26] Support and opposition were clearly regional, rather than by political party. Yet President Johnson, a Texas Democrat, anticipated that his support for the bill, and the support of a substantial number of northern democrats, could jeopardize the party loyalty of the southern democrats. The night after he signed the bill he commented to an aide, "I think we just delivered the South to the Republican Party for a long time to come."[27]

Appeal to Southern White Voters

Republicans, too, had seen the potential and, as early as 1963 when a Civil Rights bill was being discussed, had been talking about a "southern strategy" to win over disenchanted southern democrats.[28] During the 1964 presidential campaign, Johnson's opponent, Republican Barry Goldwater, emphasized states rights and touted his opposition to the Civil Rights bill. He won the five Deep South states, a first for a republican candidate. But northern voters were not ready to turn against civil rights and were concerned about Goldwater's views regarding war and the use of nuclear force. The only state outside the Deep South that he won was his home state of Arizona.[29]

In the 1968 presidential campaign, Richard Nixon, the Republican candidate, expanded the southern strategy to a racial strategy. George Wallace, the former Alabama governor, was running as an independent candidate and was polling well in the South and drawing large crowds in the North.[30] The urban unrest of the previous four years had made race a significant issue throughout the nation and Nixon saw the opportunity to appeal to the anger of southern voters and the fears of voters in the rest of the country. He emphasized the law and order rhetoric of the integration opponents of the South that also appealed to the longing for order by white voters everywhere. Though the rhetoric was also directed against the increased protests against the Vietnam war, he hedged those concerns by also promising to end the war.

26. "Roll Call Tally," National Archives.
27. Moyers, *Moyers on America*, 167.
28. Haney Lopez, *Dog Whistle Politics*, 18.
29. Ibid., 19–22.
30. Ibid., 23.

Shortly after his inauguration, during a discussion about welfare reform with his chief of staff, H. R. Haldeman, and his assistant for domestic affairs, John Ehrlichman, Nixon left no doubt about his attitude and strategy. Haldeman's diary contains the following entry regarding that meeting: "P [President Nixon] emphasized that you have to face the fact that the whole problem is really the blacks. The key is to devise a system that recognizes this while not appearing to."[31] Nixon was positioning himself as the white person's candidate and the Republican Party as the white person's party. The message was clear, though he never mentioned race or segregation.

Following the Watergate scandal, Jimmy Carter from Georgia defeated Nixon's successor Gerald Ford from Michigan, and briefly regained southern support for the Democratic Party. When Carter ran for re-election in 1980, Ronald Reagan, his Republican opponent, wasted no time in signaling that he was ready to pick up the baton from Nixon in the pursuit of Southern white voters. His first speech after his nomination at the Republican convention was given at the Neshoba County Fair, just a few miles from the Mississippi town where three civil rights workers had been murdered sixteen years earlier during the Civil Rights Movement.[32] In that setting, there could be no doubt regarding the meaning of his comment:

> I believe in states' rights; I believe in people doing as much as they can for themselves at the community level and at the private level. And I believe that we've distorted the balance of our government today by giving powers that were never intended in the constitution to that federal establishment.[33]

To Carter, a southerner, the meaning was clear and he accused Reagan of injecting racism into the campaign. Reagan claimed that he had been referring to his proposal to shift some social programs, like welfare, to the states,[34] though reporters following his campaign could not remember him using the term "states' rights" in that context on any other occasion.[35]

Stopping the Progress

Regardless of motives or intent, Reagan's presidency resulted in a significant setback to the Civil Rights Movement and set in motion policies that have

31. Haldeman, *The Haldeman Diaries*, 53; Alexander, *The New Jim Crow*, 44.
32. Haney Lopez, *Dog Whistle Politics*, 58.
33. "Transcript," The Neshoba Democrat.
34. Smith, *White House Repudiates*.
35. Herbers, *Race Issue*.

been extremely harmful to People of Color. In his first news conference, nine days after he took office, Reagan was asked whether there would be any retreat in the federal government on the government's advocacy of affirmative action programs. His answer denied any retreat, and then immediately expressed reservations about the program and connected it with the idea of "quotas," which implied discrimination against white workers: "No, there will be no retreat. This administration is going to be dedicated to equality. I think we've made great progress in the civil rights field. I think there are some things, however, that may not be as useful as they once were or that may even be distorted in the practice, such as some affirmative action programs becoming quota systems. And I'm old enough to remember when quotas existed in the United States for the purpose of discrimination, and I don't want to see that happen again."[36]

The Commission on Civil Rights had been created under the Civil Rights Act of 1957 and had the responsibility to "appraise the laws and policies of the Federal Government with respect to equal protection of the laws under the Constitution."[37] When the commission issued several reports in 1981 and 1982, which were critical of federal actions and policies in regard to civil rights, rather than addressing the concerns of the commission, Reagan began attempts to replace commission members with people who supported his policies.[38] That was clearly at odds with the legislative intent in the creation of the commission, which was to be an independent body, free from political influence.

When the commission came up for reauthorization in 1983, Congress refused to act until the commission's independence could be assured. An agreement regarding specific membership was brokered with the administration but, as soon as the reauthorization was passed, Reagan broke the agreement and appointed members supportive of his policies.[39] The commission immediately changed its focus. Instead of studying areas of continued discrimination against People of Color, it began projects such as a study of "'the adverse consequences of affirmative action programs on Americans of Eastern and Southern European descent." Its new staff director said that study was "one of our highest priorities for the new year."[40]

36. Ronald Reagan Presidential Library, *The President's News Conference January 29, 1981*.

37. "Civil Rights Act of 1957," U.S. Government Publishing Office.

38. Amaker, *Civil Rights*, 169–75; Frye et al., "The Rise and Fall," 476–80; Pear, "Reagan Ousts 3."

39. Amaker, *Civil Rights*, 174; Frye et al., "The Rise and Fall," 480; Pear, "Rift Grows Wider."

40. Pear, "New Director."

The Civil Rights Act of 1957 also created the Civil Rights Division of the Justice Department to ensure the enforcement of civil rights laws. The man Reagan appointed to be assistant attorney general of the Civil Rights Division was openly opposed to affirmative action, and in 1983 filed a brief with the Supreme Court in support of five Detroit police sergeants challenging that city's affirmative action plan.[41] By 1985, his failure to enforce civil rights laws had been so egregious that the Senate Judiciary Committee defeated his nomination for promotion to associate attorney general.[42] Yet, in news conferences, Reagan consistently claimed that his administration was prosecuting civil rights violations at record levels.[43]

"We" and "They"

Reagan was often referred to as "The Great Communicator" because of his ability to connect with his audience when he spoke. Sadly, that skill was not always used in a way that benefited all citizens. For instance, in his inaugural address in January 1981 Reagan made the following comment:

> If we look to the answer as to why for so many years we achieved so much, prospered as no other people on Earth, it was because here in this land we unleashed the energy and individual genius of man to a greater extent than has ever been done before. Freedom and the dignity of the individual have been more available and assured here than in any other place on Earth.[44]

While this might seem like harmless hyperbole to Whites, for People of Color it has absolutely no basis in fact, and is anything but harmless. Consider the impact of that last sentence on the descendents of slaves and on the descendents of the original inhabitants who were brutally driven off their land. Also, consider the impact on white people. An inaugural address was not the place to dwell on negative aspects of our history, but the blatant disregard of the experiences of People of Color raised some serious questions. Were People of Color not part of the America he was addressing? Or had they received the same freedoms and opportunities as white

41. Pear, "Administration is Hoping."

42. Williams, "Washington Talk: Q&A: William Bradford Reynolds."

43. Ronald Reagan Presidential Library, *Question-and-Answer Session February 7, 1983*; Ronald Reagan Presidential Library, *The President's News Conference, May 17, 1983*; Ronald Reagan Presidential Library, *The President's News Conference, June 28, 1983*.

44. Ronald Reagan Presidential Library, *Inaugural Address, January 20, 1981*.

people and were personal choices solely responsible for any differences in their economic situations?

His economic policies, and the way he presented them, further contributed to the divisiveness. His primary goal, to cut taxes, had broad appeal. Nobody likes paying taxes. But to justify the cuts, he had to make the case that tax money was being wasted through inefficiency and fraud. The government spending he chose to focus on was welfare and other programs designed to help the poor. Less than a month after his inauguration, when he presented his economic proposals to a joint session of Congress, he referred to "those with true need": "Those who, through no fault of their own, must depend on the rest of us—the poverty stricken, the disabled, the elderly, all those with true need—can rest assured that the social safety net of programs they depend on are exempt from any cuts."[45]

The obvious inference was that there was an undefined "other" group of citizens who were not truly in need and were abusing the system. When he spoke of specific programs, there was a suggestion of the size of that group:

> The Food Stamp program will be restored to its original purpose, to assist those without resources to purchase sufficient nutritional food. We will, however, save $1.8 billion in fiscal year 1982 by removing from eligibility those who are not in real need or who are abusing the program. . . . We will tighten welfare and give more attention to outside sources of income when determining the amount of welfare that an individual is allowed. This, plus strong and effective work requirements, will save $520 million in the next year.[46]

On other occasions, he used the example of welfare reform in California while he was governor and claimed they had reduced the number of welfare recipients in that one state by 350,000 who "weren't legitimately needy."[47] In one question and answer session with high school students he claimed that 40 percent of welfare recipients in California had misrepresented their outside income.[48] He was clearly suggesting that significant numbers of those receiving food stamps and welfare were not needy and were collecting benefits they were not entitled to.

45. Ronald Reagan Presidential Library, *Address Before a Joint Session of the Congress, February 18, 1981.*

46. Ibid.

47. Ronald Reagan Presidential Library, *Question-and-Answer Session With High School Students, January 21, 1983.*

48. Ibid.

Then he added those who were guilty of waste or fraud, specifically fraud in social programs:

> Now, let me say a word here about the general problem of waste and fraud in the Federal Government. One government estimate indicated that fraud alone may account for anywhere from 1 to 10 percent—as much as $25 billion of Federal expenditures for social programs. If the tax dollars that are wasted or misman-aged are added to this fraud total, the staggering dimensions of this problem begin to emerge.[49]

His speeches were filled with this sort of dramatic finger-pointing at unnamed others, if not emphasizing the number of offenders, then em-phasizing the individual offenses. In campaign speeches in 1976 he had regularly referred to a Chicago welfare recipient who he claimed had used eighty names, thirty addresses, and twelve social security cards to get tax-free income of over $150,000.[50] He was referring to a real person, a career criminal who was guilty of a number of crimes. But the welfare fraud she was actually tried and convicted for totaled $8,000, using only four aliases.[51] In the session with the high school students in 1983, long after the details of her case were known, Reagan again mentioned her, this time claiming she had collected welfare under 123 different names.[52]

Reagan's push for changes in welfare continued throughout his presi-dency, with the corresponding inference of a large number of abusers steal-ing taxpayers' money. Some believe he used code words to imply a racial category, though I could not find evidence of that. It was the press that first used the "welfare queen" label for the Chicago woman, which quickly be-came shorthand for any female welfare abuser.[53] And, though more Whites than Blacks received welfare benefits, welfare queens were generally por-trayed as black.[54]

Poverty did plague the segregated inner cities. But there were many rural areas and suburban residents who were also dependent on welfare benefits to get through economic difficulties. Yet, the public generally saw welfare as an urban issue and, therefore, assumed it was Blacks who were

---

49. Ronald Reagan Presidential Library, *Address Before a Joint Session of the Con-gress, February 18, 1981.*

50. " 'Welfare Queen' Becomes Issue," *New York Times.*

51. Ibid.; Levin, "The Welfare Queen."

52. Ronald Reagan Presidential Library, *Question-and-Answer Session With High School Students, January 21, 1983.*

53. Levin, "The Welfare Queen."

54. Gilliam, *The 'Welfare Queen' Experiment.*

the primary users. And because the political rhetoric emphasized welfare abuse, rather than the conditions that created the need for public assistance, the common perception was that every inner city recipient of welfare was taking advantage of the system.

Crime and the War on Drugs

The Reagan rhetoric and policies that created the most lasting harm were those relating to crime and drugs. From the very beginning, he chose to connect the topic of civil rights to the topic of crime. In his first State of the Union speech in January 1982, he commented briefly on the importance of civil rights and immediately followed with:

> So, too, the problem of crime—one as real and deadly serious as any in America today. It demands that we seek transformation of our legal system, which overly protects the rights of criminals while it leaves society and the innocent victims of crime without justice.[55]

There was no reason to place those two topics together in a forty-minute speech, unless he believed they were connected and wanted to convey that idea to his listeners. His State of the Union speech the following year contained exactly the same placement. There his brief comments about civil rights were followed with, "The time has also come for major reform of our criminal justice statutes and acceleration of the drive against organized crime and drug trafficking. It's high time that we make our cities safe again."[56]

Crime was the "law and order" theme repackaged, and Reagan proved to be an excellent salesman for it. In typical Reagan hyperbole, in a September 1982 radio address to the nation, he claimed that, "We live in the midst of a crime epidemic . . . Nine out of ten Americans believe that the courts in their home areas aren't tough enough on criminals."[57] In that speech, he spoke of a crime bill that had been "given important leadership by men such as Senator Thurmond . . . ."[58] Senator Strom Thurmond, from South Carolina, was well known as a staunch segregationist who once said: "all the laws

55. Ronald Reagan Presidential Library, *Address on the State of the Union, January 26, 1982.*

56. Ronald Reagan Presidential Library, *Address on the State of the Union, January 25, 1983.*

57. Ronald Reagan Presidential Library, *Radio Address to the Nation , September 11, 1982.*

58. Ibid.

of Washington and all the bayonets of the Army cannot force the Negro into our homes, into our schools, our churches, and our places of recreation and amusement."[59]

By the time Reagan took office in 1981, law and order were no longer of primary concern to most citizens. The urban unrest of the 1960s was past, and unemployment, high inflation, the cold war, and regional conflicts were of much more immediate concern. In every speech about crime, Reagan felt the need to first appeal to people's fears by talking about fear to walk the streets at night, fear of being awakened by a burglar or rapist, the cleaning lady being afraid to ride the subway late at night, and families' fears for the safety of their children. Repackaging law and order as crime also allowed more focus on criminals, and Reagan took full advantage, referring to "hardened criminals,"[60] and "a criminal justice system that often treats criminals better than it does their victims."[61]

He talked about drugs as a separate crisis, but also made sure the public saw the two as connected. In his radio address declaring his war on drugs, three weeks after the talk about crime, Reagan referred to drugs as "an especially vicious virus of crime."[62] In her book, *The New Jim Crow: Mass Incarceration in the Age of Colorblindness*, Michelle Alexander notes that less than 2 percent of the population considered drugs the most important issue at the time.[63] Just as with the issue of crime, public concern needed to be created. To help create that concern, Reagan asked his wife Nancy to participate in his radio addresses, and talk about her travels around the country meeting with parents whose children's lives and families had been damaged by the use of drugs. In the initial address, her first sentence set the tone: "I have to tell you that few things in my life have frightened me as much as the drug epidemic among our children."[64] Another time she warned that, "Sometimes it seems as if we could lose a whole next generation to drug abuse."[65]

In his 1983 State of the Union speech, Reagan continued the theme of protecting the children when he said, "This administration hereby declares

59. Clymer, "Strom Thurmond."

60. Ronald Reagan Presidential Library, *Radio Address to the Nation*, September 11, 1982.

61. Ronald Reagan Presidential Library, *Radio Address to the Nation, July 7, 1984.*

62. Ronald Reagan Presidential Library, *Radio Address to the Nation, October 2, 1982.*

63. Beckett, *Making Crime Pay*, 55; Alexander, *The New Jim Crow*, 49.

64. Ronald Reagan Presidential Library, *Radio Address to the Nation, October 2, 1982.*

65. Ronald Reagan Presidential Library, *Radio Address to the Nation, June 30, 1984.*

an all out war on big-time organized crime and the drug racketeers who are poisoning our young people."[66] By 1987, he was proudly announcing that spending for the drug war had tripled to nearly $4 billion.[67] Though he implied otherwise, almost all of the spending was for law enforcement. Spending for education, prevention, and treatment was dramatically reduced.[68]

His speeches consistently emphasized that the targets of law enforcement were "drug traffickers" and "drug kingpins," but most arrests were simply for possession. In his 1985 State of the Union address, he bragged about the progress of the drug war: "We've convicted over 7,400 drug offenders and put them, as well as leaders of organized crime, behind bars in record numbers."[69] Few people considered the inconsistency of 7,400 convictions with a stated targeting of traffickers and kingpins. The trend continued and, in the next fifteen years, imprisonment for drug offenses increased from approximately 41,000 to about 500,000.[70] In the first three years, incarceration of Blacks quadrupled.[71]

This review of the Reagan presidency has been fairly detailed, not to lay inordinate blame for racism on him, but to show the origin of a number of attitudes and policies that continue to affect us in the present. A number of administrations have succeeded his, and both political parties have controlled Congress in the intervening years. But the *tough on crime* and the *war on drugs* policies have endured. Very few of the setbacks to the Civil Rights Movement have been addressed.

---

66. Ronald Reagan Presidential Library, *Address on the State of the Union, January 25, 1983*.

67. Ronald Reagan Presidential Library, *Radio Address, May 30, 1987* .

68. Beckett, *Making Crime Pay*, 53, citing U.S. Office of the National Drug Control Policy, National Drug Control Strategy, (1992); Alexander, *The New Jim Crow*, 49–50.

69. Ronald Reagan Presidential Library, *Address on the State of the Union, February 6, 1985*.

70. Alexander, *The New Jim Crow*, 60.

71. Ibid., 98.

12

The Supreme Court

In many respects, the Supreme Court is the most powerful of the three branches of our federal government. Nine justices, appointed for life, have the power to interpret the Constitution and endorse or invalidate any act of Congress or the president. Some of the effects of their rulings can be overcome by legislation, but others require the much more difficult process of amending the Constitution.

Yet the actual functioning of the Supreme Court is frequently misunderstood by the public. It is common for those disagreeing with Court rulings to label those justices as "activist judges," and accuse them of *making* law rather than *interpreting* it. What is lost in that argument is that courts have always made law. All of their rulings become law, referred to as "case law." Unless Congress changes case law by one of the two methods noted above, it remains in effect indefinitely.

The following cases are not intended to be a comprehensive look at Supreme Court rulings regarding civil rights. They are simply a few obvious examples of the role the Court has played in the development and continuation of racism. The first two cases are from the past and are included to demonstrate the lasting impacts of Court rulings and the difficulty of overcoming those rulings. The next four cases are fairly current and demonstrate how access to rights guaranteed by the Constitution have hinged on how the Court interpreted a single word, or decided which party to the case had the greater burden of proving their argument.

The final case is a very recent case having to do with voting rights. That case demonstrates how fragile basic civil rights are when they are dependent on the judgment of a few individuals with immense power. A five to four majority decided that case. A single member of the majority, with a perspective more aligned with people who have had to fight for their basic rights instead of with governmental units that have a history of abridging rights, would have produced a different result.

How the Perspective of Individual Justices Affect Outcomes

The opinions of the dissent are generally as compelling as those of the majority. What differs is the perspective of the justices. The perspectives of Supreme Court candidates can be discerned with reasonable certainty from their writings and rulings while serving on lower courts. Presidents who appoint justices, and senators who confirm them, look carefully at each candidate's political views. Considering our racist past and the lingering problems of racism, it would seem obvious that equal consideration should be given to a candidate's views on matters as basic as racism and civil rights.

The following example is not intended to speak ill of the dead, but to highlight the concern. Justice Antonin Scalia was still serving on the Court when he died in February 2016. Two months before his death, during oral arguments in the case of *Fisher v. University of Texas at Austin, et al.*, a case regarding the consideration of race in admission decisions, Justice Scalia made the following statement:

> There are—there are those who contend that it does not benefit African-Americans to—to get them into the University of Texas where they do not do well, as opposed to having them go to a less-advanced school, a less—a slower-track school where they do well. One of—one of the briefs pointed out that—that most of the—most of the black scientists in this country don't come from schools like the University of Texas. . . . They come from lesser schools where they do not feel that they're—that they're being pushed ahead in—in classes that are too—too fast for them.[1]

It's obvious from the pauses that he was choosing his words carefully. Yet, without hesitation or embarrassment, he made a statement suggesting

---

1. Transcript of Oral Argument at 67, *Fisher v. University of Texas*, 579 U.S. ___ (2016) (No. 14–981).

that Black students do better in "slower-track" schools. He brought that perspective to every civil rights case that came before the Court after his appointment in 1986. Three of the cases that follow were decided while he was on the Court. He joined the majority in all three, two of which were decided by one vote. Like all of us, Justices have their biases. Because of the power of the Court, the biases of those who sit on it deserve careful scrutiny, by themselves, as well as by those who have the power to appoint them.

The Rights of Blacks under the Constitution

The case of *Dred Scott*, decided in 1857, demonstrates the potential for harm by Supreme Court rulings and the difficult process of overcoming those rulings. That case also highlights the difficulty of interpreting a document from a different time and applying the provisions of that document to situations in the present. Dred Scott was a slave who sued for his freedom based on his residency in non-slave states. The Court ruled that he was not a citizen and had no standing to bring suit. In the majority opinion, Chief Justice Roger B. Taney said this regarding the "all men are created equal" words of the Declaration of Independence:

> The general words quoted above would seem to embrace the whole human family, and if they were used in a similar instrument at this day would be so understood. But it is too clear for dispute, that the enslaved African race were not intended to be included . . . .[2]

He also included this observation regarding attitudes toward African Americans at the time the Constitution was written:

> They had for more than a century before been regarded as beings of an inferior order, and altogether unfit to associate with the white race, either in social or political relations; and so far inferior, that they had no rights which the white man was bound to respect . . . .[3]

As is clear from these excerpts, the majority was interpreting the Constitution based on the intent of the drafters at the time it was written. There was criticism of the ruling at the time, and two justices dissented because several of the states had recognized free Blacks as citizens at the time the Constitution was written. But this ruling by the majority meant that those of

2. *Scott v. Sandford*, 60 U.S. 393 (1857).
3. Ibid.

African descent had no rights under the Constitution as originally written. It required three separate amendments to the Constitution to grant citizenship, equal protection under the law, and voting rights to those of African descent.

If the original meaning of the Constitution at the time it was written is the principle under which it will always be interpreted, and some current justices and constitutional scholars feel that it should be, we are in fact governed by a racist document, which has had a band-aid applied. This is not hyperbole. Even the Fourteenth Amendment, providing for equal protection of the laws, was adopted at a time when many forms of segregation and discrimination were common.

Though this case occurred more than a century and a half ago, it raised some questions that are still pertinent today. If the biases of the past, when the Constitution and its amendments were adopted, affect interpretations today, must People of Color forever depend on the favorable rulings of judges, or the good will of legislators, for their rights? Or is a new Constitution required periodically to provide a governing document that reflects our evolving knowledge and sensitivities?

Segregation Sanctioned

An illustration of how rulings by the Supreme Court can have extremely broad and long-term consequences is provided by the 1896 case of *Plessy v. Ferguson*, which was discussed briefly in chapter 10. That ruling, by just seven men, opened the door to more than a half-century of legally sanctioned and brutally enforced gross discrimination against African Americans. Plessy, a man with one-eighth African ancestry, had sued under the equal protection provision of the Fourteenth Amendment to prevent the State of Louisiana from requiring him to sit in a segregated railroad car. The opinion of the one dissenting justice made it clear that there was no doubt about the intent of the law:

> The thing to accomplish was, under the guise of giving equal accommodation for whites and blacks, to compel the latter to keep to themselves while traveling in railroad passenger coaches. No one would be so wanting in candor as to assert the contrary.[4]

Yet the majority ruled that the law did not violate the Fourteenth Amendment and was constitutional. Their opinion included the following comment:

4. *Plessy v. Ferguson*, 163 U.S.537 (1896), Harlan, dissenting.

> Legislation is powerless to eradicate racial instincts, or to abol-
> ish distinctions based upon physical differences, and the at-
> tempt to do so can only result in accentuating the difficulties of
> the present situation. If the civil and political rights of both races
> be equal, one cannot be inferior to the other civilly or politically.
> If one race be inferior to the other socially, the constitution of
> the United States cannot put them upon the same plane.[5]

An indication of how misguided that ruling was is the fact that they were not considering legislation designed to eradicate racial instincts, or to abolish distinctions based upon physical differences. Exactly the opposite; they were considering legislation designed to *foster* racial instincts and to *enforce* distinctions based on physical differences. The plaintiff was not looking to the Constitution to put him on the same plane as white people; he was looking to the Constitution to prevent the State of Louisiana from putting him on a *lower* plane. That was the legislation the Court was considering and found constitutional.

The Supreme Court has been extremely reluctant to completely reverse previous rulings, no matter how misguided and harmful they may be. As noted in chapter 9, the Court eventually issued some rulings preventing segregation in specific situations, culminating in the 1954 ruling in *Brown v. Board of Education* prohibiting the segregation of public schools. Yet those were all very narrow and specific reversals. It required an act of Congress, passed ten years later, over strong resistance from some states, to overcome all of the other injustices sanctioned by that one ruling. The direct effects lasted almost seventy years. The indirect effects are still with us more than a century later.

The Meaning of the Word "Seizure"

Some more recent rulings have the potential to be as harmful as *Plessy*. The first ten amendments to the Constitution are commonly called the Bill of Rights because they were specifically intended to guarantee that individual rights are protected. The Fourth Amendment reads as follows:

> The right of the people to be secure in their persons, houses,
> papers, and effects, against unreasonable searches and seizures,
> shall not be violated, and no warrants shall issue, but upon prob-
> able cause, supported by oath or affirmation, and particularly

5. *Plessy v. Ferguson*, 163 U.S.537 (1896).

describing the place to be searched, and the persons or things to be seized.

Most people are not as familiar with the exact wording of that amendment as they are with some others, such as the First and Second Amendments, because for most people the Fourth Amendment is generally not in jeopardy. Yet there are many other people for whom that amendment is very much in jeopardy. This case, and the one that follows, provide two examples. In each case the ruling depended on the definition of a single word.

In 1991, a six-justice majority of the Supreme Court ruled in *Florida v. Bostick* that consent searches on interstate buses do not violate the Fourth Amendment prohibiting unreasonable searches and seizures.[6] The dissent summarized the issue:

> At issue in this case is a "new and increasingly common tactic in the war on drugs": the suspicionless police sweep of buses in interstate or intrastate travel. . . . . Typically under this technique, a group of state or federal officers will board a bus while it is stopped at an intermediate point on its route. Often displaying badges, weapons or other indicia of authority, the officers identify themselves and announce their purpose to intercept drug traffickers. They proceed to approach individual passengers, requesting them to show identification, produce their tickets, and explain the purpose of their travels. Never do the officers advise the passengers that they are free not to speak with the officers. An "interview" of this type ordinarily culminates in a request for consent to search the passenger's luggage.[7]

Broward County, Florida routinely conducted such sweeps. Bostick was a young black man riding a bus from Miami, Florida to Atlanta, Georgia. At a brief stop at Fort Lauderdale, Florida, two Broward County Sheriff's Department officers boarded the bus and, "without articulable suspicion," began to question him and obtained his consent to search his bags. They wore bright green "raid" jackets and displayed badges, while one held a pistol in a zippered pouch.[8]

The most troubling aspects of this case are the police procedures that are sanctioned and how casually the Court disposed of a basic constitutional right. The dragnet approach of suspicionless searches of the luggage of thousands of bus passengers did not concern the majority. One similar case showed that just one officer had searched over three thousand bags in

6. *Florida v. Bostick*, 501 U.S. 429 (1991).

7. *Florida v. Bostick*, 501 U.S. 429 (1991), Marshall, dissenting.

8. Ibid.

a nine-month period. Another case showed that a sweep of one hundred buses resulted in just seven arrests.[9] Assuming just fourteen passengers per bus, this would indicate that two hundred passengers were intimidated and inconvenienced to accomplish each arrest. The number of innocent passengers inconvenienced was likely much higher, but bus riders are a constituency easily dismissed by the Court. It is doubtful that the public or the Court would tolerate this approach if it was used on airplanes.

The ruling of the majority was based on a consideration of the meaning of "seizure," which was discussed extensively in the Opinion of the Court. The majority ruled that this was not an unreasonable search because Bostick had given his consent, and it was not an unreasonable seizure because "a reasonable person would have felt free to decline the officers' requests or otherwise terminate the encounter."[10] The dissent disagreed with the conclusion:

> I have no objection to the manner in which the majority frames the test for determining whether a suspicionless bus sweep amounts to a Fourth Amendment "seizure." I agree that the appropriate question is whether a passenger who is approached during such a sweep "would feel free to decline the officers' requests or otherwise terminate the encounter." What I cannot understand is how the majority can possibly suggest an affirmative answer to this question.[11]

The ruling of the majority stands. It is now the law of the land that uniformed police can board any bus and without any valid reason other than arbitrary whim question any passenger and search their luggage in these supposedly "consensual" encounters. A consideration of the reasoning of the majority is informative. They were aware that the selection of the passengers to be questioned in the sweeps was not random and that young black men were targeted, yet that fact was considered so irrelevant it was not even discussed.

They discounted the fact that one of the officers was holding a pistol in a zippered pouch because he hadn't actually threatened Bostick with it. They argued that when questioning someone in the confines of a bus holding a pistol in a zippered pouch was "the equivalent of carrying a gun in a holster."[12] They also argued that even though one of the officers was partially blocking the narrow aisle, they did not actually prevent Bostick from

9. Ibid.

10. *Florida v. Bostick*, 501 U.S. 429 (1991).

11. *Florida v. Bostick*, 501 U.S. 429 (1991), Marshall, dissenting.

12. *Florida v. Bostick*, 501 U.S. 429 (1991).

leaving the bus. They claimed that any intimidation he felt because of the close confines of the bus was of his own making because he chose to take the bus.[13] The dissent said that reasoning "borders on sophism."[14] Others might not have been so diplomatic.

The fact that this case was decided based on the definition of a single word and that, to justify their decision, the majority could so easily defy what many would see as common sense shows why few of us know exactly what the law is. It also shows the validity of the dissent's comment that: "a passenger unadvised of his rights and otherwise unversed in constitutional law *has no reason to know* that the police cannot hold his refusal to cooperate against him."[15]

Supreme Court Definition of "Consent"

The previous case centered on the definition of "seizure" because the definition of "consent," regarding the search of the luggage, had been decided in an earlier case. The case of *Schneckloth v. Bustamonte*, decided in 1973, centered on the definition of "consent." In that ruling, the majority decided that the only relevant issue was whether the consent was voluntary, and not coerced. Whether the person knew he had the right to refuse consent or that he was waiving a constitutional right was not considered relevant. Their disregard for the protections of the Fourth Amendment was so egregious that the Opinion of the Court admitted that if there was a requirement that an individual know he has a right to refuse consent, it "would, in practice, create serious doubt whether consent searches could continue to be conducted."[16]

The Opinion of the Court made this comment in regard to the ruling: "We cannot accept the position of the Court of Appeals in this case that proof of knowledge of the right to refuse consent is a necessary prerequisite to demonstrating a 'voluntary' consent."[17]

In his dissent, Justice Brennan expressed his incredulity: "It wholly escapes me how our citizens can meaningfully be said to have waived something as precious as a constitutional guarantee without ever being aware of its existence."[18] Justice Marshall put it this way: "I would have thought

13. Ibid.
14. *Florida v. Bostick*, 501 U.S. 429 (1991), Marshall, dissenting.
15. Ibid.
16. *Schneckloth v. Bustamonte*, 412 U.S. 218 (1973).
17. Ibid.
18. *Schneckloth v. Bustamonte*, 412 U.S. 218 (1973), Brennan, dissenting.

that the capacity to choose necessarily depends upon knowledge that there is a choice to be made. But today the Court reaches the curious result that one can choose to relinquish a constitutional right—the right to be free of unreasonable searches—without knowing that he has the alternative of refusing to accede to a police request to search."[19]

The difference in approach between the majority and the dissent is striking. The singular concern, by the majority, for the police, and their need and ability to investigate crime, allowed them to see only one possibility for abuse—coercion. Justice Marshall noted the importance of "a realistic assessment of the nature of the interchange between citizens and the police."[20] We are all taught that it is our obligation to always cooperate with the police, and the law frequently compels our cooperation. But the line between voluntary cooperation and required cooperation is rarely clear. The Court of Appeals had made the observation that "under many circumstances, a reasonable person might read an officer's "May I" as the courteous expression of a demand backed by force of law."[21]

The majority considered none of that relevant in any way as long as there was no coercion. They saw no harm in the fact that this police method worked only because most people are not aware of how the Fourth Amendment was included in the Bill of Rights specifically to protect against this kind of action. Their casual disregard for the rights of the individual was demonstrated by their admission that consent searches would be ineffective for the police if people knew they had the right to withhold consent.

The unfortunate thing about those Supreme Court rulings limiting the protection of the Fourth Amendment is that, like the post-Civil War laws in the South that led to convict leasing, and the Jim Crow laws that led to sixty-eight years of gross discrimination, they are seemingly race-neutral. The unforgivable thing about them is the fact that, like the post-Civil War laws and the Jim Crow laws, the only thing that made them acceptable was the common knowledge that they would only be enforced against certain people. In *The New Jim Crow*, Michelle Alexander provides numerous examples of how Blacks are being targeted for consent searches through pretext stops and bus sweeps, all in the name of the war on drugs. She also documents how this virtually "anything goes" authority has emboldened police to delay, inconvenience, intimidate, and harass individuals to gain their "consent."[22]

19. *Schneckloth v. Bustamonte*, 412 U.S. 218 (1973), Marshall, dissenting.
20. Ibid.
21. Ibid.
22. Alexander, *The New Jim Crow*, 65–69.

Because of the selective enforcement, Whites are rarely affected by the rulings, and are not even aware of what is taking place.

Supreme Court Defense of Bias in the Justice System

The case of *McCleskey v. Kemp*, decided in 1987 by a 5 to 4 margin, will also have long-term and far-reaching consequences. That case is noteworthy because of the tortured way the majority ignored statistical evidence and judicial precedent to reach the conclusion they wanted. The Opinion of the Court was essentially a tacit approval of bias in the justice system and an admission that a finding of bias in this case would open the door to charges of bias in other instances besides race.

McCleskey v. Kemp was about a death penalty sentence in a murder trial in Georgia. The petitioner, McCleskey, was a black man involved in an armed robbery in which a white police officer was killed. He appealed his death sentence based on a statistical analysis of death penalty sentences in Georgia, referred to as the Baldus study. The Baldus study, done by three University of Iowa professors, included every homicide case in Georgia from 1973 through 1978, a total of 2,484 cases.[23]

The following summary of the study was taken from the opinion of the majority, which accepted its validity. The study showed that "prosecutors sought the death penalty in 70% of the cases involving black defendants and white victims; 32% of the cases involving white defendants and white victims; 15% of the cases involving black defendants and black victims; and 19% of the cases involving white defendants and black victims."[24] The study also showed that "the death penalty was assessed in 22% of the cases involving black defendants and white victims; 8% of the cases involving white defendants and white victims; 1% of the cases involving black defendants and black victims; and 3% of the cases involving white defendants and black victims."[25] The result was that "defendants charged with killing white persons received the death penalty in 11% of the cases, but defendants charged with killing blacks received the death penalty in only 1% of the cases."[26] Two of the individuals involved in the study were law professors and the third was a statistician. The data was subjected to extensive statistical analysis, taking into account "230 variables that could have explained the disparities

23. *McCleskey v. Kemp*, 481 U.S. 279 (1987), Blackmun, dissenting.
24. *McCleskey v. Kemp*, 481 U.S. 279 (1987).
25. Ibid.
26. Ibid.

on nonracial grounds."[27] One of the models concluded that, even after taking into account "39 nonracial variables, defendants charged with killing white victims were 4.3 times as likely to receive a death sentence as defendants charged with killing Blacks."[28] It was on the basis of that disparity that McCleskey challenged his sentence as violating the Eighth and Fourteenth Amendments of the Constitution.

The Eighth Amendment prohibits cruel and unusual punishments, which the Court has interpreted to mean arbitrary imposition of acceptable penalties. Justice Brennan's dissent noted the standard that had been used by the court previously and how that applied to McCleskey:

> Defendants challenging their death sentences thus never have had to prove that impermissible considerations have actually infected sentencing decisions. We have required instead that they establish that the system under which they were sentenced posed a significant risk of such an occurrence. McCleskey's claim does differ, however, in one respect from these earlier cases: it is the first to base a challenge not on speculation about how a system *might* operate, but on empirical documentation of how it *does* operate.[29]

Yet in a lengthy opinion, which claimed that "the traditional discretion that prosecutors and juries necessarily must have" is the "very heart of our criminal justice system," and which included an extensive discussion of the "safeguards"[30] in the Georgia capital sentencing system, the majority rejected the documented proof of significant bias in the actual operation of discretion within the system with a single sentence:

> McCleskey asks us to accept the likelihood allegedly shown by the Baldus study as the constitutional measure of an unacceptable risk of racial prejudice influencing capital sentencing decisions. This we decline to do.[31]

The Fourteenth Amendment guarantees equal protection under the law to all citizens. This ruling by the Court concerning the Fourteenth Amendment extends far beyond McCleskey's capital sentencing case and now affects every other claim of unequal protection of the laws. The Court ruled that:

27. Ibid.
28. Ibid.
29. *McCleskey v. Kemp*, 481 U.S. 279 (1987), Brennan, dissenting.
30. *McCleskey v. Kemp*, 481 U.S. 279 (1987).
31. Ibid.

To prevail under the Equal Protection Clause, McCleskey must prove that the decision makers in *his* case acted with discriminatory purpose. He offers no evidence specific to his own case that would support an inference that racial considerations played a part in his sentence.[32]

The proof offered by the Baldus study was clear, and the majority had to admit that there was precedent for the use of "statistics as proof of intent to discriminate."[33] But instead of following precedent, they sought to change precedent by limiting the use of statistical analysis of outcomes to the earlier cases. Their attempt to distinguish the earlier cases from *McCleskey* and other subsequent cases was not particularly logical or convincing, and Justice Blackmun offered an effective rebuttal. Justice Blackmun began his dissent with an expression of his disappointment with the Court's ruling "because of its departure from what seems to me to be well-developed constitutional jurisprudence."[34] This departure from precedent, and the new standard established, has great significance. Alexander describes the ultimate effect of the ruling:

> The very evidence that the Court demanded in *McCleskey*—evidence of deliberate bias in his individual case—would almost always be unavailable and/or inadmissible due to procedural rules that shield jurors and prosecutors from scrutiny. This dilemma was of little concern to the Court. It closed the courthouse doors to claims of racial bias in sentencing.[35]

The case that follows will contrast how the burden of proof was exactly the opposite; it was initiated by a white man challenging an affirmative action admission policy at a medical school.

As troubling as many of the aspects of the *McCleskey* ruling are, the most shocking is the shameless admission by the majority that their specific intent was to limit the protections of the Constitution, and their suggestion that this was essential to preserve the principles that underlie the criminal justice system:

> McCleskey's claim, taken to its logical conclusion, throws into serious question the principles that underlie our entire criminal justice system. The Eighth Amendment is not limited in application to capital punishment, but applies to all penalties. Thus, if

32. Ibid.
33. Ibid.
34. *McCleskey v. Kemp*, 481 U.S. 279 (1987), Blackmun, dissenting.
35. Alexander, *The New Jim Crow*, 111.

we accepted McCleskey's claim that racial bias has impermissibly tainted the capital sentencing decision, we could soon be faced with similar claims as to other types of penalty. Moreover, the claim that his sentence rests on the irrelevant factor of race easily could be extended to apply to claims based on unexplained discrepancies that correlate to membership in other minority groups, and even to gender.[36]

In his dissent, Justice Brennan said, "Taken on its face, such a statement seems to suggest a fear of too much justice."[37] Justices can use any reasoning they choose to justify their opinions, but this concern that a finding of bias would throw into question "the principles that underlie our entire criminal justice system" must make one wonder exactly what those principles are in their minds. Their fear that a finding of bias in this case could lead to an examination of other types of bias in the system was seen as a greater danger than ignoring the biases that have been proven. It is difficult to conclude that their statement was anything other than a defense of bias.

Difference of Black and White Burden of Proof

Justice Brennan ended his dissent of the previous case with this astute warning: "The way we choose those who will die reveals the depth of moral commitment among the living."[38] Comparing that case with an affirmative action case, *Regents of the University of California v. Bakke*,[39] decided in 1978 nine years before *McCleskey*, provides a clear demonstration of the moral commitment among the living referred to by Justice Brennan. Justice Powell wrote both majority opinions. As noted above, the majority had unequivocally placed the burden of proof on McCleskey. ". . . to prevail under the Equal Protection Clause, McCleskey must prove that the decision makers in *his* case acted with discriminatory purpose."[40]

In the affirmative action case, a white man, Bakke, claimed to have been discriminated against when he was denied admission to the University of California, Davis School of Medicine. Yet, unlike McCleskey, the majority did not expect Bakke to offer any proof that decision makers in *his* case acted with discriminatory purpose. Instead, they accepted his expectation

---

36. *McCleskey v. Kemp*, 481 U.S. 279 (1987).

37. *McCleskey v. Kemp*, 481 U.S. 279 (1987), Brennan, dissenting.

38. Ibid.

39. *Regents of the University of California v. Bakke*, 438 U.S. 265 (1978).

40. *McCleskey v. Kemp*, 481 U.S. 279 (1987).

that without the affirmative action program he would have been admitted, and the burden fell to the university to prove that he would not have been:

> With respect to respondent's (Bakke's) entitlement to an injunction directing his admission to the Medical School, petitioner (University of California) has conceded that it could not carry its burden of proving that, but for the existence of its unlawful special admissions program, respondent still could not have been admitted.[41]

The obvious discriminatory bias against People of Color inherent in the regular admissions process, which the affirmative action process was intended to counter, received no consideration by the majority. In the four years ending with the year of Bakke's rejection, the Davis School of Medicine regular admissions process included 1 Black and 6 Latinos in the 336 total admissions. The affirmative action special admissions process included 21 Blacks and 30 Latinos in the total of 64 special admissions.[42] The combined total of 58 Blacks and Latinos was 14.5 percent of the total admissions, well below the percentage of Blacks and Latinos in the total population. Justice Brennan, in his dissent in this case, noted the significance of those numbers:

> If it was reasonable to conclude—as we hold that it was—that the failure of minorities to qualify for admission at Davis under regular procedures was due principally to the effects of past discrimination, then there is a reasonable likelihood that, but for pervasive racial discrimination, respondent would have failed to qualify for admission even in the absence of Davis' special admissions program.[43]

The Regents of the University of California recognized that the Davis School of Medicine's regular admissions process, which had every appearance of being objective and fair, had a built in bias since it resulted in Blacks and Latinos representing less than 2 percent of total admissions. Its special admissions program was intended to offset that bias, and was moderately successful in doing so, though admissions of Blacks and Latinos was still below their proportion to the total population. Still, five justices decided that it was a white man who had been discriminated against because the university could not prove that in a hypothetical situation he would still have been denied admission.

41. *Regents of the University of California v. Bakke*, 438 U.S. 265 (1978).

42. Ibid.

43. *Regents of the University of California v. Bakke*, 438 U.S. 265 (1978), Brennan, concurring in judgment, dissenting in part.

Nine years later, some of those same justices decided that McCleskey, a black man facing execution, had not been discriminated against despite uncontested statistical evidence that Blacks were almost three times as likely as Whites to receive the death penalty when the victim was white. The difference in the approach of the Supreme Court's five-justice majorities to the Fourteenth Amendment claims of those two men is significant, and the long-term effects of that difference and the resulting rulings must not be ignored or discounted.

Disregard for the Protection of Voting Rights

One final case, *Shelby County v. Holder*, decided in 2013, demonstrates the power of the Supreme Court to overturn actions of Congress regardless of how much support those actions have. In this case, a five-justice majority overturned a critical part of Congress' 2006 Reauthorization of the 1965 Voting Rights Act. With an unusual show of bipartisan support, Congress had approved reauthorization of the Act by votes of 390 to 33 in the House of Representatives and 98 to 0 in the Senate.[44] Clearly, those 488 members of Congress viewed the constitutionality of the law differently than the five justices who ruled it unconstitutional.

Part of the Voting Rights Act consisted of identifying those states and political subdivisions that had a history of implementing obstacles to voting by Blacks and requiring those states and political subdivisions to get federal approval before implementing any changes to their voting laws or procedures, a process called "preclearance." That section of the Act was originally set to expire in five years, but it was reauthorized by succeeding Congresses several times before coming up for reauthorization again in 2006.

That reauthorization was clearly not routine. Prior to reauthorizing the Act in 2006, both houses of Congress held extensive hearings, heard from witnesses, and received many reports and documents regarding the issues. The reports showed that, between 1982 and 2006, over seven hundred voting changes had been blocked based on a determination that the changes were discriminatory. In the same period, over eight hundred proposed changes were withdrawn or modified following requests for more information by the Department of Justice prior to a ruling.[45]

The majority ruled that singling out states for preclearance violated the principle of state sovereignty, which is that states cannot be treated differently by the federal government. Justice Ginsburg's dissent, joined by

44. *Shelby County v. Holder*, 570 U.S. ___ (2013), Ginsburg, dissenting.
45. Ibid.

three other justices, claimed that the principle of state sovereignty had very limited application, and that the Court had recognized those limitations in previous rulings. She argued that applying that principle to this Act was in error and noted that the majority offered no explanation for their departure from precedent.

Yet with questionable and incomplete justification, five justices were able to overturn legislation approved by a unanimous Senate and a 390 to 33 majority in the House of Representatives. The Fifteenth Amendment, the third amendment adopted after the Civil War, guarantees everyone the right to vote and specifically authorizes Congress to "enforce this article by appropriate legislation." Justice Ginsburg's dissent argued that the Voting Rights Act conformed to that provision of the Constitution and that the majority had erred "egregiously by overriding Congress' decision." She added: "Hubris is a fit word for today's demolition of the VRA."[46]

The success of the preclearance part of the Voting Rights Act had shown how much more effective a proactive approach could be than a reactive approach in combating racism. The difficulty in dealing with the complex problem of racism and its effects is that it has proven to be very effective at adapting when necessary. Legislation as a remedy has proven generally ineffective because of that ability of racism to adapt. Each time a law was passed to prevent a specific abuse, an alternative means was found to accomplish the same purpose. In her dissent, Justice Ginsburg pointed out why this legislation was unique and effective:

> Unlike prior statutes, which singled out particular tests or devices, the VRA is grounded in Congress' recognition of the "variety and persistence" of measures designed to impair minority voting rights. In truth, the evolution of voting discrimination into more subtle second-generation barriers is powerful evidence that a remedy as effective as preclearance remains vital to protect minority voting rights and prevent backsliding.[47]

The data showed the positive effects of that process. By 2004, the percentage of eligible voters who were registered was essentially equal between Blacks and Whites in the six states originally subject to preclearance. The majority saw that as proof that preclearance was no longer needed.[48] The dissent saw the majority view as "throwing away your umbrella in a rainstorm because you are not getting wet."[49] By negating that part of the Act,

46. Ibid.
47. Ibid.
48. *Shelby County v. Holder*, 570 U.S. ___ (2013).
49. *Shelby County v. Holder*, 570 U.S. ___ (2013), Ginsburg, dissenting.

the Supreme Court has made future use of proactive approaches difficult, if not impossible. Because the ruling was based on an interpretation of the principle of state sovereignty, unless the Court reverses itself at some later date, it will require the difficult process of a constitutional amendment to restore this important tool in the struggle against racism.

PART III

The Present and Future

13

Racism in the Present

This chapter will not be a list of examples of racism. There will be some familiar examples, but primarily this chapter will suggest a new way of looking at those examples to better understand racism. Looking at racism as fundamentally the ranking of groups of people, rather than as specific acts committed against individuals or groups, requires a different focus. Using that definition of racism, there is a difference between racism and the manifestations and effects of racism.

Because we have been conditioned to subconsciously think in terms of race, our actions based on that conditioning are often referred to as racism. But it is important to recognize that it is the nature of the conditioning that is the true racism, and that must be countered before actions will change. The manifestations and effects of racism are by no means unimportant, because they do affect the daily lives of millions of people. But they are the symptoms of racism and treating symptoms can only produce limited and temporary results.

If I use a racial slur or discriminate against someone, I have caused that person harm. But generally my intent was not specifically to harm. I simply viewed the other person as less worthy. Granted, racism can, and does, reach such an emotional level that hatred and intent to cause harm occur. If my view of the ranking of groups of human beings is so strong that I see every group as having a set place in society, intense emotions and hatred can be aroused when I see people defying what I see as the proper social order. Actions based on those emotions can be extremely harmful and even deadly, but it is the misguided view of a set social order that must be changed to ensure permanent change.

Of course, this way of looking at racism presents an immediate problem. We can't see conditioning, or in more familiar terms, socialization—how we have been taught to see the world and the people around us. We can't see socialization directly, but we can see it indirectly. That will be the focus of this chapter. Connecting the past to the present and looking at the socialization process provides a road map for looking for the effects of that process on each of us. The socialization process also included rationalizations to justify conditions that we would otherwise reject immediately. That aspect of socialization must also be addressed before we can be honest about what we are seeing.

Following a review of the process of socialization, there will be some examples of the effects of racism. At that point it is important to remember that the effects are only part of the problem. The examples cited must be used as an indicator of the underlying attitudes that allow people to act in ways that are not only improper, but also contrary to what we would expect from rational social human beings. The examples should be viewed as symptoms that guide us in a diagnosis of the underlying invisible illness that is racism.

Finally, an important part of looking at racism in the present is an awareness of the significance of whiteness in racism. Racism is about difference. While we don't think about it, and probably would deny it if we did, subconsciously we white people generally think of white people as the norm and People of Color as different. For many of us, racism is about People of Color. In reality, racism is about all groups including those of us who are identified as white. Whiteness in racism will be discussed in the following chapter.

Connecting the Past to the Present

In his dissent to a Supreme Court decision in 1987, Justice William Brennan wrote, "We remain imprisoned by the past as long as we deny its influence in the present."[1] An important part of identifying the influence of the past in the present is making that direct connection. In his book, *Lies My Teacher Told Me*, historian James W. Loewen makes the following observation: "As we college professors get older, we grow ever more astonished at what our

---

1. *McCleskey v. Kemp*, 481 U.S. 279 (1987), Brennan, dissenting.

undergraduates don't know about the recent past."[2] He goes on to say that the failure of textbooks to adequately cover the recent past makes it "hard for students to draw connections between the study of the past, their lives today, and the issues they will face in the future."[3]

The recent past and the present directly involve us, which means we are unable to look at them with the same detachment we have with distant history. If we are defensive about the actions of our historic figures, how much more defensive will we be about our own actions? Yet, if we honestly follow the progression of attitudes and events through time, we will have a more objective—and more accurate—view of our own attitudes. Defensiveness gives way to a desire to learn more about what we have been conditioned not to see.

Defensiveness is a natural reaction. Sometimes, though, it is so automatic that there is no opportunity to rationally consider the perceived threat. This is often the case in discussions about racism. Defenses such as *I never owned slaves, I never discriminated against anybody*, and *I'm colorblind* aren't responses to accusations, but they effectively shut off any discussion. What they all say in so many words is, *I'm not responsible.*

Why do so many white people feel the need for this preemptory defense? It is because, despite the good things accomplished in the Civil Rights era, there were some unintended consequences. One was making racism about blame, the idea that racism could be eliminated by identifying the racists. The first thing we need to do as we look at racism in the present is to rid ourselves of that mindset. We are not looking for racists; we are looking at the effects of a system that was intentionally implemented centuries ago and now operates in the background of our minds and our institutions. None of us is responsible for its creation. If we ignore this legacy of the past, we are all responsible for its continuation.

Some Misunderstandings about Racism

When looking at the present, it is important to guard against some traps that sound reasonable, but are really designed to let white people off the hook. This is not about blaming white people but about being honest about how we are all involved.

The first trap is viewing racism as something that is natural. This chronological review makes it clear that racism was created; it is not a natural fear of that which is different. The connection between human beings

2. Loewen, *Lies My Teacher Told Me*, 240.

3. Ibid., 252.

is instinctive and is extremely strong. One has only to look at the instantaneous emotional response to the victims of natural disasters, even those in other countries and on other continents, to see the manifestation of that natural connection. Armies are well aware of the need to de-humanize their enemies before soldiers can bring themselves to kill other human beings. The slang names given to the enemy are used specifically to de-humanize them. While there are real and obvious differences of skin color and other physical features between people from the various parts of the world, their shared humanity is equally obvious and the human bond between them is automatic.

If the separation of people because of their physical differences were natural, there would have been no need for laws prohibiting marriage between different groups of people. Yet, in almost every state such laws were passed.[4] There would have been no need for the Jim Crow laws segregating rail cars, schools, lunch counters, and even water fountains in the South. There would have been no need for restrictive covenants in housing developments throughout the North and West. The truth is that laws had to be passed, and vigorously enforced, to keep people separated.

The second trap consists of defining racism in ways that exclude ourselves and most of the inequities we see. Prejudice is often used as a synonym for racism, and in his book, *Dog Whistle Politics*, Ian Haney Lopez notes that most people think of racism as hate.[5] Anyone can be prejudiced, bigoted, or hateful to people of a different color or ethnicity than their own, and it's not illogical to call that racism. But individual prejudice, bigotry, and hate are not what caused the unemployment rate and the poverty rate for African Americans to be twice that of Whites. It's not what caused the incarceration rate to be five times that of Whites. Even organized bigotry and hate, such as the white supremacists or the KKK, are not to blame for those disparate outcomes.

The results of racism can be measured, and statistics are readily available. Most of the cases discussed in the chapter on the Supreme Court contained statistical evidence. There are a few more examples in this chapter. But unfortunately, for many white people statistics showing disparate outcomes actually reinforce their belief in the fairness of the system and the appropriateness of the results.[6] They recognize that it is no longer acceptable to blame the victims directly, but they do so indirectly by blaming lack of education, lack of parental control, gangs, or any of dozens of other

4. Haney Lopez, *White by Law*, 82.
5. Haney Lopez, *Dog Whistle Politics*, 42.
6. Ibid., 35–36.

rationalizations that allow us white people to deny any responsibility. So it's important to take a closer look at outcomes.

A good analogy is an oval running track with eight lanes. The standard track is 400 meters long, measured around the inside lane, so a 400-meter race would consist of one lap around the track. A race with eight runners who were required to run the entire race in their assigned lanes that all had the same starting line and finish line would obviously not be a fair race. Our ability to measure the length of each lane makes it easy to adjust for the differences with staggered starting lines. But assuming the unadjusted starting line, how many race results would we need before the outcomes alone would convince us that there was something inequitable about the arrangement? Would one or two exceptional runners winning in the outside lane be sufficient to prove that the system was fair?

Life cannot be measured like a physical track. Consider the connection between smoking and lung cancer. Because that connection had to be made solely by analyzing outcomes, it took some time before most people were convinced. We find ourselves in the same situation regarding racism. Except that we have too much concrete evidence of cause and effect and have been collecting and analyzing data for far too long to retain any doubts about the connection between racism and disparate outcomes. The continued insistence on considering alternative explanations is just one indication of the state of racism in the present.

The third trap is the need to emphasize the good parts of our past because of the misguided view that looking more thoroughly at the bad parts is the equivalent of hating our country. If, because of pride or embarrassment, we lie about the past or relegate it to the dustbin, we cannot be honest about the present. It should be obvious that true love for our country naturally demands that our love be based on the truth. Love of our country should also include the sincere desire that she continue to improve and become better. Defending love of country with lies, or partial truths, or with the idea of perfection, suggests that the truth, or less than perfection, is not worthy of our love.

Every Fourth of July we celebrate the words of the Declaration of Independence that "We hold these truths to be self evident, that all men are created equal" while we celebrate the birth of our nation. We can love our country and celebrate its founding without perpetuating the lie that it was founded on the principle contained in those words. We can love our country and at the same time honestly admit that it never has lived up to that noble ideal. It is a noble ideal, and definitely should be our goal. But we must treat it as a goal, not a reality. By addressing our failures we will make progress toward our goal.

Mount Rushmore honors four of our most influential presidents. All of those presidents demonstrated by their words and actions that they had fallen prey to the myth of superior and inferior human beings. They were influential men who, it must be acknowledged, played a role in advancing the myth. We can honor our past leaders and at the same time recognize what they left undone and where they actually contributed to the current problem of racism. We can also admire the amazing work that honors those men and at the same time recognize that its location in the Black Hills of South Dakota is on sacred land of the Lakota Sioux that was protected by a treaty in 1868. The U.S. Government broke that treaty less than a decade later when gold was discovered on the land.[7]

The fourth trap is the tendency to doubt what we don't see or experience. The Civil Rights era of the 1950s and 1960s marked the end of blatant government-sanctioned discrimination. As brutal and shocking as the process was, and as significant as the external changes were, the effect on racism was not as significant as we would like to believe. It was no longer acceptable to be openly racist, so openly racist comments and actions became the definition of racism.

Other than members of the various white supremacist groups, white people became very good at policing their words and actions. Because the white supremacist groups were open about their attitudes toward Blacks and other People of Color, they became the face of racism. And because their numbers were relatively small, many white people became convinced that racism had been substantially reduced and virtually eliminated.

In a CBS *60 Minutes* interview during his presidency, Reagan was asked about the concerns of the Black community regarding his policies. His response suggested that racism was not a significant problem and questioned the motivations of the leaders expressing the concerns. "Sometimes I wonder if they really want what they say they want, because some of those leaders are doing very well leading organizations based on keeping alive the feeling that they're victims of prejudice."[8]

That line of thinking was not unique to Reagan, and continues to be the initial reaction of many Whites who don't experience racism and who

---

7. Rose, "Native History: Construction of Mount Rushmore"; Brown, *Bury My Heart at Wounded Knee*, 273–313.

8. Rosenthal "Reagan Hints Rights Leaders."

form conclusions based on their own experience. We expect proof when People of Color tell about their experiences. We need to see blatant acts of racism, a "smoking gun." When we see white supremacist groups openly promoting their cause, we accept that as the extent of racism.

There are many other overt forms of racism, but they are easily denied and we accept the denials without question. A biased criminal justice system presents examples of overt racism at every level: police, prosecutors, and judges. Overt racism exists in our schools with consistent grading and graduation gaps and unequal punishments. Overt racism has been demonstrated in housing, health care, job applications, and promotions.[9] But unless someone has used a racial slur, white people are happy to accept the denials of racism. Believing there is no problem is much easier than dealing with the complex reality.

A Reminder about the Realities of Racism

Racism was created specifically to support slavery and, while it gets its name from race, it actually predates the concept of "race." The idea of race, or races of humanity, was a convenient justification for the ranking of human beings that was being used to justify slavery. In his book, *Brainwashed, Challenging the Myth of Black Inferiority*, Tom Burrell, founder of the very successful advertising company Burrell Advertising, made the following observation about the process:

> As a marketing professional who respects and admires brilliantly conceived and deftly executed propaganda, I eventually recognized that one of the greatest propaganda campaigns of all time was the masterful marketing of the myth of black inferiority to justify slavery within a democracy. . . . The early American ruling class used every available tool—religion, law, politics, art, literature, even the nascent field of science—as tools of their sales promotion and PR strategy.[10]

The ranking of human beings proved to be a very effective tool for justifying slavery. And a secondary result was that it also provided an effective means of creating competition and friction between other groups of people. Those who benefited most had all of the control, including the control of information, education, law, and police power. The brief overview of scientific

9. Feagin and McKinney, *The Many Costs*, 26–38; DiAngelo, *What Does It Mean*, 56–59, 109–23.

10. Burrell, *Brainwashed*.

racism shows the willing participation of scientists and doctors in building and propagating the myth of inferior and superior groups of people. First through the universities, and ultimately through primary and secondary schools as well, the myth of distinct races was taught to virtually every child for generations. The lessons took root, and throughout history, up to and including the present time, this tool of racism has served its master well.

It is also important to look at the intentional way we continue to misinform each succeeding generation about our past. One of the first books I read when I began this work was *From Slavery to Freedom, A History of African Americans* by John Hope Franklin and Alfred A. Moss, Jr.[11] The first thing that struck me was the fact that the book was not just about African Americans, but included European Americans and Native Americans in equal measure. They could not tell the story of African Americans without including the context of everything that was going on around them. That suddenly seemed so obvious. Yet our children's history books presume to tell United States history with only an occasional mention of Native Americans, African Americans, and slavery.

Much of our past is ugly, but we do our children no service by pretending that it did not happen or by minimizing it. Our educators are certainly capable of presenting all of our history in age-appropriate ways and including information about how we have made efforts to do better. But we must not expect a positive for every negative. Our children need to know about our failures as well as our successes. They will soon be the adults charged with the task of completing our unfinished work. Starting them off with faulty and incomplete knowledge hurts their chances for success.

We must also recognize that a more complete telling of our history would make students aware that Native Americans, African Americans, and all People of Color were an integral part of all of our history—the good as well as the bad. From Native Americans we learned much about agriculture, medicine, and use and conservation of our natural resources. Contrary to what many of us were taught, this continent was not a barren wasteland when the Europeans arrived. Throughout North America, there were thriving towns, large agricultural fields, roads, and trade and political connections between communities and nations.[12] Native Americans taught us about democracy, and the confederation of six tribes in the northeast served as a model for the original confederation of the thirteen colonies.

11. Franklin and Moss, *From Slavery to Freedom*.

12. Dunbar-Ortiz, *An Indigenous Peoples' History*, 15–31; Wilder, *Ebony & Ivy*, 174–76; Zinn, *A People's History*, 18–19.

African Americans brought farming skills from Africa, and their skill and hard work produced the crops that fed the nation and provided the trade commodities that made the United States an economic powerhouse. They built the White House[13] and the Capitol Building.[14] A slave brought the science of vaccination from Africa to America when he informed his master that prior to his capture "a tiny amount of pus from a smallpox victim had been scraped into his skin with a thorn, following a practice hundreds of years old that resulted in building up healthy recipients' immunities to the disease."[15]

From the very beginning, Native Americans and free Blacks interacted with European Americans in every aspect of social and political life. By leaving them out of our history books, we make them outsiders in their own country. Is it any wonder that relations among different groups of people are so awkward and strained? Since very few of us are exposed to any history beyond high school, we go through our entire lives oblivious to how our incomplete exposure to the past has skewed our perception of the present.

A New Way to Look for Racism

Before we can expect to see and understand racism, we must look within ourselves to understand the effect of our socialization on how we interpret what we see. We must ask ourselves why we find the consistent anecdotal evidence of People of Color so easy to discount or ignore. How can we view something as pervasive as the disproportionate stopping and ticketing of black drivers that has become known as *driving while black* and still accept the denial of racism? How can we hear the same stories from People of Color hundreds of times and still question whether they really are experiencing racism?

We find it easy to doubt the stories of People of Color, and we must ask ourselves why. Only then will we be able to see how centuries of conditioning regarding "us" and "them," "superior" and "inferior," has distorted our perspective and clouded our vision regarding the racism that exists today. In the present day, when virtually everyone is consciously aware that there are no distinct races, we all retain the subconscious sense of superiority and inferiority. In his book, Mr. Burrell, who is black, shared this candid personal account:

13. White House Historical Association, *Did slaves build the White House?*
14. Robinson, *The Debt*, 3–5.
15. Kendi, *Stamped from the Beginning*, 71.

Early indoctrination into my own inferiority fueled a determination to succeed. I remember coming to a conscious decision when I reached adulthood that, rather than continue internalizing the hurt and humiliation, "I'd just show them."

I tried to deal with it in a variety of ways . . . Ultimately, I chose the "fake it until you make it" approach, spoofing the public until I was financially secure enough to retire into a category of my own design. This line of thinking continued until I was more than 40 years old, well after I'd established my marketing firm.

. . . At some point it dawned on me that I was not faking. I was, indeed, just as smart, just as brave, just as disciplined, and just as beautiful as what I thought I was pretending to be. The more I learned about the origin of my own issues, which had been festering from the legacy of chattel slavery, the more I was able to see the same wounds in others.

It was then I realized that I, like most Americans, had been brainwashed.[16]

Mr. Burrell is absolutely correct. We have all been brainwashed. But, when the process took place over generations and over centuries, reversing it, or even stopping it will not be simple. An absolutely essential first step is that we white people actively look for the brainwashing within ourselves.

The People's Institute for Survival and Beyond refers to this brainwashing as "internalizing racial oppression," and to the two components of it as "internalizing racial inferiority" and "internalizing racial superiority."[17] In their workshops, they have found that white people are more receptive to the concept of internalized racial superiority if they hear about it from another white person. Five years after attending my first workshop, I attended another, and the following year I attended my third. At that third workshop, the white trainer was delayed or was unavailable for this segment, and I was asked to lead it. I had been working with the other trainers in various organizations and on various events since attending my first workshop. But I had never really come to an understanding of internalized racial superiority. I was repulsed by the KKK and white supremacists and their doctrine of white superiority. How could I have internalized their message of superiority?

I was given some talking points prepared by another white trainer, and I stumbled through that segment of the workshop. Though I participated as a trainer in several subsequent workshops, I was never satisfied with my understanding of internalized racial superiority—until I realized I was looking

16. Burrell, *Brainwashed*, 5–6.

17. Chisom and Washington, *Undoing Racism*, 22.

in the wrong place. The messages I was getting and internalizing were the same messages People of Color were receiving about their inferiority. But by definition, any message of the inferiority of People of Color contains a corresponding message of white superiority. And since the messages are ostensibly about People of Color, we white people never realize we are getting and internalizing those messages about us. Once I started looking at it from that perspective, I could see all sorts of ways I had internalized those messages, starting with the idea that this was something I was doing to help People of Color with their problem and that white people could understand racism and make changes without ever consulting with the people whose daily lives are affected by it.

In his book, *The Heart of Whiteness: Confronting Race, Racism, And White Privilege*, Robert Jensen, a white man, shared his personal story. He was at a book festival discussing a chapter he had contributed to a book called *When Race Becomes Real: Black and White Writers Confront Their Personal Histories*.[18] Also on the panel was a black writer, Les Payne, who had contributed a chapter, as well. Jensen describes his initial reaction:

> As I walked to my seat, I was well aware of Payne's impressive record. I had read his work, and I knew he was a more experienced journalist who had won more prizes and written more important stories than I. Payne had traveled more widely and reported on more complex subjects. He was older and had done more in his life than I had. I also had heard Payne speak before and knew that he was a more forceful and commanding speaker.
>
> So as I sat down at my seat, I did what came naturally. I felt superior to him.[19]

Jensen goes on to say that he wasn't even conscious of his feelings as he sat down or while he was speaking to the audience. It wasn't until Payne began to speak about the feelings of inferiority he had to overcome that Jensen became aware of his own feelings of superiority. He was so shaken by this sudden awareness that he found it difficult to get through the rest of the program.

If Mr. Burrell, Mr. Payne, and other People of Color can recognize the internalization of the indoctrination of their inferiority, how naïve are we white people to believe that we have not also internalized that indoctrination? In fact, as Jensen points out, part of the reason it is so hard for African Americans to overcome their feeling of inferiority is "because white people are so often expressing, through their behavior as well as words, a feeling of

18. Singley, *When Race Becomes Real*.
19. Jensen, *The Heart of Whiteness*, 67.

superiority."[20] On a conscious level I would never accept the idea of white superiority, or behave in a way that would suggest feelings of superiority. But on a subconscious level, I had to be influenced by the messages I received my entire life about the inferiority of some people; and if I'm not conscious of those feelings, how logical is it that they would not affect my actions?

We keep looking for the few "bad apples" that are the racists, so we have someone to blame. But it is not about blaming individuals; it is about recognizing the environment we live in and how we are all affected. In her book, *Why Are All the Black Kids Sitting Together in the Cafeteria?*, Beverly Tatum describes what is taking place:

> None of us would introduce ourselves as "smog breathers " . . . but if we live in a smoggy place, how can we avoid breathing in the air? If we live in an environment in which we are bombarded with stereotypical images in the media, are frequently exposed to the ethnic jokes of friends and family members, and are rarely informed of the accomplishments of oppressed groups, we will develop the negative categorizations of those groups that form the basis of prejudice.[21]

The internalized feelings of inferiority and superiority discussed in this section are currently referred to as *implicit bias*. Implicit biases apply to any subconscious preferences, but in the case of racism they effect how we relate to other people. The Kirwan Institute for the Study of Race and Ethnicity at Ohio State University identified some key characteristics of implicit bias, including:

- Implicit biases are *pervasive*. Everyone possesses them, even people with avowed commitments to impartiality such as judges.
- The implicit associations we hold *do not necessarily align with our declared beliefs* or even reflect stances we would explicitly endorse.[22]

This last point is particularly important. Because we are not consciously aware of our implicit biases they can lead to attitudes and actions that on a conscious level we would avoid. Learning about racism and working to overcome it doesn't automatically change the implicit biases that have developed over our lifetime. That requires a conscious effort. And once again, this is not about blame. We all live in a society that has evolved from a racist past.

20. Ibid., 68.
21. Tatum, *Why Are All the Black Kids Sitting Together*, 6.
22. Kirwan Institute, *Understanding Implicit Bias*.

The lingering effect of centuries of misinformation is the racism of the present. We are all affected and we are all involved. The inability of Whites to see those effects, or see a need to look for them, is a major part of the problem. This lingering effect of the past that is racism resides in each of us and in all of our institutions, but it is not visible. What we can see and must look for are the effects of that racism, the manifestations of it rather than the racism itself. The results are very visible.

Economic Effects of Racism

One of the difficulties for many white people is that their own economic situation makes it difficult for them to see themselves in a privileged position. They struggle economically and feel powerless to change policies that they see as holding them back. Yet privilege is a relative matter. The enactment of the Virginia slave laws of 1705 was the beginning of allocated privilege. Those laws included legal rights and protections for indentured servants, while expressly denying any rights or protections to slaves. Indentured servants were still poorly treated and inadequately compensated, but they could feel good that they were not slaves and they had some rights.

After slavery ended, industrialists in the northern states encouraged freed slaves to come to work in the factories because they could be paid less than the white workers who were beginning to organize into unions.[23] In the mines in the South, leased convicts were brought in to replace striking free workers.[24] The wealthy land owners and industrialists, who were exploiting all workers for their own personal gain, were seen as benefactors for providing jobs, while the white workers blamed black workers for keeping wages low. Ian Haney Lopez refers to this as strategic racism. "Because strategic racism is strategic, *it is not fundamentally about race.* The driving force behind strategic racism is not racial animus for its own sake or brutalizing nonwhites out of hate; it is the pursuit of power, money, and/or status."[25]

The process was, and continues to be, hugely successful for the very wealthy. The top 1 percent of citizens, whose average net worth is over $18 million, collectively own 36.7 percent of the wealth in the United States.[26] The bottom 40 percent, 120 million people, collectively own no total wealth;

23. Massey and Denton, *American Apartheid*, 28.
24. Curtin, *Black Prisoners and Their World*, 75; Blackmon, *Slavery by Another Name*, 72–73, 90.
25. Haney Lopez, *Dog Whistle Politics*, 48.
26. Wolff, "Household Wealth," 50–51; Domhoff, "Wealth, Income, and Power."

their debts exceed the value of everything they own.[27] So white people
who struggle economically and feel powerless really do have much more
in common with the very poor than with the very wealthy. But, as with
the indentured servants and the slaves, this system of allocating benefits
among the many for the benefit of the few continues to separate people who
would have much to gain by working together. Before we can work together,
though, Whites must recognize the benefits we have been accorded, which
have been denied to People of Color, and the significant impacts of that
disproportionate allocation. Median household wealth for Whites in 2013,
though a relatively modest $116,000, including the value of their home, was
more than fifty times that of Blacks and Latinos.[28]

Reparations

When looking at the very real economic effects of racism, spanning the
centuries from slavery to segregation, a consideration of the subject of reparations naturally follows. There is precedent in our recent past. Reparations
were paid to the Jews in Germany and to the Japanese internment victims
after the Second World War. But due to the significant elapsed time since
slavery, and the difficulty of identifying specific victims and appropriate
sources of reparations funds, most people see no point in even considering
the subject. There is also the problem of the uncertainty about the amount
of damages and the potential for it to be in the trillions of dollars. For people
with modest incomes, this immediately brings to mind the prospect of substantial new taxes levied only against white people.

But the fear of new taxes and the complexity of identifying recipients
must be set aside to first look at the wider issue. If we made the effort to
calculate the value of lost wages by all of the slaves in our history, and added
the value of interest for the hundreds of years to the present, we might well
find that the damages were in the trillions of dollars. Just having that information would cause us to think differently about wealth distribution in
this country today. That much money in the hands of slaves and their heirs
instead of in the hands of slave owners and their heirs would have resulted
in very different conditions in the present. The slaves created great value in
this country, and were never paid. This is a debt that is owed. It doesn't go
away because of the passage of time or the difficulty of locating heirs.

In addition to lost wages there are consequential damages, harm that
was caused as an indirect result of slavery. In his book, *The Debt: What*

27. Ibid.

28. Wolff, *A Century of Wealth*, 400–401; Domhoff, "Wealth, Income, and Power."

America Owes To Blacks, Randall Robinson points out that "whole peoples lost religions, languages, customs, histories, cultures, children, mothers, fathers."[29] The loss of connection to homeland, ancestors and culture, in addition to opportunities for stable family relationships, had psychological effects that continue to the present.[30] There is a cost to recovery from that.

We must also think about the harm done by decades of segregation, restrictive covenants, and red lining. The lost opportunities for home ownership and capital appreciation had significant effects on wealth accumulation. When we stop to consider the many ways African Americans were harmed, we become more aware of the ways they continue to be harmed, and we get a better perspective on the causes that underlie current problems.

The discussion must also include harm done to Native Americans. Every bit of land in the United States, and all of its resources, were stolen from the original inhabitants. How would the economics be different today if the Europeans had come here as immigrants rather than as conquerors? Just having these discussions improves our understanding of current conditions. And the discussions do inevitably lead to a consideration of remedies, none as simple as writing a check. The issue of reparations is much more that a question of who is owed a check, and from whom.

Tough on Crime and the War on Drugs

It's easy to look back critically at segregation and the people who fought to justify it and continue the discrimination. We must be equally critical of the current incarnation of racism and the people who use and justify it. The defenders of segregation changed the discussion from segregation to "states' rights." This is now the standard language of racism. Whether it's immigration issues, or attempts at voter disfranchisement through voter ID laws, or limited voting days and long lines, the seemingly innocuous term "states' rights" really indicates an expectation that discrimination is still possible state by state where it is not acceptable on the national level.

The phrase "law and order" came into use as a thinly disguised attempt to shift attention from the injustice of Jim Crow laws to the civil disobedience used by protesters as the only available weapon against Jim Crow. As the urban unrest of the 1960s brought to light other inequities that needed to be addressed, the law and order rhetoric quickly morphed into "tough on crime," emphasizing crime and criminals. Politicians in both political

29. Robinson, *The Debt,* 208.

30. Ibid., 201–234; DeGruy Leary, *Post Traumatic Slave Syndrome,* 184–217; Feagin and McKinney, *The Many Costs,* 28–34, 94–105; Burrell, *Brainwashed,* 20–34, 213–27.

parties embraced the new language because the distraction was easier to deal with than the centuries-old underlying problems. Since Reagan successfully sold the ideas of a crime epidemic and a "liberal approach of coddling criminals,"[31] no politician has dared to appear "soft on crime." The disproportionate effect on People of Color has been devastating and continues to grow.

Studies have consistently shown that white people use and sell drugs at exactly the same rate as other groups.[32] Yet, African Americans and Latinos, who make up about a quarter of the population, represent three-quarters of those sent to prison for drug offenses.[33] In nearly a third of the states, Blacks are imprisoned on drug charges at rates more than twenty times that of Whites. In some states the rate is more than fifty times.[34] Incarceration is just the first step. Once convicted, a person is labeled a criminal, so even after release from prison they are forever viewed as undesirables to be feared and avoided. Drug offenses are felonies, so those convicted bear the additional label of felon, and can be legally discriminated against in employment, housing, and government benefits. In most states they lose the right to vote, sometimes permanently.

As in the days of convict leasing, the laws are neutral, but the outcomes are far from neutral. And as in the days of convict leasing, the disproportional conviction of Blacks supports the argument that they are inclined to crime and lawlessness. The impact on the general public is significant and is reflected in the tendency of many to cross the street rather than encounter a black man, and of women tightly clutching their purses or cowering in fear when sharing an elevator with a black man.[35]

The inevitable results of the terribly misguided war on drugs and tough on crime policies have finally reached a level that can no longer be tolerated by those who are directly affected—and can no longer be disregarded by those of us who are not. Police departments nationwide have become military units rather than public safety organizations. The preposterous level of militarization is demonstrated by these statistics provided by Michelle Alexander:

31. Ronald Reagan Presidential Library, *Radio Address on Proposed Crime Legislation, February 18, 1984.*

32. Alexander, *The New Jim Crow,* 99.

33. Ibid., 98; Mauer and King, "Schools and Prisons," 3.

34. Human Rights Watch, *Punishment and Prejudice*; Alexander, *The New Jim Crow,* 98.

35. Lowe, "A Day in the Life"; McCall, *What's Going On,* 149–53.

According to the Cato Institute, in 1997 alone, the Pentagon handed over more than 1.2 million pieces of military equipment to local police departments. Similarly, the *National Journal* reported that between January 1997 and October 1999, the agency handled 3.4 million orders of Pentagon equipment from over eleven thousand domestic police agencies in all fifty states.[36]

Under that program, the Pentagon had transferred over $4.3 billion of equipment to police departments between 1997 and 2013. In 2013 alone it transferred almost a half billion dollars of equipment, including armored tactical vehicles, night vision rifle scopes, camouflage fatigues, M16 automatic rifles, and grenade launchers.[37] Predictably, the availability of that military equipment dramatically changed policing methods. Special Weapons and Tactics (SWAT) team raids increased from a few hundred in 1972[38] to forty thousand in 2001.[39] The average number of SWAT raids in recent years has been estimated to be as high as eighty thousand.[40]

In addition to changing police methods, the war on drugs and tough on crime campaigns changed police focus. As noted above, though the level of illegal drug use is equal among all groups of people, three-quarters of those incarcerated on drug charges are People of Color, primarily Blacks. This disparity is not accidental, but reflects police emphasis. Of the SWAT raids, at least 54 percent were against People of Color and 68 percent of those were for drug searches.[41] The result has been the criminalization of young black men. According to Alexander, "One in three young African American men will serve time in prison if current trends continue, and in some cities more than half of all young adult black men are currently under correctional control—in prison or jail, on probation, or parole."[42]

For the police, those statistics have made every young black man a criminal or a suspect, and a threat. The growing number of unarmed young black men killed by police, including a twelve-year-old boy with a toy pistol,[43] could no longer be ignored by the press and the public. A

36. Alexander, *The New Jim Crow*, 74.

37. Ingraham, "The Pentagon"; Wofford, "How America's Police Became an Army."

38. Epstein, *Agency of Fear*, 224; Ericson, "Commando cops."

39. Alexander, *The New Jim Crow*, 75; Balko, *Overkill*, 11; Kraska, "Militarization and Policing."

40. "The Excessive Militarization," American Civil Liberties Union; Balko, "Shedding light."

41. Ibid.

42. Alexander, *The New Jim Crow*, 9.

43. Fitzsimmons, "Boy Dies."

police shooting of an unarmed black teen in Ferguson, Missouri, whose body was left in the street for four hours, resulted in a mass protest that received extensive national news coverage. The paramilitary police response to the nonviolent protest, including the use of armored vehicles, tear gas and stun grenades, and military rifles firing rubber bullets, caught the nation's attention.

Subsequent reporting highlighted the huge racial disparities between police forces and the communities they operate in, and the significant number of police departments nationwide that have been found by the Justice Department to be guilty of biased policing and unreasonable use of force. Additional research and reporting disclosed widespread use of traffic fines and court fees disproportionately levied against People of Color and the poor, to provide as much as 30 percent of municipal revenues.[44]

The Media

Though the myth of race is no longer taught in schools, and the ranking of human beings is no longer promoted by scientists, the lessons linger and we subconsciously pass them on. Outside of our education system, the press and other forms of media are the primary means by which we receive information. Reporters, editors, writers, movie producers, entertainers, and all members of the media are just people and they reflect the broader society. They pass along the same stereotypes and misinformation that we all carry from the past. And because they reach so many people they help reinforce those stereotypes and misinformation within ourselves.

One of those stereotypes is the way we view individuals within different groups, emphasizing the individuality of Whites and identifying Blacks as a group. For example, though there have been a number of deadly school shootings by white students, the news reporting always centers on trying to understand why he, or they, went astray. The focus is always on the individual, never a suggestion that the problem is white students in general. The one group element that entered into the reporting on several of the school shootings occurred when the shooter was a victim of bullying. The effect of that reporting was to emphasize the separation of the shooter from the group, and as acting individually. The actions of the group, the students doing the bullying, while unacceptable, were seen as separate from the violence.

By contrast, whenever a Black youth is involved in a shooting incident there is almost always a reference to gangs. If a connection to a gang is

44. "Edmundson takes stand," *St. Louis Post-Dispatch.*

known it is reported. If no connection is known, the story will still refer to gangs by stating that it is unknown whether there is a connection to a gang. Black youth violence is as troubling as White youth violence. But it is also as complex as the individuals involved. By portraying every incident involving a Black as gang-related, the focus is always on the group, and the group is always connected to violence.

As noted earlier, the Justice Department has found that cities across the country have engaged in biased policing; and grossly unequal enforcement of our drug laws has resulted in Blacks and Latinos disproportionately imprisoned for drug offenses. Yet, news reports of encounters between police and People of Color almost always present the police version of events as factual, and include the criminal record of the Person of Color, whether it is relevant to the story or not.

A recent event in Seattle provides an example. On a Sunday a black man was shot by two white police officers. The Monday newspaper report had few details but did refer to the victim as a "known felon," and said he was armed.[45] The opening line in Tuesday's paper was: "The felon who was fatally shot by two Seattle police officers Sunday reached for a handgun after ignoring commands to show his hands and get on the ground, Seattle police (SPD) said Monday."[46] On Wednesday, there was a report that the local NAACP disputed the police account of the shooting. The opening line of that report was: "Expressing outrage, the president of the Seattle King County NAACP on Tuesday called the fatal shooting of an African-American man by Seattle police 'cold-blooded murder.'"[47]

There was a difference between the ways the information was presented in the two reports, but unless we are looking for it, we don't even notice. The placement of the attributions is different, and that does have an impact. In the Tuesday report, the attribution is after the information provided. In the Wednesday report, the attribution is before the information. The impression we are left with is that the Tuesday report gave us facts provided by the police, while the Wednesday report gave us the NAACP president's opinion. The truth is that until there is a thorough investigation, we don't know the facts. But because of the way the story was reported we think we already do.

The actual information provided also had an impact. The Tuesday report, which drew heavily on a detailed description of the incident provided by the police,[48] referred to the victim as a "convicted violent felon" and said

45. Cornwell, "Police say man shot was armed."
46. Miletich, "SPD: Man killed by cops."
47. Miletich, "NAACP labels fatal shooting."
48. Miletich, "SPD: Man killed by cops."

that he had in his possession suspected crack cocaine and black tar heroin. The police report did not give the names of the officers.[49] It wasn't until Friday that the police released the names of the officers, one of whom had been involved in a controversial 2013 fatal shooting of a young Native American man.[50] Multiple witnesses to that shooting had contradicted the police account of the incident.[51]

We don't notice the biases because these kinds of reports are so familiar. But if we pause, we have to ask how reasonable is it to expect that the police can conduct an impartial investigation when their first priority was to make public the officers' accounts and to highlight the victim's criminal record and drug possession, while withholding the information about the previous controversial shooting by one of the officers? The reporters did what reporters do; they brought the story. But they also saw it appropriate to do extensive research and reporting on the victim's criminal record and to include the fact of his drug possession. When they reported the officers' names, the reporter did refer to the 2013 shooting but made no mention of the controversy, despite the drastic differences between the witnesses' accounts and that of the police.

Differences in what news is presented and how it is presented are everywhere, but we don't notice. When we do notice, we think of it as an aberration, rather than the tip of the iceberg. A striking example happened in 2005 in the aftermath of hurricane Katrina when two similar pictures were circulated by two different news services. One, showing a black man, carried the caption: "A young man walks through chest-deep flood waters after looting a grocery store in New Orleans." The other, showing a white couple, had the caption: "Two residents wade through chest-deep water after finding bread and soda from a local grocery store in New Orleans." This wasn't intentional racism. The pictures came from two separate news services. Yet the messages were sent that the black man was a looter and the white couple was resourceful. The captions had an impact, though they might never have reached our consciousness except that Yahoo News ran both pictures at the same time, causing someone to notice.[52]

Katrina provides other examples, as well. For days the news reports coming out of New Orleans centered on looting, violence, and lawlessness by the trapped residents. The truth about the reports being mostly based on

49. Ibid.

50. Clarridge, "'Black Lives Matter' protesters."

51. Roman Nose, "Neighbors Dispute Police Account"; Green and Clarridge, "Man killed by Seattle police."

52. Ralli, "Who's a Looter?"

rumors and exaggerations did not come out until years later. On the other hand, incidents of white vigilantes and police blocking bridges and shooting people trying to escape the flooded city were not reported at all until years later when the Justice Department began conducting investigations and filing charges.[53]

Impressions made in the initial days of news events are not easily changed after the fact when people feel they have the information they need, and they stop following the story as closely. This is particularly true when the initial stories conform to our preconceived ideas. The above are just a few examples. In his book, *Brainwashed*, Tom Burrell gives an excellent illustration of how the constant images of crime and poverty shown with black faces, alternating with images of successful black athletes, entertainers, and even President Obama, reinforce the idea that success or failure are simply a matter of choice.[54] These images and the biases in their presentation occur in every form of media, not just news reports. When they occur in the entertainment media they are even more likely to be subconscious, since we are less inclined toward conscious and critical evaluation of what we are seeing in those situations.[55]

The problem with citing examples is not that they are hard to find. On the contrary, the problem is that examples are everywhere and selecting a few draws the focus off the magnitude of the problem. The issue isn't about dealing with a few cited examples. The issue is that we need to learn to notice how pervasive bias in the media is. No matter how many examples are cited, there will always be alternative explanations and perspectives that are offered. But we must not fall into the trap of debating specific examples.

We must set aside our natural skepticism and defensiveness and become proactive in seeking our own examples in the media and in all of our institutions. What seems very subtle and virtually invisible becomes embarrassingly obvious if we care enough to look. There is nothing to be defensive about. We are trying to learn. We are also not looking for intentional racism. We are just learning to recognize how the misinformation of the past continues to impact all of our institutions, and all of our thinking, in the present.

53. Lee, "Rumor to Fact."

54. Burrell, *Brainwashed*, 1–5.

55. Kendi, *Stamped from the Beginning*, 299–300, 343–44, 400–401, 419–23; DiAngelo, *What Does it Mean*, 168–75, 320–21.

14

White

In the process of looking at racism it is helpful, especially for white people, to look at whiteness and how we got here. We all know that "white" as it relates to human beings is an artificial concept, and we often find ourselves embarrassed by it. Many white people prefer the term *Caucasian* because it sounds less arbitrary. The reality though, as shown in the chapter on scientific racism, is that the term Caucasian is as artificial as "white," created and perpetuated specifically to give scientific support to the lie of separate races.

And though "white" is an artificial and arbitrary concept, it is also very real because of racism. For more than two centuries it has been a matter of law, included in both federal and state laws. In looking at those laws, and their effects, it is important to note that the specific purpose of all laws designating "Whites" was to exclude Non-Whites. The current segregation in our cities and the lack of diversity in small towns and rural areas are a direct result of police and court enforcement of those laws of exclusion.

The denial of rights to People of Color was no different than the granting of special rights to Whites. Those laws are past, but the privileges for white people remain. Those of us who meet the arbitrary definition of "white" continue to receive benefits that are denied to others. We receive the benefits as individuals; but we receive them because we are members of the group called "Whites." We Whites rarely think of ourselves as a collective. But in racism there is a white collective, and we receive benefits because of our membership in that collective.

The Creation of Whiteness

The first legal reference to people as "white" appeared late in the seventeenth century in colonial laws preventing white persons from marrying black, mixed race, or Native American persons.[1] In his book *White By Law*, Ian Haney Lopez notes that almost every state had laws prohibiting intermarriage between Whites and Blacks.[2] As recently as 1967, when the Supreme Court ruled that laws prohibiting intermarriage were unconstitutional, sixteen states still had those laws on their books.[3] Other Jim Crow laws regarding segregation used the term "white" as well. But what constituted "white?" Haney Lopez provides this summary:

> Thus, in the years leading up to *Brown [v. Board of Education of Topeka]*, most states that made racial distinctions in their laws provided statutory racial definitions, almost always focusing on the boundaries of Black identity. Alabama and Arkansas defined anyone with one drop of "Negro" blood as Black; Florida had a one-eighth rule; Georgia referred to "ascertainable" non-White blood; Indiana used a one-eighth rule; Kentucky relied on a combination of any "appreciable admixture" of Black ancestry and a one-sixteenth rule; Louisiana did not statutorily define Blackness but did adopt via its Supreme Court an "appreciable mixture of Negro blood" standard; Maryland used a "person of Negro descent to the third generation" test; Mississippi combined an "appreciable amount of Negro blood" and a one-eighth rule; Missouri used a one-eighth test, as did Nebraska, North Carolina and North Dakota; Oklahoma referred to "all persons of African descent," adding that the "term 'white race' shall include all other persons"; Oregon promulgated a one-fourth rule; South Carolina had a one-eighth standard; Tennessee defined Blacks in terms of "mulattoes, mestizos and their descendants, having any blood of the African race in their veins"; Texas used an "all persons of mixed blood descended from Negro ancestry" standard; Utah law referred to mulattos, quadroons, or octoroons; and Virginia defined Blacks as those in whom there was "ascertainable any Negro blood" with not more than one-sixteenth Native American ancestry.[4]

1. Battalora, *Birth of a White Nation*, 20–22.
2. Haney Lopez, *White by Law*, 82.
3. *Loving v. Virginia*, 388 U.S. 1 (1967).
4. Haney Lopez, *White by Law*, 83.

It is glaringly obvious from the summary that "white" was a totally arbitrary classification. It also becomes obvious, but it bears emphasizing, that there is no definition for "white." In all of the state definitions, whiteness was determined by what it was *not*. A one-eighth rule meant that having just one black great-grandparent, out of eight, made you black. A one-sixteenth rule meant having just one out of sixteen great-great-grandparents who was black. Being one-sixteenth black, just over 6 percent, meant that you were no longer "not black" and were therefore not white. One drop of black blood meant that you were no longer "not black." Only because the purpose was for exclusion did such illogical definitions make sense.

Whiteness in Federal Law

As noted in chapter 6, whiteness was a part of federal law for over one hundred and sixty years from the very founding of our country. The naturalization act passed by the first congress in 1790 allowed for the naturalization of "any alien, being a free white person." The law did not define a "white person," so the courts were left to deal with that question.

Various courts, including the United States Supreme Court, decided a total of fifty-one cases on this question.[5] Though the courts used a variety of approaches in their attempts to arrive at a positive definition for "white person," the end result was no less vague and arbitrary than the various state definitions, and ultimately was resolved by what white was *not*, as well. The first court to deal with the question was the Circuit Court of California in 1878, hearing the case of a man, Ah Yup, born in China, in which the judge made the following observation:

> The words "white person," as well argued by petitioner's counsel, taken in a strictly literal sense, constitute a very indefinite description of a class of persons, where none can be said to be literally white, and those called white may be found of every shade from the lightest blonde to the most swarthy brunette.[6]

His decision finally rested on a combination of scientific categories and common usage. "As ordinarily used everywhere in the United States, one would scarcely fail to understand that the party employing the words "white person" would intend a person of the Caucasian race."[7] In ruling against Ah Yup, he said, "I am, therefore, of the opinion that a native of

5. Ibid., 35.

6. *In re Ah Yup*, I F.Cas. 223 (C.C.D.Cal. 1878).

7. Ibid.

China, of the Mongolian race, is not a white person within the meaning of the act of congress."[8]

Haney Lopez provides a table of all fifty-one cases, showing the decisions and the basis used in forming the decisions.[9] The inconsistent findings for persons born in the same country, and the tortured justifications used, demonstrate the difficulty of finding an objective definition of "white person." Two cases decided by a unanimous U.S. Supreme Court three months apart, in November 1922 and February 1923, show that despite the positive language of the law regarding who was to be included, the law was primarily intended to exclude certain groups, and the Court struggled with a definition that was specific enough for legal application but not so specific that undesirable groups could not be excluded. In Takao Ozawa v. United States, the Court looked to science for the easy answer:

> Beginning with the decision of Circuit Judge Sawyer, in *In re Ah Yup*, 5 Sawy, 155 (1878), the federal and state courts, in an almost unbroken line, have held that the words "white person" were meant to indicate only a person of what is popularly known as the Caucasian race. . . . With the conclusion reached in these several decisions we see no reason to differ.[10]

This excluded the appellant, Ozawa, who had been born in Japan, and solved the Court's problem in that case. But the Court also realized that this definition might be too broad and inclusive, so they left themselves an out:

> The determination that the words "white person" are synonymous with the words " a person of the Caucasian race" simplifies the problem, although it does not entirely dispose of it. Controversies have arisen and will no doubt arise again in respect of the proper classification of individuals in border line cases. The effect of the conclusion that the words "white person" mean a Caucasian is not to establish a sharp line of demarcation between those who are entitled and those who are not entitled to naturalization, but rather a zone of more or less debatable ground outside of which, upon the one hand, are those clearly eligible and outside of which, upon the other hand, are those clearly ineligible for citizenship.[11]

8. Ibid.
9. Haney Lopez, *White by Law*, 163–67
10. *Takao Ozawa v. United States*, 260 U.S. 178 (1922).
11. Ibid.

Three months later, in United States v. Bhagat Singh Thind, the Court took advantage of that out by departing from the scientific definition of "Caucasian" and turning to what they saw as the "popularly understood" definition. Thind was Hindu, born in India, considered at that time by the scientific community as belonging to the Caucasian race. Though the court continued to rely on the scientific terminology to support their decision, they first mocked the scientific definition and then provided their own:

> The word "Caucasian" is in scarcely better repute. It is at best a conventional term, with an altogether fortuitous origin, which, under scientific manipulation, has come to include far more than the unscientific mind suspects. According to Keane, for example . . . it includes not only the Hindu but some of the Polynesians, (that is the Maori, Tahitians, Samoans, Hawaiians and others), the Hamites of Africa, upon the ground of the Caucasic cast of their features, though in color they range from brown to black. We venture to think that the average well informed white American would learn with some degree of astonishment that the race to which he belongs is made up of such heterogeneous elements.

. . .

> What we now hold is that the words "free white persons" are words of common speech, to be interpreted in accordance with the understanding of the common man, synonymous with the word "Caucasian" only as that word is popularly understood.[12]

This odd approach was all that was left to them. In Ozawa, they had eliminated a color test in favor of a race test:

> Manifestly, the test afforded by the mere color of the skin of each individual is impractical as that differs greatly among persons of the same race, even among Anglo-Saxons, ranging by imperceptible gradations from the fair blond to the swarthy brunette, the latter being darker than many of the lighter hued persons of the brown or yellow races.[13]

A pure race test, though, was too broad for their comfort, and the reality was that science was never able to arrive at standard definitions for each of the "races." Country of origin, as a determinant of whiteness, was a moving target, as noted in Thind:

---

12. *U.S. v. Bhagat Singh Thind*, 261 U.S. 204 (1923).
13. *Takao Ozawa v. United States*, 260 U.S. 178 (1922).

The words of familiar speech, which were used by the original framers of the law were intended to include only the type of man whom they knew as white. The immigration of that day was almost exclusively from the British Isles and Northwestern Europe, whence they and their forbears had come. When they extended the privilege of American citizenship to "any alien, being a free white person," it was these immigrants—bone of their bone and flesh of their flesh—and their kind whom they must have had affirmatively in mind. The succeeding years brought immigrants from Eastern, Southern and Middle Europe, among them the Slavs and the dark-eyed, swarthy people of Alpine and Mediterranean stock, and these were received as unquestionably akin to those already here and readily amalgamated with them. It was the descendants of these, and other immigrants of like origin, who constituted the white population of the country when section 2169, reenacting the naturalization test of 1790, was adopted; and there is no reason to doubt, with like intent and meaning.[14]

What was left was essentially *we know it when we see it* or, as they stated in Ozawa, deciding individual cases, "as they arise from time to time by what this Court called, in another connection, 'the gradual process of judicial inclusion and exclusion.'"[15] That federal law of inclusion and exclusion was not changed until 1952.

White Privilege

"White" was an integral part of the laws of our country from its founding and for most of our past, until very recently. Yet "white" was always a matter of what it was not, rather than what it was. Is it any wonder that white people have difficulty seeing themselves in a discussion of racism? But, the reality is that those who were not excluded were the recipients of very real and significant benefits. And, though the laws are gone, their effects remain, and white people continue to receive unearned benefits.

In current language, this is referred to as "white privilege," and it is very real. Peggy McIntosh has written an article that is an excellent introduction to white privilege. The article, "White Privilege: Unpacking the Invisible Knapsack," is a personal account of her recognition of white privilege in her

14. *U.S. v. Bhagat Singh Thind*, 261 U.S. 204 (1923).
15. *Takao Ozawa v. United States*, 260 U.S. 178 (1922).

life.[16] As aware as she is now of her white privilege, she had to intentionally look for it, and that is the position we all find ourselves in.

In their workshops, The People's Institute for Survival and Beyond conduct a session asking each individual, "What do you like about being . . . (Black, Latino, Native American, White, etc.). People of Color reply with "family," "food," "music," etc., things related to community and culture. White people find it difficult to respond because we rarely think about our group identity. We want to be viewed as individuals. A typical initial response from white people is, "I never thought about it." Not having to think about race in a society that is plagued by racism is clearly a privilege for white people.

People of Color all have experiences of being followed around stores while shopping, of being stopped and questioned by police for no valid reason, of being treated unfairly or disrespectfully where they work or shop, of being expected to condone or condemn the actions of every person who looks like them. Every one of those situations that white people don't have to deal with is a privilege, and eventually the workshop discussion brings them up. But it takes some probing to bring this to the consciousness of most white people.

White people feel entitled to enter any public space or event and to be treated with respect there. We expect our views and ideas to be given a fair hearing and to be respected. People of Color have been denied these basic courtesies far too frequently to feel any such entitlement.

White people expect to be comfortable. For many white people, racism is only a problem when it makes them uncomfortable. We've all heard white people say words to the effect that *racism wouldn't be a problem if People of Color didn't keep bringing it up*. We've even given ourselves the privilege of telling People of Color what is, or is not, racism.

McIntosh's account is not an exercise in blaming white people, and she distinguishes between earned privilege that should be available to everyone, and unearned privilege that gives advantages to one group at the expense of other groups:

> I want then, to distinguish between earned strength and unearned power conferred systemically. Power from unearned privilege can look like strength when it is in fact permission to escape or to dominate. But not all of the privileges on my list are inevitably damaging. Some, like the expectation that neighbors will be decent to you, or that your race will not count against you in court, should be the norm in a just society. Others, like

16. McIntosh, "White Privilege."

the privilege to ignore less powerful people, distort the humanity of the holders as well as the ignored groups.[17]

Whiteness, though a construct of laws and never formally defined consistently, continues to provide advantages to people who meet this artificial
standard, and set at a disadvantage people who do not. Because of racism,
white people most definitely have a group identity, and our membership in
the group affects our experiences and our perspective. We cannot run away
from the past, or from the present inequity, by attempting to disown the
designation "white." We must understand it and own it and then work to
change it.

Owning our whiteness is one of the most effective tools in understanding and combating racism. When we accept that racism gives Whites a group
identity, and the only thing we have in common is appearance, we begin to
appreciate that all of the group identities assigned by racism have no more
significance than common appearance. If groups were based on hair color,
or eye color, or height, they would be no less superficial and meaningless.

17. Ibid.

15

An Opportunity

Current events have once again brought us to a crossroads. The signing of the Declaration of Independence in the eighteenth century, the ending of slavery in the nineteenth century, and the Civil Rights Movement in the twentieth century were all missed opportunities to create true equity in this country. Our present situation presents one more opportunity, and it must not be missed. The disastrous consequences of the paranoia-induced wars on drugs and crime and the corresponding shameful distortion of our criminal justice system have created a crisis that cannot be ignored.

The massive "Black Lives Matter" movement built quickly as a result of current events, but it must also be viewed as a response to the long history of devaluing Black lives. Beginning with throwing overboard the bodies of thousands who died on slave ships and laws such as the 1669 "Act about the casual killing of slaves," there has been a long history of devaluing the lives of people of African descent. In 1901, a U.S. Senator shamelessly called for the killing of one thousand Blacks "to get them back to their places," and widespread mob killings and lynchings followed. The present mass incarceration and criminalizing of black men and the disproportionate killing of black men by police is a continuation of that history.

What Can Be Done?

There are some who have studied racism for years and who believe it cannot ever be eliminated.[1] While I hope that is not the case, nobody can know

1. Bell, *Faces at the Bottom of the Well*, 13–14, 197–200; Haney Lopez, *Dog*

for sure. What I do know is that pessimistic viewpoint is not without basis. This brief review shows how racism endured for several centuries. The review was intentionally quite condensed, intended to give a snapshot view of where we are and how we got here. But the reality of racism is in the details, obvious and available for anyone who cares enough to look. We must never delude ourselves about the magnitude of the problem of racism. Undoing the results of centuries of misinformation will take a very long time and it will take the commitment of individuals, scholars, and politicians. Whether we can find the commitment within ourselves and create the motivation in our institutions and politicians is unknown, and I suspect the primary reason for skepticism. What we can do is try.

We must start with recognition of what has been done in the past and what is being done in the present. While new ideas are always helpful, the most important element is more awareness of the realities of racism and more participation in actions already underway. People should be aware that amazing efforts are taking place in the struggle to overcome racism. Many of those efforts are by institutions and experts in their fields. More people need to be aware of those efforts so they can learn from them, but also in order to support them and create new expectations when those efforts are insufficient or misguided.

There are also many grassroots actions that arise in response to specific events. The success of those actions is often dependent on the number of people who participate. Just being a face in the crowd can be extremely helpful, particularly when there are thousands in the crowd. Because of the realities of racism, white faces in gatherings and protests related to racism are very important. Racism has its victims, without doubt. And we must accept their leadership in the efforts to bring about the changes that have direct effects on their lives. But racism is an illness that infects our entire society. All citizens must be involved in the campaign to create a just society.

The effort that can have the biggest impact is the internal work we do regarding identifying and addressing our own implicit biases that result from the socialization of the past. That was covered in chapter 13 in the discussion of how we view racism. Because this must be a continual effort, it will be discussed here with regard to how we move forward. Moving forward requires action, but actions must be based on an accurate picture of where we are and where we are going. The misinformation of the past is still with us, and we are continually exposed to new misinformation generated by those who hope to benefit from the divisions fostered by racism. We must change ourselves as we work to change society.

Whistle Politics, x–xii.

Current Status of Anti-racism Efforts

In his book, *Ebony and Ivy*, Craig Steven Wilder acknowledges the work of many universities in documenting their past connections to slavery.[2] For our universities, which were among the most influential institutions in the establishment of racism, this is important work, but we should be expecting much more. All acknowledgement of history is helpful, but must also lead to a study of the impact of that history on the present situation. Most importantly, the universities must lead in seeking appropriate means for countering and reversing those impacts. Such research must take into account the magnitude of the task, with a corresponding anticipation of push back and a commitment to follow-through.

Unquestionably, some of the pushback comes from benefactors of the universities. Funding is always a major concern for universities striving to provide quality research and education services. But the definition of quality must emphasize honesty and integrity. Difficult decisions often carry a price, and our universities must be leaders in demonstrating the importance of doing the right thing, regardless of cost. The complexity of reversing the effects of centuries of misinformation must be given full consideration, to avoid safe and simplistic approaches that are actually counterproductive and cause further harm to People of Color.

The natural sciences, which created the primary support for the ranking of groups of people, have also been taking a more active role in highlighting and speaking out against the errors of the past. Many members of the scientific community now recognize that the word "race," as applied to human beings, cannot be rehabilitated. Prior to its use on human beings, the word had been used occasionally on domestic animals, but in the sense of "pedigree" or "bloodline."[3] It is no longer used on animals, in any sense, and its use on human beings has been so flawed from the beginning that any use of the word continues the myth of the ranking of human beings.

There are many differences among human beings, and advances in science are making the identification and study of those differences possible. But none of those differences correspond with the flawed idea of race, and anthropologists have terminology that is better and more descriptive to identify groups of people to whom those differences apply.[4] The total discontinuation of the use of the word "race" by the scientific community is

---

2. Wilder, *Ebony & Ivy*, 289–90.

3. Montagu, *Man's Most Dangerous Myth*, 47.

4. Smedley and Smedley, *Race in North America*, 289–304.

essential. Eliminating the foundation of racism is paramount in the effort to eliminate racism.

At the same time, there must be awareness that change presents risks, as noted by Eduardo Bonilla-Silva in his book, *Racism without Racists*:

> If race disappears as a category of official division, as it has in most of the world, this will facilitate the emergence of a plural racial order where the groups exist in *practice* but are not officially recognized—and anyone trying to address racial divisions is likely to be chided for racializing the population.[5]

Despite being the namesake of a myth, racism is very real. Destroying the myth of race will not eliminate the reality of racism, though unquestionably many would try to make the case that it had. Decreasing the emphasis on race must be accompanied with an increased emphasis on racism, and terminology would be needed to support that increased emphasis. Appropriate language would also be needed to give recognition to the growing complexity of racism, as the rankings of human beings become even more fluid than in the past. The more informed we become about the realities of racism, and the more broadly that information is disseminated, the less effective the deniers will be at impeding the significant efforts of scholars, policy makers, and the public that will be needed to undo this sad legacy of our past.

The social sciences have also done much research regarding racism. In order to find solutions, more must be understood about how this system that ultimately handicaps the vast majority of people could be so effectively and permanently implemented. Scholars must understand—and recommend the most effective means to counter—the self-sustaining nature of racism, which can be reinforced and reinvigorated with a few words by a politician, or by media focus on current events.

At every turning point in history, when the fallacy of racism might have been exposed, racism itself was the tool used to keep it in place. When those seeking power use racism as a tool, they also become tools of racism. A butcher, sharpening his knife to make it a more effective tool, is at that time being a tool of the knife. The difference is that racism is a tool that becomes sharper with use. Each use of racism refuels the hate and distrust that support it. Even challenging the barely disguised uses of racism generally ends up reinforcing it by validating the underlying myth of separate races when the debate centers on whether or not a given "race" was maligned.

5. Eduardo Bonilla-Silva, *Racism without Racists*, 232.

Lawmakers have always played a significant role in enabling the continuation of racism, and unquestionably still do. Because racism remains an effective tool for politicians, some will always use it. For the rest, it is not enough just to refrain from its use. To be part of the solution, lawmakers must take an active role in helping the public see the subtle appeals that are used to exploit our subconscious conditioning.

But most importantly they must take an active role in monitoring the effects of legislation. They must take an honest look at neutral laws that are enforced in ways that produce very unequal results. Changing the way those laws are enforced would be an easy solution, but an objective look at racism and subconscious attitudes regarding the inferiority of some people tells us that an easy solution is not possible. Rewriting or re-wording some laws might provide a solution. But lawmakers must recognize that some laws may have to be eliminated altogether in order to guarantee equal protection under the law. We don't need laws to connect us, but we need to end laws that separate us. The courts should not be the only recourse when laws produce unequal results.

Critical Race Theory

A significant new approach to addressing racism on the institutional level is critical race theory. Legal scholars began critical race theory in the 1970s, initially to apply the principles of critical legal studies to the study of racism.[6] The basic idea is a critical examination of law from its many perspectives: political, social, the conflicting interests of the parties affected, etc. Summarizing the origins of the critical race theory movement in their book, *Critical Race Theory: An Introduction*, Richard Delgado and Jean Stefancic described one of the first steps:

> From critical legal studies, the group borrowed the idea of legal indeterminacy—the idea that not every legal case has one correct outcome. Instead, one can decide most cases either way, by emphasizing one line of authority over another, or interpreting one fact differently from the way one's adversary does.[7]

The differing opinions offered by the majority and the dissent in the cases reviewed in the Supreme Court chapter demonstrate that fact, and how outcomes would have been different with a change of one or two votes. This critical scholarly approach to law and racism is desperately needed

6. Delgato and Stefancic, *Critical Race Theory*, 4.

7. Ibid., 5.

to better understand outcomes that historically have favored Whites and harmed People of Color and to find ways to counter the disparate results of the past.

A very important aspect of critical race theory is the coordination that it promotes among the various areas of study and society. Though racism got its start in law, the more than 300 years of its existence has resulted in its permeating every aspect of our society, our institutions and our lives. Eliminating it is not simply a matter of law, and critical race theory recognizes the interconnectedness of politics, law, society and all of the institutions that impact our lives. Delgado and Stefancic put it this way:

> The movement considers many of the same issues that conventional civil rights and ethnic studies discourses take up, but places them in a broader perspective that includes economics, history, context, group- and self-interest, and even feelings and the unconscious. Unlike traditional civil rights, which stresses incrementalism and step-by-step progress, critical race theory questions the very foundations of the liberal order, including equality theory, legal reasoning, Enlightenment rationalism, and neutral principles of constitutional law.[8]

It should be noted that, however slowly, progress has been made. We don't have to continually start over, and scholars and activists are able to build on the past. A significant lesson of the past is the durability of racism and its adaptability to overcome efforts to end it. The incremental approaches of the past allowed for persistent backsliding. The holistic approach of Critical Race Theory does not lend itself to easy steps or easy answers, but it holds the promise of more comprehensive and more permanent progress toward social justice.

We Are All Involved

As important as it is to be aware of institutional efforts to overcome racism, individual efforts are equally important. Throughout my life, as I tried to understand racism, I saw it as something involving People of Color as the victims of racism and white racists who were the problem. I saw the white racists as two groups: the white supremacists who were outspoken about their racism; and closet racists, many of whom might not even have been aware of their racist views. I saw myself as an outsider looking in. I wanted to be an objective observer who might help make things better. My

8. Ibid., 3.

involvement was to be like that of a cancer researcher who studies cancer—not because he has it, but in order to help those who do.

Many white people feel this way, and we are encouraged to do so by a press that loves to do "gotcha" stories about people who make racist remarks. By identifying the racists we can distinguish ourselves from them. Unfortunately, making racism about blame has become one of the biggest problems in combating it. The key to combating racism is addressing a racist system, not searching out racist individuals.

Our racist system affects all of us who live in it. We are all affected by the environment we live in, and we, in turn, affect that environment. An essential first step for white people who want to work for change is to develop an understanding of how each of us is affected by racism and the role we play in allowing this legacy of the past to continue.

At every point in history there were thousands of individuals working to overcome racism and to promote true equality. But it was the millions who were indifferent who allowed it to flourish. Those in power have always controlled the flow of information, so the indifference often was, and continues to be, due to a lack of knowledge. Distractions and feel-good stories about our "glorious" past promote ignorance, and ensure no change. We must resist calls for patriotism and love of country that depend on partial truths and untruths.

We must demand honesty. An honest look at our past, while frequently sad and embarrassing, must not be equated with blame or guilt. No one living today was responsible for slavery or the racism it spawned. Our responsibility is for the time we live in and for our impact on the future. The better we understand the present, the better we are able to overcome the past and work for a more just and equitable future.

As we do this work, we must be deliberate about distinguishing between the myth of race and the reality of racism. Because of the misinformation passed down for centuries, the ranking of groups of people has become internalized by all of us. This ranking of groups, not just how we identify those groups, must be countered before we can finally end racism.

Since the ranking began with slavery, people of African descent have always occupied the lowest rank and those of European descent have always occupied the highest, while other People of Color occupied the ranks in between. Acknowledging this, we must also acknowledge the impossibility of something called "reverse racism." The general misunderstanding of racism that allows terms like "reverse racism" to appear reasonable speaks to the magnitude of the task. But developing a better understanding does not begin with a debate about words. It begins with looking more closely at our social and political environment and seeing how this ranking is manifesting itself. White people must commit themselves to seeing what we have been conditioned not to see, but which People of Color see all the time because it affects their lives every day.

Conversations about Racism

We must never be defensive or apologetic about speaking about racism. Contrary to the views of those Whites who are uncomfortable hearing about racism, discussions about the subject do not create, or add to, the problem of relations between groups of people. Racism exists. Racism should make us uncomfortable.

After attending my first Undoing Racism® workshop it took two weeks for me to process the information I had received. Or rather, that is what I thought was happening. I've since come to realize that what really happened was that it took two weeks for me to figure out how to make myself comfortable again. The ability of Whites to make ourselves comfortable by denying or ignoring racism is a major reason it has endured. Again, we *should* be uncomfortable about racism. Not as a penance, but because there is something wrong. Making ourselves comfortable by ignoring that wrong does not make it right.

Conversations with others are an important part of the process. And in talking about the subject, we are forced to organize our own random thoughts, many of which are buried in our subconscious. But part of white socialization has been that it is improper to talk about racism, and consequently it is difficult for white people to have these conversations. This was noted in the report of a 1998 study, titled *Time To Move On*, which examined White and Black parents' attitudes regarding issues of race in public education:

> One of the earliest observations in this project was that it was far easier for a white moderator to talk with an all-black group about race and schools than for a white moderator to discuss these issues with an all-white group.
>
> . . .
>
> The reticence of white parents to talk explicitly means their fears and anxieties remain beneath the surface, not easily vetted in public. One consequence is that while the views of African-American parents are resolved and focused, the views of whites about race and the schools often seem murky and ambivalent, replete with twists and turns in attitudes that are difficult to

unravel because they are sometimes hidden—sometimes not worked through—and rarely discussed.[9]

Because white people rarely discuss the subject of racism—other than in regard to specific incidents in the news—we are not comfortable doing so. Part of that discomfort is the recognition that what we say might not sound quite right. So we choose our words carefully, and often struggle to find words, or the correct words, since our first attempts at putting our thoughts into words don't always sound sufficiently non-racist. The constant policing of ourselves as we speak results in the twists and turns mentioned in the report, leading to a level of incoherence noted by Eduardo Bonilla-Silva. He gives several examples including the following response of a university student to a question on interracial marriage:

> I mean, personally, I don't see myself, you know, marrying someone else. I mean, I don't have anything against it. I just I guess I'm just more attracted to, I mean, others. Nothing like, I could not and I would never, and I don't know how my parents would—just on another side, I don't, like, if my parents would feel about anything like that.[10]

One of the white parents in the 1998 study was quoted as saying, "Whites have to walk on egg shells."[11] It probably didn't occur to him that the risk for white people is not that we might be misunderstood, but that our implicit biases might be exposed. The topic of subconscious feelings, or implicit bias, was discussed in chapter 13. One of the key characteristics of implicit bias identified by The Kirwan Institute for the Study of Race and Ethnicity at Ohio State University was the following: "The implicit associations we hold *do not necessarily align with our declared beliefs* or even reflect stances we would explicitly endorse."[12]

The fact that our implicit biases are often contrary to our conscious principles is one of the reasons white people find it difficult to express their thoughts on race and racism. Because our implicit biases are in our subconscious, we are not really aware what they are. This is the discovery we need to make about ourselves. But, as awkward, embarrassing, and disconcerting as it is to expose those biases, even to ourselves, searching out and changing them within ourselves is an essential early step for all white people. Doing so will not only change our own actions but will also allow us to see the

9. Farkas et al., *Time To Move On*, 23–24.

10. Bonilla-Silva, *Racism without Racists*, 116.

11. Farkas et al., *Time To Move On*, 23.

12. Kirwan Institute, *Understanding Implicit Bias*.

subtle messages that flood our environment, though we have been conditioned not to see them. Often those messages are not messages at all, but rather what is *not* said or noticed.

Non-racist or Anti-racist

White people rarely see their own experiences from a racial perspective. We see our predominantly white communities, schools, and work places as normal. Only in those more rare instances when we see communities, schools, and worksites with significant numbers of People of Color do we think of race. This distorted perspective on race and racism leads to a widespread assumption, noted by Derrick Bell in his book *Faces at the Bottom of the Well: The Permanence of Racism*, that:

> Blacks, unlike whites, cannot be objective on racial issues and will favor their own no matter what. This deep-seated belief fuels a continuing effort—despite all manner of Supreme Court decisions intended to curb the practice—to keep black people off juries in cases involving race. Black judges hearing racial cases are eyed suspiciously and sometimes asked to recuse themselves in favor of a white judge—without those making the request even being aware of the paradox in their motions.[13]

Our separation from People of Color is a lingering effect of the past. This isolation has denied us regular contact and social interaction with People of Color and made us susceptible to believing the stereotypes that have evolved. Whether we think about it or not, we make judgments about people based on those stereotypes. We want to be non-racist, but we also have to be honest about how we have been affected by our environment. Bonilla-Silva urges, "a personal and political movement away from claiming to be 'nonracist' to becoming 'antiracist'," an idea he credits to Eileen O'Brien, a sociology professor at the State University of New York-New Paltz:[14]

> Being an antiracist begins with understanding the institutional nature of racial matters and accepting that all actors in a racialized society are affected *materially* (receive benefits or disadvantages) and *ideologically* by the racial structure. This stand implies taking responsibility for your unwilling participation in

13. Bell, *Faces at the Bottom of the Well*, 113.
14. Bonilla-Silva, *Racism without Racists*, 15, 24, note 82.

these practices and beginning a new life committed to the goal
of achieving real racial equality.[15]

Seemingly insignificant differences in terminology can actually be very
significant, as they reflect our thoughts and communicate those thoughts to
others, and even to ourselves. The subtle difference between "non-racist"
and "anti-racist" influences how we think about ourselves, how we think
about the issue, and how we view our role in affecting change. The word
non-racist suggests that our internal work is done. The word *anti-racist*
acknowledges we are all personally involved in a racist system, have been
affected by it, and have a role both personally and collectively in the work
of making things better. It also reflects the recognition that this will require
a lifetime commitment, not just a passive interest on Martin Luther King's
birthday or during Black History Month.

We do manifest our implicit bias, but we don't see it because it seems
normal. People of Color see it all the time, because this is their experience
with racism. White people need to learn how to see it too. But we don't learn
by an occasional query to a Person of Color. We do it by caring enough to
do our own research. We do it by taking every accusation of racism seri-
ously and struggling to see what we don't see. People of Color have been
telling white people about racism for years. They have written books, made
speeches, and been quoted in news reports. The resources are available; we
have to care enough to look. We have to be willing to listen in order to
learn, not in order to find a defense. The more open we become, the more
capable we become of seeing what we have been conditioned not to see. Just
consider how dramatically our perspective changes when we recognize and
overcome the tendency to deny or diminish the experiences reported by
People of Color; when we see every experience they share as an opportunity
for us to learn.

More Than Inclusion

Understanding our implicit biases, where they come from and how they
affect us is just the first step. The next step also takes place within ourselves.
It involves understanding our subconscious responses to our implicit biases
and our conscious responses as we become aware of them. In their book,
Beyond Inclusion, Beyond Empowerment, Leticia Nieto, et al. discuss five
levels of response by members in any dominant group—Whites in the case

15. Ibid., 15.

of racism. The five levels are Indifference, Distancing, Inclusion, Awareness, and Allyship.[16]

The first two occur when we see no need to be involved. Indifference refers to the response characterized by the statement: "This doesn't concern me, I'm not interested in it." This is the level of not caring to know anything about racism or even having to admit that it exists. Distancing recognizes differences and separates ourselves from the "other." Distancing can be negative, as in white supremacy: "Those people are the problem." Or it can be neutral, as in "I don't care what those people do as long as I'm not bothered." Finally, distancing can even show a positive attitude toward the "other" group, while maintaining separation. Examples include admiring Native Americans for their spirituality or viewing people of Asian descent as exotic.

It is the third level, Inclusion, which we need to consider in some detail. As the title suggests, this level recognizes that we are all the same and should be treated equally. It has the appearance of being the goal, although it does fall short. We are all the same, but because of racism we have very different life experiences. We also have different cultures, some aspects of which date back millennia to ancestral homelands.[17] Diversity training and tolerance emphasize inclusion and center on welcoming others into our lives, generally, however, with the unstated assumption that they will assimilate. This of course means adopting the dominant culture.

In his book, *A Country of Strangers,* David K. Shipler tells of a workshop he attended where the leader asked how many of the participants found that they had to leave their "culture at the door when [they] went to work?" He said the Blacks, Latinos, and Asians all stood. The Whites remained seated.[18] Obviously People of Color want to be included in everything this country has to offer. But they shouldn't have to conform to our expectations in order to be included.

In his book, *Stamped From The Beginning: The Definitive History of Racist Ideas in America,* Ibram X. Kendi presents the history not as two opposing ideologies, but as three. His three categories are segregationists, assimilationists, and antiracists. His book clearly demonstrates that assimilationist ideology did much more to weaken antiracist efforts than to support them.[19] This was because the failure of People of Color, and Blacks in

---

16. Nieto, et al., *Beyond Inclusion, Beyond Empowerment,* 102–40.

17. Nichols, "The Philosophical Aspects of Cultural Difference."

18. Shipler, *A Country of Strangers,* 560.

19. Kendi, *Stamped from the Beginning.*

particular, to assimilate was inevitably blamed on their inability to conform to expected standards.

That was a predetermined outcome. The standards set for People of Color to assimilate have never been the same as those expected of Whites. From the colonial period to the present, People of Color have always been expected to assimilate, not as equals, but into a social order that expected them to subordinate themselves to Whites. Every refusal of Whites to accept People of Color as equals, for whatever arbitrary reason, was blamed on their inability to assimilate.

Awareness

We seize on words such as Martin Luther King, Jr.'s dream of the day his children "will not be judged by the color of their skin but by the content of their character,"[20] and see simplistic answers like being "colorblind" as the goal. We delude ourselves into believing that is all Dr. King asked. Reading the entire speech, not just those few words, makes it obvious he was asking much more. Claiming to be "colorblind" is the equivalent of "I don't discriminate." It absolves us of any responsibility regarding the racism that exists in the society we are a part of. It disregards the experiences of People of Color regarding racism. It totally ignores the existence of institutional racism and how it significantly impacts some people. We must see color to understand the experience of People of Color. This is the meaning of awareness, and this is the critical element that is lacking in simple inclusion.

Whites can never truly feel the experience of People of Color. But we can take every opportunity to hear and honor what they say when they tell us about their experience. We can read all of Dr. King's speeches and writings in order to learn, not to find phrases we can twist into absolution. We need an awareness of how racism works and how people are being affected before we can participate in creating solutions. People of Color do not want to be "tolerated." They expect to be respected for who they are. That's all any of us expect. People of Color do not expect to be included for the sake of diversity. Diversity exists. Including People of Color does not create diversity; excluding them defies our existing diversity. We work to overcome racism, not as a service to People of Color, but to create a better and more just society for us all.

20. King, "I Have A Dream."

Allyship

Thus far, the discussion has been about the internal work that white people must do. We have lifetimes of exposure to misinformation to overcome. Much of the misinformation had its origins long before we were born. But the misinformation continues, and we must always be on our guard and expect to always continue learning. At the same time, we must keep in mind that it takes action to create change.

Action without a clear understanding of the problem can be ineffective at best, and counterproductive at worst. This is especially true regarding racism. Racism has a very real effect on millions of people every day of the year. Any actions regarding racism affect those people's lives. No matter how well-intentioned our actions, if we fail to consider the impacts on People of Color we risk causing them additional harm.

Further, it is one of the unfortunate realities of racism that People of Color are always judged as a group. The actions of individuals are inevitably associated with the group. This is particularly the case regarding actions that some people find objectionable. Whites, on the other hand, expect to be, and are, judged as individuals. Oddly, because racism is identified with People of Color, even actions by white people in attempts to counter racism, can be blamed on People of Color.

This is why accountability to People of Color is so important in this work. This is the meaning of Allyship. That does not mean that we cannot take independent action. We cannot expect People of Color to hold our hands or tell us what to do. White people are still the majority in this country. The existence of racism ensures that we still have the most power. We must be willing and able to commit ourselves to the work of stopping racism.

The way I received that message is actually a fond memory from a number of years ago when I was relatively new to the work. A group of anti-racist Whites that I belonged to was asked to support a group of People of Color who were presenting a list of demands to the local school board. Over one hundred white people attended the school board meeting. About two months later, two young women and I represented the White anti-racist group at the monthly meeting of that particular organization of People of Color to talk about our support of their cause. One of the first responses we received was, "But what have you done since then?"

Their demands to the school board concerned the fact that their children were not being treated equitably, and many would not be graduating on schedule. They had hoped that our support would have been more than attending one meeting and that we would have responded as if it had been our own children who were being shortchanged on their education. Understandably, since they were talking about their children's futures, they spoke with a lot of passion when they expressed their concerns to us. When a member of their group came to our defense with "Maybe they were afraid of doing something wrong," the immediate response was "If they do something wrong, we will tell them." Despite the emotion and passion directed at us, their response showed trust. They assumed we cared. We did, and I learned a lot.

Taking risks is never easy. But we must never forget that the risks for white people are significantly less than for People of Color. People have lost jobs, been beaten and killed because of their struggle against racism. Students during the Civil Rights Movement faced fire hoses and police dogs. Any risks we face are minor by comparison. We might embarrass ourselves occasionally by doing the wrong thing. But if we hold ourselves accountable, we will learn from our mistakes. We can also mitigate that risk by showing some humility, doing our research, listening to People of Color, and establishing relationships with People of Color through our anti-racism work.

Another risk is that family, friends, and co-workers might object to what we are doing. There too, humility helps because we know we don't have all the answers. We also know that it's not a matter of identifying racists, but recognizing that we are all affected. So family members and acquaintances who don't have the level of awareness we do are no different than we were not long ago. We have no reason to offend people by flaunting our new awareness. If we engage them respectfully, we might even learn from them as their responses remind us of biases we still have not addressed in ourselves. And gradual exposure to our new perspective might eventually help shift their perspective. Reaching out to the white community is some of the most important work we do.

What We Can Do as Individuals

In our lives, we each play many roles as employees, managers, community members, church members, voters, and interested bystanders. We have varying degrees of influence in each of those roles. In some cases we have decision-making power. If we make opposing racism a priority, we can notice it in all of our roles and commit ourselves to working for change. The work of course must be strategic. Although we want to start immediately, we can't expect lasting change to happen in weeks or months. There is no undiscovered secret that will allow us to end racism by changing a few policies or procedures. It's important to recognize this as a lifetime commitment.

And while in some situations we can and must work independently, we will generally be most effective when we work with others. In our workplaces, we can begin organizing efforts. But in the broader community, there are likely already organizing efforts in place and we can be most helpful by joining those organizations.

Many people lack the time or emotional energy to participate in organized anti-racism activities. Still, small individual efforts do help. Getting on email lists or Facebook groups so we receive notification of rallies or protests allows us to participate with minimal personal time commitment. There is strength in numbers, and large crowds draw the attention of the media and politicians. There is strong inertia in the status quo. The demonstration of commitment to change by large numbers of citizens is often the only thing that will overcome that inertia. Participation in group demonstrations can be very helpful without the time or emotional demands of doing the organizing.

Social media can also alert us to calls for specific assistance. Because of my accounting background, I am occasionally in a position where I can use my experience to help organizations doing anti-racism work. For example, with just a few hours of my time each year, I am able to assist a local organization with the tax reporting required to maintain their tax exempt status, which enables them to secure the funding they need to do their important work. All of us have work and personal skills that can be helpful in given situations. If we are prepared to heed the call when those specific needs arise, that assistance can be invaluable.

Our conversations with family and friends in which we share what we see and learn are also very helpful to the cause. News reports, textbooks, books, movies, music, and television are all susceptible to bias and stereotypes. Learning to recognize that bias, and sharing what we see is helpful. There is a natural defensiveness that results from the idea of blame and guilt, which has been the traditional approach to racism. But if we don't see every example of racism or racial bias as an accusation, we can become more objective. We become more aware of the ways the racism of the past continues to influence the thinking of reporters, writers, producers, and the people they cover in their reporting or depict in their storytelling.

It is also helpful to notice and discuss the impact of racism on politics and the political process. Politicians, intentionally and unintentionally, appeal to our fears and biases. Their legislation and appointments and/or confirmations of judges frequently reflect those same fears and biases. The political process has been driven by fear for so long that it seems normal. The injustices of the wars on drugs and crime exist because we, and our representatives, allow them to. We accept that black politicians will represent the interests of the black community, but when white politicians do so they are viewed suspiciously. There is a real need for public awareness and conversation about this connection between our implicit biases and the creation and application of our laws. The conversations with family, friends and neighbors add to the general awareness. Letters by individuals or groups to news outlets and politicians also have an impact.

Every parent should monitor school curriculum and particularly *the history* being taught to our children. Issues as basic as school names and mascots also often reflect past disregard for People of Color and must be addressed. Discussions with other parents about school issues are important. Also important is attedance at parent/teacher organizations and school board meetings where discussions related to racism occur. If our circle of friends does not include People of Color, public meetings are often our best opportunity to hear their viewpoints and concerns. Obviously, People of Color won't always agree on the issues any more than white people. But on matters of racism, white people should value all perspectives from People of Color.

Joining and Supporting Organizing Efforts

For those who have the time and energy to participate in anti-racism organizing, local Martin Luther King Day events and Black History Month activities present opportunities to become familiar with the activities of various groups and to support their efforts. Anti-racism organizations recognize the benefit of coordinating their efforts; joining one organization always leads to opportunities to participate in others as well. This is hard work and can become disheartening. Finding an organization that focuses on an area that fits our interest makes the commitment a bit less of a chore. Being around other volunteers whom we find compatible provides the support we all need.

Some organizing efforts grow into movements, such as the Civil Rights Movement and the Black Power Movement. The current "Black Lives Matter" movement is the latest example. Movements *do* lead to major change, but they require hard work and a major commitment by participants. There is a role for white people, but we must be willing to take leadership from People of Color and be accountable to them. Large, visible movements attract the most organized opposition. Our silence aids the opposition. We dare not be silent, but we must inform ourselves before we speak out.

Without the myth of "race," we are all one. The differences that are a part of our reality are a distortion of our humanity resulting from the myth of intrinsic differences. All lives matter, and the fact that some among us must start a movement just to be included is an indication of how much we remain imprisoned by the past. Racism is stealing the lives of some of us and has stolen some of the humanity from all of us. For the simple reason of our common humanity, we must all be a part of this movement, and all those that follow, until this scourge from the past is recognized and destroyed.

Time to Move On?

The past is past. It's time to move on. Consider that statement in the aftermath of a multi-car collision on a freeway. Dozens of damaged cars, some on their sides, scattered everywhere. Bumpers, fenders, twisted pieces of metal, broken glass littering the highway from edge to edge for hundreds of yards. Can we just walk away from the mess because *It's time to move on?*

Of course not. But that is what we have attempted to do in the case of racism. Racism wasn't an accident; it was vandalism. But the effects are the same. For centuries we have been negotiating around the wreckage and pushing forward over the debris. The convoluted and troubled path has caused additional wreckage to accumulate in each succeeding decade. Some of the wreckage is so old it is no longer recognizable. But it is still there, still impeding our path. And then we wonder why the road is so rough.

Don't dwell in the past, we are told. How logical is that when the past dwells in us, when the wreckage of the past is all around us? The past is not past. Until we clean up the debris, the past remains forever in the present. We did not create the mess. But can we honestly say we did not contribute some of the more recent debris, however unintentionally? And regardless of who is responsible for the mess, we either assume responsibility for the clean up, or it is again left for future generations. That is the choice. That will be *our* legacy.

Bibliography

"Abraham Lincoln. [March 1861] (First Inaugural Address, Final Version)." Library of Congress. http://memory.loc.gov/cgi-bin/query/r?ammem/mal:@ field(DOCID+@lit(d0773800)).

Adams, Edward M. "Edward M. Adams to John E. Wilkie, Chief of Treasury Secret Service investigators, June 24, 1904," ff 13098, Department of Justice, Peonage Files, Record Group 60, National Archives, Washington, D.C.

"African Americans in World War II." The National WWII Museum. http://www. nationalww2museum.org/assets/pdfs/african-americans-in-world.pdf.

Alexander, Michelle. *The New Jim Crow: Mass Incarceration in the Age of Colorblindness.* New York: New Press, 2012.

Almanac of Theodore Roosevelt. "America's Part of the World's Work," Lincoln Club Dinner in New York City, February, 13, 1899. http://www.theodore-roosevelt. com/images/research/txtspeeches/610.pdf.

———. "The Complete Presidential Pardons granted by Theodore Roosevelt." http:// www.theodore-roosevelt.com/trpardons.html.

Amaker, Norman C. *Civil Rights and the Reagan Administration.* Washington, D.C.: Urban Institute Press, 1988.

"Andrew Johnson, Third Annual Message, December 3, 1867," University of California, The American Presidency Project. http://www.presidency.ucsb.edu/ ws/?pid=29508.

Arber, Edward, and A. G. Bradley, eds. *Travels and Works of Captain John Smith.* 2 vols. Edinburgh: John Grant, 1910. https://archive.org/details/travelsworksofca02smit.

Balko, Radley. "Overkill: The Rise of Paramilitary Police Raids in America." *Cato Institute,* 2006. https://www.cato.org/publications/white-paper/overkill-rise-paramilitary-police-raids-america.

———. "Shedding light on the use of SWAT teams." *Washington Post,* February 17, 2014. https://www.washingtonpost.com/news/the-watch/wp/2014/02/17/ shedding-light-on-the-use-of-swat-teams/.

Banished. Directed by Marco Williams. United States: Center for Investigative Reporting and Two Tone Productions, 2007. DVD, 84 min.

Barton, R. T. *Virginia Colonial Decisions.* Boston: Boston Book Company, 1909. https:// archive.org/details/virginiacolonial01virg.

Battalora, Jacqueline. *Birth of a White Nation: The Invention of White People and Its Relevance Today,* Houston: Strategic, 2013.

Baum, Bruce. *The Rise and Fall of the Caucasian Race: A Political History of Racial Identity*, New York: New York University Press, 2008.

Beckett, Katherine. *Making Crime Pay: Law and Order in Contemporary American Politics*. New York: Oxford University Press, 1997.

Beckman, Gail McKnight, ed. *The Statutes at Large of Pennsylvania in the Time of William Penn, Vol. 1*, 1680–1700, New York: Vantage, 1976.

Bell, Derrick. *Faces at the Bottom of the Well: The Permanence of Racism*. New York: Basic Books, 1992.

Bender, Diana, et al. "European-Americans Against Racism," letter to the editor, *Seattle Times*, October 31, 1999.

Bendyshe, Thomas, ed. *The Anthropological Treatises of Johann Friedrich Blumenbach*. London: Longman, Green, Longman, Roberts, & Green, 1865. https://archive.org/details/anthropologicaltooblum.

———. "The History of Anthropology." In *Memoirs Read Before the Anthropological Society of London, 1863-4*, Vol. I, 335–458. London: Trubner, 1865. https://archive.org/details/b21937412_0001.

"Birmingham Campaign of 1963." Encyclopedia of Alabama. http://www.encyclopediaofalabama.org/face/Article.jsp?id=h-1358.

Blackmon, Douglas A. *Slavery by Another Name*. New York: Anchor Books, 2008.

Bonilla-Silva, Eduardo. *Racism Without Racists: Color-Blind Racism and the Persistence of Racial Inequality in America*. Lanham, MD: Rowman & Littlefield, 2014.

Bridges, Roger D. "The Illinois Black Codes," *Northern Illinois University Libraries, Illinois Periodicals Online*. http://www.lib.niu.edu/1996/iht329602.html.

Broca, Paul. "Sur les crânes de la caverne de l'Homme-Mort (Lozère)." *Revue d'Anthropologie 2, 1–53*.

———. "Sur les proportions relatives du bras , de l'avant bras et de la clavicule chez les nègres et les européens." *Bulletin Societe d'Anthropologié Paris*. vol.3, part 2.

Brown, Dee. *Bury My Heart at Wounded Knee: An Indian History of the American West*. New York: Henry Holt and Company, 1970.

Browne, William Hand. *Archives of Maryland: Proceedings and Acts of the General Assembly of Maryland, October 1678—November 1683*, Vol. 7. https://archive.org/details/archivesofmarylao7brow.

Burrell, Tom. *Brainwashed: Challenging the Myth of Black Inferiority*. New York: Smiley Books, 2010.

Camper, Petrus. *The Works of the Late Professor Camper, on the Connexion Between the Science of Anatomy and the Arts of Drawing, Painting, Statuary*, A New Edition. Translated by T. Cogan. London, 1821. https://archive.org/details/b21305122.

Candler, Allen D., ed. *Colonial Records of the State of Georgia*. Atlanta: Franklin Printing and Publishing, 1904. https://books.google.com/books?id=yEgOAAAAIAAJ&pg=PA574&dq=The+Colonial+Records+of+the+State+of+Georgia,+vol.+1&hl=en&sa=X&ved=0ahUKEwiOzISAlKbYAhUB_WMKHbTzAZkQ6AEIMzAD#v=onepage&q=The%20Colonial%20Records%20of%20the%20State%20of%20Georgia%2C%20vol.%201&f=false.

Cao, Lan and Himilce Novas. *Everything You Need to Know About Asian American History*. New York: Plume, 1996.

Chisom, Ronald and Michael Washington. *Undoing Racism: A Philosophy of International Social Change*. New Orleans: The People's Institute Press, 1997.

"Civil Rights Act of 1957, September 9, 1957." U.S. Government Publishing Office. https://www.gpo.gov/fdsys/pkg/STATUTE-71/pdf/STATUTE-71-Pg634.pdf.

Clarridge, Christine. "'Black Lives Matter' protesters call for chief to be fired over killing." *Seattle Times,* February 26, 2016, B1.

Clymer, Adam. "Strom Thurmond, Foe of Integration, Dies at 100." *New York Times,* June 27, 2003.

Cobb, "History of the Penitentiary, (Special Message of Gov. Cobb), November 27, 1882." In *First Biennial Report of the Inspectors of Convicts to the Governor. From October 1, 1884, to October 1, 1886*, 348–66. Montgomery: Barrett & Co., 1886. https://books.google.com/books?id=lsBGAQAAMAAJ&pg=PA348&lpg=PA348&dq=History+of+the+Penitentiary,+Special+Message+of+Gov.+Cobb,+1882&source=bl&ots=uJh2g5hC9U&sig=PirxobwsAppL6zoyCzydmvoJ6Uo&hl=en&sa=X&ved=0ahUKEwiWgpHE8LLYAhUSS2MKHVZoAOEQ6AEILDAC#v=onepage&q&f=false.

Colonial Laws of New York From the Year 1664 to the Revolution, Vol. I. Albany: James B. Lyon, 1894.

"Constitution of 1816." *Indiana Historical Bureau.* http://www.in.gov/history/2460.htm.

"Constitution of 1851 as Originally Written." *Indiana Historical Bureau.* http://www.in.gov/history/2473.htm.

"Constitution of the State of Illinois, 1818." *Illinois Digital Archives.* http://www.idaillinois.org/cdm/ref/collection/isl2/id/12600.

Cornwell, Paige. "Police say man shot was armed." *Seattle Times,* February 22, 2016, B1.

Curtin, Mary Ellen. *Black Prisoners and Their World, Alabama*, 1865–1900. Charlottesville: University Press of Virginia, 2000.

Daniel, Pete. *The Shadow of Slavery: Peonage in the South. 1901–1969*, Urbana: University of Illinois Press, 1972.

Davenport, Frances Gardiner, ed. *European Treaties bearing on the History of the United States and its Dependencies to 1648*. Washington, DC: Carnegie Institution of Washington, 1917. https://archive.org/details/europeantreatieoopaulgoog.

"The Dawes Act 1887," nebraskastudies.org. http://www.nebraskastudies.org/0600/frameset_reset.html?http://www.nebraskastudies.org/0600/stories/0601_0200.html.

DeGruy Leary, Joy. *Post Traumatic Slave Syndrome: Amrica's Legacy of Enduring Injury and Healing*. Milwaukie, OR: Uptone Press, 2005.

Delgato, Richard, and Jean Stefancic. *Critical Race Theory: An Introduction*. New York: New York University Press, 2012.

DiAngelo, Robin. *What Does It Mean to be White?: Developing White Racial Literacy*, Revised Edition. New York: Peter Lang, 2016.

"Documented History of the Incident Which Occurred at Rosewood, Florida in January 1923, Submitted to the Florida Board of Regents December 22, 1993," displaysforschools.com. http://www.displaysforschools.com/rosewoodrp.html.

Domhoff, G. William. "Wealth, Income, and Power." Who Rules America? http://whorulesamerica.net/power/wealth.html.

Du Bois, W. E. B. *Black Reconstruction in America.* in *The Oxford W. E. B. Du Bois*, edited by Henry Lewis Gates. New York: Oxford University Press, 2007.

———. *The Souls of Black Folk*. New York: Barnes & Noble Classics, 2003.

Dunbar-Ortiz, Roxanne. *An Indigenous Peoples' History of The United States.* Boston: Beacon, 2014.

"Edmundson takes stand against measure that would limit traffic fines to 10 percent of budget." *St. Louis Post-Dispatch*, March 13, 2015. http://www.stltoday.com/news/local/govt-and-politics/edmundson-takes-stand-against-measure-that-would-limit-traffic-fines/article_74d0d07d-86a1-5519-8291-01572b1e5df5.html.

Epstein, Edward Jay. *Agency of Fear: Opiates and Political Power in America.* New York: Putnam, 1977.

Ericson, Edward Jr. "Commando cops." *Orlando Weekly*, May 7, 1998.

"The Excessive Militarization of American Policing." American Civil Liberties Union https://www.aclu.org/files/field_document/ACLU%20-%20%20Militarization%20of%20Policing.pdf.

Farkas, Steve, et al. *Time To Move On: African-American And White Parents Set An Agenda For Public Schools.* A Report from Public Agenda, 1998. http://www.publicagenda.org/files/time_to_move_on.pdf.

Faust, Drew Gilpin. "Death and Dying." National Park Service, http://www.nps.gov/nr/travel/national_cemeteries/death.html.

Feagin, Joe R., and Karyn D. McKinney. *The Many Costs of Racism.* Lanham, MD: Rowman & Littlefield, 2005.

"Federal naturalization laws (1790, 1795)." Indiana University Bloomington. http://www.indiana.edu/~kdhist/H105-documents-web/week08/naturalization1790.html.

Finch, Stanley W. "Stanley W. Finch to Frank Strong, General Agent, Department of Justice, June 23, 1903," Peonage Files (5280), ff 9927, Department of Justice, Peonage Files, Record Group 60, National Archives, Washington, D.C.

Fitzsimmons, Emma G. "Boy Dies After Police in Cleveland Shoot Him." *New York Times*, November 24, 2014.

Fletcher, Robert. "Paul Broca and the French School of Anthropology," The Saturday Lectures Delivered in the Lecture-room of the U.S. National Museum Under the Auspices of the Anthropological and Biological Societies of Washington in March and April 1882. Washington, DC: Judd & Detweiler, 1882, 113–42, available at http://www.biodiversitylibrary.org/item/67734#page/1/mode/1up.

Fluehr-Lobban, Carolyn. *Race and Racism: An Introduction.* Oxford, UK: AltaMira Press, 2006.

"The Founding Fathers and Slavery." *Encyclopædia Britannica.* https://www.britannica.com/topic/The-Founding-Fathers-and-Slavery-1269536.

"Fourth Debate: Charleston, Illinois, September 18, 1858." National Park Service. https://www.nps.gov/liho/learn/historyculture/debate4.htm.

Franklin, Benjamin. *Observations Concerning the Increase of Mankind, Peopling of Countries, &c.* Reprint. Tarrytown, NY:William Abbatt, 1918. https://archive.org/details/increasemankindoofranrich.

Franklin, John Hope, and Alfred A. Moss, Jr. *From Slavery to Freedom: A History of African Americans.* 8th ed. New York: Alfred A. Knopf, 2000.

Fredrickson, George M. *The Black Image in the White Mind: The Debate on Afro-American Character and Destiny 1817–1914*, Middletown, CT: Wesleyan University Press, 1987.

Frye, Jocelyn C., et al. "The Rise and Fall of the United States Commission on Civil Rights." Harvard Civil Rights-Civil Liberties Law Review, Vol. 22, No. 2 (Spring 1987), 450–505.

Galbraith, John Kenneth. *A Journey Through Economic Time: A Firsthand View.* New York: Houghton Mifflin, 1994.

Gilliam, Franklin D., Jr. "The 'Welfare Queen' Experiment." *Nieman Reports,* Summer 1999, http://niemanreports.org/articles/the-welfare-queen-experiment.

Goldenberg, David M. *The Curse of Ham: Race and Slavery in Early Judism, Christianity, and Islam,* Princeton: Princeton University Press, 2003.

Gould, Stephen Jay. *The Mismeasure of Man,* New York: W. W. Norton & Company, Inc., 1996.

Green, Sara Jean, and Christine Clarridge. "Man killed by Seattle police was mentally ill, neighbors say." *Seattle Times,* February 28, 2013.

Haldeman, H. R. *The Haledman Diaries: Inside the Nixon White House.* New York: Putnam, 1994.

Haller, Jon S., Jr. *Outcasts from Evolution: Scientific Attitudes of Racial Inferiority, 1859–1900,* Carbondale, IL: Southern Illinois University Press, 1995.

Haney Lopez, Ian. *Dog Whistle Politics: How Coded Racial Appeals Have Reinvented Racism and Wrecked the Middle Class.* New York: Oxford University Press, 2014.

———. *White By Law: The Legal Construction of Race.* New York: New York University Press, 2006.

Haynes, Stephen R. *Noah's Curse: The Justification of American Slavery,* New York: Oxford University Press, 2002.

Hening, William Waller. *Statutes at Large; A Collection of all the Laws of Virginia.* Vol. I. New York: R. & W. & G. Bartow, 1823. https://books.google.com/books/reader?id=yDIMAQAAMAAJ&printsec=frontcover&output=reader#v=onepage&q&f=false.

———. *Statutes at Large; A Collection of all the Laws of Virginia.* Vol. II. Richmond: Samuel Pleasants, Junior, 1810. https://books.google.com/books/reader?id=SkIVAAAAYAAJ&printsec=frontcover&output=reader&pg=GBS.PR1#v=onepage&q&f=false.

———. *Statutes at Large; A Collection of all the Laws of Virginia.* Vol. III. Philadelphia: Thomas Desilver, 1823. https://books.google.com/books/reader?id=rTQMAQAAMAAJ&printsec=frontcover&output=reader#v=onepage&q&f=false.

———. *Statutes at Large; A Collection of all the Laws of Virginia.* Vol. V. Richmond: Franklin Press, 1819. https://books.google.com/books/reader?id=wD8VAAAAYAAJ&printsec=frontcover&output=reader#v=onepage&q&f=false.

Herbers, John. "Race Issue in Campaign: A Chain Reaction." *New York Times,* September 27, 1980.

Higginbotham, A. Leon, Jr. *In the Matter of Color: Race & The American Legal Process: The Colonial Period.* New York: Oxford University Press, 1980.

"How many of the signers of the Declaration of Independence owned slaves?" *www.mrheintz.com.* http://www.mrheintz.com/how-many-signers-of-the-declaration-of-independence-owned-slaves.html.

Human Rights Watch. *Punishment and Prejudice: Racial Disparities in the War on Drugs.* HRW Reports, Vol.12, No. 2 (May 2000). https://www.hrw.org/legacy/reports/2000/usa.

Ingraham, Christopher. "The Pentagon gave nearly half a billion dollars of military gear to local law enforcement last year." *Washington Post*, August 14, 2014.

Jefferson, Thomas. *Notes on the State of Virginia*, Richmond: J. W. Randolph, 1853. https://archive.org/details/notesonstateofvio1jeff.

Jensen, Robert. *The Heart of Whiteness: Confronting Race, Racism, And White Privilege*. San Francisco: City Lights, 2005.

Jordan, Winthrop D. *White Over Black: American AttitudesToward the Negro* 1550–1812, Williamsburg: University of North Carolina Press, 1968.

"Judge Scores Alabama Jury." *New York Times*, July 13, 1903.

Kendi, Ibram X. *Stamped From The Beginning: The Definitive History of Racist Ideas in America*, New York: Nation Books, 2016.

King, Martin Luther, Jr. "I have a dream." Speech at "March on Washington," Lincoln Memorial, Washington, D.C. , August 28, 1963. http://www.thekingcenter.org/archive/document/i-have-dream-1#.

Kipling, Rudyard. "The White Man's Burden." *McClure's Magazine*, Vol. XII, No. 4, February, 1899. https://babel.hathitrust.org/cgi/pt?id=mdp.39015030656113;view=2up;seq=314.

Kirwan Institute for the Study of Race and Ethnicity, Ohio State University. *Understanding Implicit Bias*. http://kirwaninstitute.osu.edu/research/understanding-implicit-bias.

Kraska, Peter B. "Militarization and Policing—Its Relevance to 21st Century Police." *Policing: A Journal of Policy and Practice*, Vol. 1, Issue 4, 1 January 1, 2007, 501–13. https://doi.org/10.1093/police/pam065.

Lee, Trymaine. "Rumor to Fact in Tales of Post-Katrina Violence." *New York Times*, August 26, 2010.

Levin, Josh. "The Welfare Queen." *Slate*, December 19, 2013. http://www.slate.com/articles/news_and_politics/history/2013/12/linda_taylor_welfare_queen_ronald_reagan_made_her_a_notorious_american_villain.html.

Levy, Andrew. *The First Emancipator: The Forgotten Story of Robert Carter, the Founding Father Who Freed His Slaves*, New York: Random House, 2005.

Linnaeus, Carl. *Systema naturae*, 1735. The Digital Library of the Royal Botanic Garden, http://bibdigital.rjb.csic.es/ing/Libro.php?Libro=1359&Pagina=13.

———. *Systema naturae*, 1766. Biodiversity Heritage Library, http://biodiversitylibrary.org/bibliography/68927#/summary.

The Linnean Society of London, "Who Was Linneaus?" https://www.linnean.org/education-resources/who-was-linnaeus.

Loewen, James W. *Lies My Teacher Told Me: Everything Your American History Textbook Got Wrong*. New York: Touchstone, 1996.

———. *Sundown Towns: A Hidden Dimension of American Racism*. New York: New Press, 2005.

Lopresti, Robert. "Which U.S. Presidents Owned Slaves?" http://pres-slaves.zohosites.com.

Lowe, Frederick H. "A Day in the Life of Black Men: Microaggressions, a Subtle Form of Racism." *NorthStar News Today*, March 29, 2015. http://www.northstarnewstoday.com/news/a-day-in-the-life-of-black-men-microaggressions-a-subtle-form-of-racism.

Lynch, Hollis R. *The Black Urban Condition: A Documentary History*, 1866–1971, New York: Crowell, 1973.

Malcomson, Scott L. *One Drop of Blood: The American Misadventure of Race.* New York: Farrar, Straus and Giroux, 2000.

Massey, Douglas S. and Nancy A. Denton. *American Apartheid: Segregation and the Making of the Underclass.* Cambridge, MA: Harvard University Press, 1993.

Mauer, Marc, and Ryan Scott King. "Schools and Prisons: Fifty Years After Brown v. Board of Education." *The Sentencing Project.* https://static.prisonpolicy.org/scans/sp/brownvboard.pdf.

McCall, Nathan. *What's Going On: Personal Essays.* New York: Random House, 1997.

McCarthy, Colman. "Malcom's message to the end: violence." *Seattle Times,* November 27, 1992.

McIlwaine, H. R., ed. *Minutes of the Council and General Court of Colonial Virginia 1622–1632, 1670–1676.* Richmond, VA: Colonial Press, 1924. https://archive.org/details/minutesofcounciloovirg.

McIntosh, Peggy. "White Privilege: Unpacking the Invisible Knapsack." *Peace and Freedom,* July/August 1989, 10–12.

McPherson, Edward. *The Political History of the United States of America During Reconstruction, (From April 15, 1865, to July 15, 1870).* Washington, D.C.:Philp & Solomons, 1871. https://archive.org/details/politicalhistoryoolcmcph.

Miletich, Steve. "NAACP labels fatal shooting by police 'coldblooded murder.'" *Seattle Times,* February 24, 2016.

———. "SPD: Man killed by cops reached for gun." *Seattle Times,* February 23, 2016.

Montagu, Ashley. *Man's Most Dangerous Myth: The Fallacy of Race,* Cleveland: The World Publishing, 1964.

Montejano, David. *Angelos and Mexicans in the Making of Texas, 1836–1986.* Austin, TX: University of Texas Press, 1987.

Moyers, Bill. *Moyers on America: A Journalist and His Times.* New York: New Press, 2004.

National Archives and Records Administration. *Signers of the Declaration of Independence.* https://www.archives.gov/files/founding-docs/declaration_signers_gallery_facts.pdf.

Nichols, Edwin. "The Philosophical Aspects of Cultural Difference." Keynote address at the African Nova Scotian Mental Health & Addictions Initiative Conference, Dartmouth, NS, November 27, 2014. http://haac.ca/ans_mhai_conference/.

Nieto, Leticia, Margot F. Boyer, Liz Goodwin, Garth R. Johnson, and Laurel Collier Smith. *Beyond Inclusion, Beyond Empowerment: A Developmental Strategy To Liberate Everyone.* Olympia, WA: Cuetzpalin, 2010.

Nokes, Greg. "Black Exclusion Laws in Oregon." *The Oregon Encyclopedia.* https://oregonencyclopedia.org/articles/exclusion_laws.

"Ohio Constitution of 1803 (Transcript)," *Ohio History Central.* http://www.ohiohistorycentral.org/w/Ohio_Constitution_of_1803_%28Transcript%29?rec=1858.

"Original 1857 Constitution of Oregon." *Oregon Blue Book.* http://bluebook.state.or.us/state/constitution/orig/const.htm.

O'Sullivan, John L. "The True Title." *New York Morning News.* December 27, 1845

Pear, Robert. "Administration is Hoping to Force Court to Confront Racial Quotas." *New York Times,* December 5, 1983.

———. "New Director of U.S. Rights Panel Calls for Major Change of Course." *New York Times,* January 6, 1984.

————. "Reagan Ousts 3 From Civil Rights Panel." *New York Times*, October 26, 1983.

————. "Rift Grows Wider Over Rights Panel." *New York Times*, December 9, 1983.

Pratt, Julius W. "The Origin of 'Manifest Destiny.'" *The American Historical Review*, Vol. 32, No. 4, (Jul. 1927): 795–98. http://www.jstor.org/stable/1837859.

Ralli, Tania. "Who's a Looter? In Storm's Aftermath, Pictures Kick Up a Different Kind of Tempest." *New York Times*, September 5, 2005.

Reese, Ty M. "The Slave Trade and Slavery." In *Converging Worlds: Communities and Cultures in Colonial America*, edited by Louise A. Breen, 344–75. New York: Routledge, 2012.

Reese, Warren S., Jr. "Reese to Knox, June 15, 1903," ff 5380–03, Department of Justice, Peonage Files, Record Group 60, National Archives, Washington, D.C.

Renschler, Emily S., and Janet Monge. "The Samuel George Morton Cranial Collection—Historical Significance and New Research." *Expedition*, 50:3 (Winter 2008): 30–38. http://www.penn.museum/sites/expedition/?p=8547.

Report of the National Advisory Commission on Civil Disorders. New York, NY: Bantam Books, 1968.

Robinson, Randall. *The Debt: What America Owes to Blacks*. New York: Dutton, 2000.

"Roll Call Tally on Civil Rights Act 1964, June 19, 1964." National Archives, The Center for Legislative Archives. http://www.archives.gov/legislative/features/civil-rights-1964/senate-roll-call.html.

Roman Nose, Renee. "Neighbors Dispute Police Account of Shooting of Native Man in Seattle." *Indian Country Today*, April 3, 2013. http://indiancountrytodaymedianetwork.com/2013/04/03/neighbors-dispute-police-account-shooting-native-man-seattle-148519.

Ronald Reagan Presidential Library & Museum. *Address Before a Joint Session of the Congress on the Program for Economic Recovery, February 18, 1981*. https://www.reaganlibrary.gov/sites/default/files/archives/speeches/1981/21881a.htm.

————. *Address Before a Joint Session of the Congress Reporting on the State of the Union, January 26, 1982*. https://www.reaganlibrary.gov/index.php?option=com_content&view=article&id=952:12682c&catid=30:1982.

————. *Address Before a Joint Session of the Congress on the State of the Union, January 25, 1983*. https://www.reaganlibrary.gov/index.php?option=com_content&view=article&id=2047:12583c&catid=31:1983.

————. *Address Before a Joint Session of the Congress on the State of the Union, February 6, 1985*. https://www.reaganlibrary.gov/index.php?option=com_content&view=article&id=4305:20685e&catid=33:1985.

————. *Inaugural Address, January 20, 1981*. https://www.reaganlibrary.gov/index.php?option=com_content&view=article&id=9662:inaugural-address-january-20-1981&catid=29:1981.

————. *The President's News Conference January 29, 1981*. https://www.reaganlibrary.gov/index.php?option=com_content&view=article&id=116:12981b&catid=29:1981.

————. *The President's News Conference, May 17, 1983*. https://www.reaganlibrary.gov/index.php?option=com_content&view=article&id=2406:51783e&catid=31:1983.

————. *The President's News Conference, June 28, 1983*. https://www.reaganlibrary.gov/index.php?option=com_content&view=article&id=2553:62883f&catid=31:1983.

————. *Question-and-Answer Session With High School Students on Domestic and Foreign Policy Issues, January 21, 1983.* https://www.reaganlibrary.gov/index.php?option=com_content&view=article&id=2038:12183c&catid=31:1983.

————. *Question-and-Answer Session With Local Television Anchors on Domestic and Foreign Policy Issues, February 7, 1983.* https://www.reaganlibrary.gov/index.php?option=com_content&view=article&id=2090:20783a&catid=31:1983.

————. *Radio Address to the Nation on Crime and Criminal Justice Reform, September 11, 1982.* https://www.reaganlibrary.gov/index.php?option=com_content&view=article&id=1605:91182a&catid=30:1982

————. *Radio Address to the Nation on Drug Abuse, June 30, 1984.* https://www.reaganlibrary.gov/index.php?option=com_content&view=article&id=3682:63084a&catid=32:1984.

————. *Radio Address to the Nation on Drug Abuse and Trafficking, May 30, 1987.* https://www.reaganlibrary.gov/sites/default/files/archives/speeches/1987/053087a.htm

————. *Radio Address to the Nation on Federal Drug Policy, October 2, 1982.* https://www.reaganlibrary.gov/index.php?option=com_content&view=article&id=1702:100282a&catid=30:1982.

————. *Radio Address to the Nation on Law Enforcement and Crime, July 7, 1984.* https://www.reaganlibrary.gov/index.php?option=com_content&view=article&id=3699:70784a&catid=32:1984.

————. *Radio Address to the Nation on Proposed Crime Legislation, February 18, 1984.* https://www.reaganlibrary.gov/index.php?option=com_content&view=article&id=3259:21884a&catid=32:1984.

Rose, Christina. "Native History: Construction of Mount Rushmore Begins." *Indian Country Today,* October 4, 2013. https://indiancountrymedianetwork.com/history/events/native-history-construction-of-mount-rushmore-begins.

Rosenthal, Andrew. "Reagan Hints Rights Leaders Exaggerate Racism to Preserve Cause." *New York Times,* January 14, 1989.

Seattle Civil Rights and Labor History Project, University of Washington. *Racial Restrictive Covenants.* http://depts.washington.edu/civilr/covenants.htm.

————. *Racial Restrictive Covenants: Enforcing Neighborhood Segregation in Seattle.* http://depts.washington.edu/civilr/covenants_report.htm.

Shipler, David K. *A Country of Strangers: Blacks and Whites in America.* New York: Alfred A. Knopf, 1997.

Singlely, Bernestine, ed. *When Race Becomes Real: Black and White Writers Confront Their Personal Histories.* Chicago: Lawrence Hill, 2002.

Singletary, Loretta, and Staci Emm. "Working Effectively with American Indian Populations: A Brief Overview of Federal Indian Policy," University of Nevada Cooperative Extension. https://www.unce.unr.edu/publications/files/ag/2011/fs1134.pdf.

Slotkin, J. S., ed. *Readings in Early Anthropology,* Chicago: Aldine, 1965.

Smedley, Audrey, and Brian D. Smedley. *Race in North America: Origin and Evolution of a Worldview.* Boulder, CO: Westview, 2012.

Smith, Marian L. "Race, Nationality, and Reality: INS Administration of Racial Provisions in U. S. Immigration and Nationality Law Since 1898," *Prologue Magazine,* Summer, 2002, Vol. 34, No. 2, http://www.archives.gov/publications/prologue/2002/summer/immigration-law-1.html.

Smith, Terence. "White House Repudiates Andrew Young Remarks." *New York Times*, October 16, 1980.

Stearn, W. T. "The Background of Linnaeus's Contributions to the Nomenclature and Methods of Systematic Biology," *Systematic Zoology* 8:1 (March 1959) : 4–22. https://www.jstor.org/stable/2411603?seq=1#page_scan_tab_contents.

Takaki, Ronald. *A Different Mirror: A History of Multicultural America*. New York: Back Bay, 2008.

Tatum, Beverly Daniel. *"Why Are All the Black Kids Sitting Together in the Cafeteria?" And Other Conversations About Race*. New York: Basic Books, 2003.

"Third Biennial Report of the Inspectors of Convicts to the Governor, From Oct. 1, 1888, to Sept. 30, 1890." Montgomery: Brown Printing, 1890. https://books.google.com/books?id=4bNGAQAAMAAJ&pg=PP7&lpg=PP7&dq=Third+Biennial+Report+of+the+Inspectors+of+Convicts,+Oct1,+1888+to+Sept.+30,+1890&source=bl&ots=SXBOpuoObp&sig=waLw7OF7kAHLyllr97IVJf8hSMA&hl=en&sa=X&ved=0ahUKEwjqsp-Vm7PYAhULwWMKHdsrAU0Q6AEILzAD#v=onepage&q&f=false.

"Transcript of Ronald Reagan's 1980 Neshoba County Fair speech." The Neshoba Democrat On The Web. http://neshobademocrat.com/main.asp?SectionID=2&SubSectionID=297&ArticleID=15600&TM=60417.67.

Trump, Donald. "Read: Donald Trump's Acceptance Speech," *U.S. News & World Report*, July 21, 2016. Accessed Feb. 23, 2017. https://www.usnews.com/news/articles/2016-07-21/read-donald-trumps-nomination-acceptance-speech-at-the-republican-convention.

"Tulsa Race Riot: A Report by the Oklahoma Commission to Study the Tulsa Race Riot of 1921, February 28, 2001," Oklahoma Historical Society, http://www.okhistory.org/research/forms/freport.pdf.

Verlie, Emil Joseph, ed. *Illinois Constitutions*, Springfield: Illinois State Historical Library, 1919. https://archive.org/details/illinoisconstituooverlrich.

" 'Welfare Queen' Becomes Issue in Reagan's Campaign." *New York Times*, February 15, 1976.

"What is Genocide?" United States Holocaust Memorial Museum http://www.ushmm.org/confront-genocide/defining-genocide.

White House Historical Association. *Did slaves build the White House?* https://www.whitehousehistory.org/questions/did-slaves-build-the-white-house.

Wilder, Craig S. *Ebony & Ivy: Race, Slavery, and the Troubled History of America's Universities*, New York: Bloomsbury, 2013.

Wilkerson, Isabel. *The Warmth of Other Suns: The Epic Story of America's Great Migration*. New York: Vintage, 2010.

Williams, Lena. "Washington Talk: Q&A: William Bradford Reynolds; Perception and Reality on Civil Rights." *New York Times*, January 4, 1987.

Wofford, Taylor. "How America's Police Became an Army: The 1033 Program." *Newsweek.com*, August 13, 2014. http://www.newsweek.com/how-americas-police-became-army-1033-program-264537.

Wolff, Edward N. *A Century of Wealth in America*. Cambridge, MA: Belknap, 2017

———. "Household Wealth Trends in the United States, 1962–2013: What Happened Over the Great Recession?," Working Paper 20733. National Bureau of Economic Research. http://www.nber.org/papers/w20733.

Woodward, C. Van. *The Strange Career of Jim Crow*. New York: Oxford University Press, 1974.

Zinn, Howard. *A People's History of the United States: 1492-Present*. New York: Harper Perennial, 1995.

Index of Subjects

Index of Names